D1320502

A Poet Before The Cross

PAUL CLAUDEL

OF THE FRENCH ACADEMY

When Paul Claudel died in Paris at the age of eighty-seven, on February 23, 1955, it was generally recognized that the era in French letters dominated by the great "masters"—Proust, Valéry, Gide, and their fellows—had come to an end. Even before Claudel's death, and particularly since World War II, the critics have been attempting to "place" Claudel and disagreeing among themselves. While T. S. Eliot hails Claudel as the greatest poetic-dramatist of our century, the leading French conservative critic, Henri Massis, has written that Claudel is "disorderly" and "incommunicable." Although many Catholic literary figures think of Claudel as the finest Catholic writer of contemporary times, others have criticized him bitterly for being "too subjective" in his art. Whatever the final verdict on Claudel the writer, few can deny his "extraordinary range, his consciousness of the world outside himself, his intensity of feeling, and his sense of the deep mystery and significance of love and suffering."

Paul Claudel

OF THE FRENCH ACADEMY

A
Poet
Before
The
Cross

Wallace Fowlie,
translator

HENRY
REGNERY   CHICAGO
COMPANY   1958

Published as *Un Poète Regarde La Croix*
Librairie Gallimard, Paris, France, 1938

The Biblical quotations used in this translation are taken from the
Ronald Knox translation of The Holy Bible,
Sheed and Ward: New York, 1956.

© 1958 Henry Regnery Company
Manufactured in the United States of America

CLAUDEL, PAUL, 1868-1955. A poet before the cross. Wallace
Fowlie, translator. Chicago, H. Regnery Co., 1958. 269 pp.
22 cm. 1. Jesus Christ—Seven last words. 2. Jesus Christ—
Meditations. 1. Title. *Full name:* Paul Louis Charles Marie
Claudel. BT455.C4213 (232.958) 58-12407 ‡

Contents

Introduction

AT THE END of the manuscript of *A Poet Before the Cross*, almost as if the work were a journal he had been keeping, Claudel inscribed the date of its inception, April 1933, and the date of its conclusion, April 1935. The book was begun, therefore, when the poet had just completed his ambassadorship at Washington (1927-1933). In April 1933, he was already in New York, and the opening paragraph refers to his leaving the New World. There are references, especially in the first part of the book, to Saint Patrick's Cathedral. The work was completed at the end of the two years he lived in Brussels, as French ambassador, in April 1935, and was first published in 1938.

A Poet before the Cross, written when Claudel was in his middle sixties (he was born in 1868), marks the beginning of what was almost a new career. By 1933, his career of poet and playwright was practically over. What lay ahead were the several volumes of Biblical exegesis which were to be published during the last twenty years of his life: the studies on *The Song of Songs, Emmaus, The Apocalypse*. If the writing of these books was reserved for the latter part of his life, their preparation had been going on for much longer. From the time of his early voyage to China, in 1895, until his death, in 1955, Claudel was a fervent and assiduous reader of Holy Scripture. All of his writings, and especially his letters (to Jammes, Gide, Suarès and countless others) testify to the fact that he spent much of his life in religious meditation directed by his daily reading of The Bible.

He calls *A Poet Before the Cross* "not an original exposition, but a diligent classification of texts." He often speaks directly to his reader, as if the two of them were working side by side in a communal effort to study the mystery of the cross. At one point he says that he expects his reader to have his Bible opened before him and to make constant reference to it.

Claudel reminds us that God is revealed in Scripture and in the world of His own Creation. One of Claudel's basic ideas concerning the poet occurs often on these pages where he defines man as God's representative, as the one capable of translating things into language. Visible things are made by the poet into intelligible things. Man as explicator is the avowed mission of Paul Claudel in this book.

One of the beauties of *A Poet before the Cross* (and one of its difficulties as well) is the confusion of voices we hear and the chronological confusion. The meditation is so intense at times that Claudel becomes one of the speakers. His own voice of commentator is merged with the voice of the actors. Thus both Pilate and Claudel can speak in the same sentence, and the reader can find himself within the same sentence simultaneously at Pilate's court and Saint Patrick's Cathedral, New York City. But these are not "confusions" in any literal sense, they are the natural consequences of what is perhaps the fundamental study of the book, the abundant suggestive analogies which the poet finds between the Old and the New Testaments. In many of the longer passages of this book, that on Joseph, for example, and the one on Absolom, Claudel employs a method closely associated with the Fathers of the Church, in which the Old Testament is seen to be the prefiguration of the New. The books which best lend themselves to this kind of exegesis, Genesis, Book I of Kings, Job, Psalms, Isaias, are abundantly used by Claudel. He returns often to certain chapters and passages of which he is constantly reminded and which offer him both inspiration and illustration for his thoughts: the chapter on Wisdom in the Book of Proverbs, chapter 17 in the Gospel of Saint John, and certain metaphorical details in the two books from which he seems to draw almost uninterruptedly: The Song of Songs and The Apocalypse.

Claudel is not a painstaking theological reasoner. He is a poet whose method, more vigorously apparent in this book than in others, is forcefulness and unshakable conviction. He forces, at least temporarily, the reader's adherence. He speaks at length in order to engage and hold the active attention of the reader. His array of sentences and his elaborately constructed paragraphs are intended first to arrest the reader and so change the focus of his thinking that at the end, he will pass beyond words and arguments and the complex arsenal of Biblical references. Claudel's goal is surely to help the reader move beyond the poignancy and the conviction of the poet's own text, to that other kind of communication which he would doubtless characterize as silence or prayer. He has written in his *Introduction à l'Apocalypse*, "I have always studied the Bible, but as a poet, not as an exegete . . . I am only a poet and a believer."

In the chapter on the harrowing of hell, Claudel quotes from Rimbaud's *Season in Hell*. There are a few other references to Rimbaud who is spoken of with gratitude. Other French writers are referred to harshly and vituperatively, Voltaire and Renan especially, whom Claudel has throughout all of his work used as typifying the modern apostasy. In speaking of certain individual writers, of Renan in particular, and in some of the passages on Protestants and Jews, Claudel demonstrates a lack of tolerance. In fact, in one passage he states that he is proud of being intolerant. His severity toward the Jews, because of their rejection of Christ, is somewhat offset by a deeply mystical passage on Judaism. His castigation of Protestants is more unremitting. Claudel's anger flares up quickly, and quickly subsides. He is as harsh on the Jews as the Old Testament prophets were, and as scathing on the Protestants as Calvin was and some of the great divines of the eighteenth century. It is the closeness of Judaism and Protestantism to the Catholic Church which irritates Claudel the most. He seems to be saying: "They are so close, why don't they submit and end their stubbornness?"

The Word on the cross gives fulfillment to the words of the prophets. This is Claudel's belief. It is the foundation both of his faith and his poetry. He is fully aware of the gravity and the cosmic proportions of such a position. This book, written after the dramas and the major poems, offers a fuller explanation of the ideas which initiated and penetrated the earlier works. His preoccupation in the writing of *A Poet Before the Cross* was twofold: the recording of his personal meditations on the final events in the life of Our Lord and the explanation in a carefully ordered intellectual form of his conception of the universe of sin and redemption. The meditations are cast very deliberately in the present tense, but this clarity of the poet's metaphysical vision allows him to understand his attachment to the past, his involvement in all the events of the past and the over-powering fact of his continuity. Elsewhere Claudel has stated this belief in succinct form: "Il y a en nous un certain regard métaphysique sur le présent où notre personne puise l'aliment de sa continuité." (*Présence et Prophétie*).

In these pages, Claudel appears as a man fully reintegrated with the physical universe and with the detailed extensive drama of man unfolding around him. This latter-day prophet, for whom truth is to be found within a precious body of doctrines, wants first to make us feel close to the original creation, to have us move far back in time to the original act of love by which the world exists and by which we exist in the world. Then, Claudel would make us, by the power of his word, witnesses to the waywardness of man, to his fall and to the loss of grace, and finally to the act of redemption on the cross.

The book, taken as a whole, is a vibrant strong testimony to the poet's faith. In these meditations on the cross and on the last seven words of Our Lord, Claudel's faith is presented not as something which can be fully understood, but as a force which is able to embrace and conquer all of creation. He is the type of man who found in his religion the coherence and the completeness which his nature and his mind needed. It is impossible to read these meditations without seeing Claudel standing close beside the Jewish patriarch who counts his flock and worries over the delinquents. He speaks always in the present tense. All the stories of the Bible are one with his own. The person of Claudel is episodic in this book, but that is because he is fully present in all the characters he calls up. The history of the Israelites is precisely the history of the modern world for Claudel. Each event in history has a double meaning: the literal historical truth it represents and the mystery it conceals. Endless is the meaning throughout history of such events as: the fall of Adam, the blood of Abel, the nakedness of Noah, the father's curse on his son.

The mystery of the cross is the central preoccupation on every page of this book, but Claudel does not attempt to organize a treatise on the subject. The title chosen is explicit and accurate. The poet is contemplating the cross. The last seven words are examined in turn and initiate meditations on seven phases of suffering. To understand something of the supernatural meaning of suffering is the goal of these meditations. The story itself of the crucifixion and the justification it offers to countless Old Testament texts teach the poet that Christ did not come in order to destroy suffering, but to suffer with us. He did not come in order to destroy the cross, but to place Himself on it. Suffering, then, is the fundamental characteristic of human nature. Through the experience of suffering, man reaches some understanding of the absolute and universal value of life. The suffering of each man is necessary, and he is not free to escape it or reject it. Like grace itself, it comes to man without his willing it, without his asking for it. The saint is the type of sufferer whom God does not leave in peace.

Throughout this book, in the introductory chapter on the cross, in each of the meditations on the last seven words, in the prayers and the appendix, Claudel writes as if he were convinced that by the act of writing he would learn more about some of the mysteries with which he is concerned. He feels a great need to understand. To love God is very much bound up with some degree of understanding God. He derives pleasure from his own speech, even from his own loquaciousness. Everything serves to illuminate his reactions and those of his readers: theological references, mystical intuitions, personal memories and anecdotes, the chance remark, old antipathies.

In the composition of this book, Claudel draws upon all his multiple resources of writer and poet. There are instances of prolonged metaphors, lists of verbs used to enforce a single idea, examples of colloquialisms and slang, explosions of vehemence. This poet's faith, which is without secrets and without hesitations, is consubstantial with his life. He looks upon himself as the guardian of that metaphysical power bequeathed by the Fathers of the Church, which he must expose again and call upon in the defense of his position. He is the opposite of the modern French poets, often referred to as the *poètes maudits,* who find no satisfaction in their destiny and who rebel against the order of things in the world and in society. Whereas the *poète maudit* looks upon all of society as inimical, Claudel has very specific enemies whom he names with scorn and vehemence. After insulting them to their faces, he continues his way. He is more peremptory and far more absolutistic in his ideas than the *poètes maudits.* The most obvious enemies of Claudel's ideas and manner of speech would be the pure Rationalists who would discount all mystical experience, the Jansenists who would emphasize morality in their religious life, Gallicans who would stress the autonomy of the French Church, the disciples of Gide who would cultivate their rights of doubt and hesitation, the Surrealists who would emphasize the powers of the subconscious and the dream world, and finally, perhaps, the strict grammarians who would be irritated by Claudel's violation of rules.

With such a theme as the crucifixion, Claudel may well give the impression that he is embracing the entire world in order to make intelligible what for Christians is the central event in the world's history. The gigantic figure of the cross is a perpetual manifestation of the Host. The poet looks upon it as the one dazzling sign which is able to pierce our blindness. In it he sees manifested the total simplicity of truth, the one symbol strong enough to defeat man's skepticism and bitterness. Thanks to the cross, the universe is filled with a Presence which gives it its equilibrium, its meaning and its unity. The principal vision seen by this poet before the cross coincides with the vision of the *Odes* of Claudel, in which the world ceases to be an enigma and becomes a text that can be read and understood.

WALLACE FOWLIE

Part One

A Poet Before The Cross

ONCE AGAIN, in this thirty-third year of the nineteenth centenary of our redemption, the Church is taking out the huge prophetic tapestries from the treasures of her art and, in the midst of the shuffling of feet and the murmuring of a people gathered in the darkness, is raising, under the light of funeral candles, in the choir itself, the special cloth and the instrument of our salvation. Outside of time and almost outside of space (for in this New World which I am now planning to leave, the entourage and the setting, consequences of the immediate will of man rather than of history and of racial necessity, have a certain quality of reflection, of a reality transcribed and continued, reduced by a part of its natural weight) I watch the long Sacrifice eternally prescribed *in the middle of the earth*. The contrite attentive public moving about and expanding between the pillars is doubtless not very different from the public which filled Jerusalem in that month of Nizan, thirty-seven years before Titus. But in the choir, the group of priests around the old archbishop, in the exercise of the ceremonies and the solemn exchange of intoned conver-

3

sations, mingled with the invisible celebrants of the Upper Chamber and Calvary, resumes contact with the initial Event once more perpetrated in its liturgical form, and restores at the foot of the altar the source of the sacraments: the bread, the wine, the fire and water, the balsam and oil.

Is not that good odor which filled the banquet hall when Mary Magdalen had broken the pot of precious ointment and poured it over the Saviour's head, the same which the priests two by two are going to recover and inhale on Maundy Thursday from the golden ampullas which the Pontiff's hand has consecrated? *Nardi spicati*, the Gospel of Saint Mark tells us. An oil we have to buy on trust and on the word of the merchant, because, for fear lest it evaporate, it is given to us in a vessel without an opening: the sealed up fountain of our delight, an hermetic guaranteed paradise, an entire garden concentrated in alabaster. And another text demonstrates the lesson of the spikenard distilled, not from the leaf, but from the spike itself—grains which have hoarded the most delicate perfume of the flower. This is the royal ampulla broken and streaming from the fingers of Magdalen, like an opened rose, like a heart bursting, in the midst of that committee of judges and professors around the unrecognized guest, like a great sudden effusion of joy and tears. This burial of Jesus which completes the burial of baptism is the Gospel escaping in every direction from the sacrificed container and filling the entire Church and the entire earth. For His baptism Christ had the holiest of the children of woman, but for His consecration, preceding His supreme enthronement, He chose a sinful woman.

Let us continue attentively and meticulously to follow the office and note down on a sheet of paper everything that strikes us.

First, it is that strange bugbear Mark alone mentions. Who

4

effusion, we considered its vertical efflorescence, we should see that different fibers are twined on that vital stem, like a vein upon an artery. The Chalice is both a root pointing below[4] and a cup dilated toward the summit. The *summit* is God according to these words of Scripture. *I am from on high*, and *Delight in what is on high*, and *below* is all that is not God, all that from the depths of the Void is called by Him into existence, all that which in relation to Him is difference, all that which—on his invitation, on solicited commotion—is both means and obstacle. Seen in this light, the Chalice is the instrument by which God put His lips to His Creation and communicates with what is different from Him, and what, O Lord, is more different than evil and sin? It is this particular bitterness which is our specific work and which we bring to Him to taste. A bitterness so terrible that in Gethsemane sacred Humanity thrust it aside with fright, and on the Cross, after tasting the infamous sponge impregnated and dripping with it, He turned his head aside.[5]

But the Chalice which is the instrument of communication is also that of intoxication, of that expanded confused state where the soul forgets its boundaries and its differences, and which, related to love, is both desire and sleep: Adam's sleep and Noah's, the sleep of Our Lord Himself on the gallows. That is why the Psalmist, wishing to depict the Lord in that somewhat scandalous state of transgression of His own limitations, does not fear using this unusual image: *Like some warrior that lay bemused with wine* (Ps. 77:65). But if the bounds can be passed by God as concerns man, He allowed them to be passed in the other direction, in accord with the magnani-

4. *Poisonous shoot* (Hebr. 12:15). *Take care that no poisonous shoot is allowed to spring up.*

5. *Deep thy cup shall be as hers, wide as hers (sister's).* (Ezechiel 23:32). *Sororis.* cf. *My bride, my true love.* (Song of Songs 4:12).

9

mous answer of James and John to the Saviour's question: *Whether they can drink from His cup?—We can.—You can in truth!* Consider the beauty and the awesomeness of this Chalice which from every side is borne to our lips![6] Consider the reactions of sin, original and superadded, under grace which is mingled with it so astonishingly[7]—I almost said, is assimilated with it! Consider the fundamental bitterness which is served to us ingeniously so that we taste completely, to the dregs, by turning the glass around, in order not to lose any of the penitential medicinal[8] power of this mixed drink where the poisoned residue is combined with the congenital mire! But this supreme flower, this opened crater which we use for offering up, is also that gaping thing which asks and receives, according to the words of the psalm (80:11), *Open thy mouth wide, and thou shalt have thy fill.* *Vena vitae,* other texts taken from Proverbs tell us, *fovea profunda.* It is the supreme kiss in which the soul, forgetful of *the house of its father* (Ps. 44:11), opens up through all its pores *to this vein of divine counsel,* to the direct operation on it of the infused Cause which proceeds to its restoration. *We have a cup that we bless; is not this cup we bless a participation in Christ's blood?* (I Cor. 10:16). It is a double reciprocal benediction. We open ourselves and Christ descends between the walls of our being.

There is another feature of the Chalice. It is both inexhaustible and measured, a finite container capable of an infinite

6. *Well filled my cup.* (Ps. 22:5). *A round for thee, now, from yonder cup the Lord holds in his hand.* (Hab. 2:16).

7. *In the Lord's hand foams a full cup of spiced wine.* (Ps. 74:9).

8. *Thou hast drunk deep of a cup that numbs the senses.* (Is. 51:17). *Thou shalt drain it to the dregs.* (Jer. 49:12). *Drink it thou shalt, ay, drain it to the dregs.* (Ezechiel 23:34). *He drew me up out of a deadly pit.* (Ps. 39:3).

content, the whole which has become our part, according to the astonishing word of psalm 72:26, *God will be eternally my inheritance.* Without ceasing to be itself, the Expression of Divinity takes our form and measure, and adapts the inexhaustible to our own capacity.

And since the shadow of the adorable recipient continues to project itself on this empty paper, why should I not profit from it to write out under this august sign a few hazardous ideas which finally command the attention of the reader of the one Book? The agnostic, positivist, materialist and minimist bias applied to Scripture has resulted in disappointing and grotesque conclusions. You will have to read a few books of Bible criticism to realize the degree of madness, stupidity, absurdity and arbitrariness which human vanity, goaded on by the Baal of flies, has driven the souls of pedants. It is the moth which imagines it is studying a tapestry while devouring simultaneously its form, color and substance. Rather than following the Letter in the Holy Books, the crass textual criticism, the pseudo-historical fantasies, the gratuitous hypotheses which are usually inept, on the psychology and intention of the writers, we should humbly admit with the Church and the Fathers that the Bible is the word of God, and the Holy Spirit is the constant inspirer who from one end to the other guided the pen and mobilized the vocation of diverse writers. And then immediately what broadening of horizon there is, what an interest in this direct work of God, comparable to the work we bring to the accomplishments of nature, what wealth in the sense of a vast number of references and comparisons! If the Bible is really the *Word of God*, with what total respect, fervent attention, ingeniousness in bringing to it reinforcements and favorable resonances, should we study its intonations, styles of composition and developments, and, above all, the intention in the multiple game of allusions and correspondences! What joy to be at the foot of the Logos and to listen with all of one's soul and intelligence to that speech! These are not the archives of the earth placed at our disposal to explore as well as possible with the miner's pick and the chemist's test-tube. This is the History of the Universe considered from God's viewpoint and released to our examination. It is not a chaos of facts which condition a wobbly obscure explanation, but the very meaning which attracts and harmonizes events and coordinates secondary causes into a continuous teaching, into a *Suite*. We have not here before us the bric-à-brac of a bazaar, a vast number of small incoherent objects which must be reduced to powder by obstinate labor, but vast synclinal areas, a maze of different strata appearing and disappearing, and, upset by emersions, a huge school of testimonials worked upon by movements comparable only to geological crackings and recoveries: a limitless significance! It is God himself who, with one hand crumples, shapes, composes the matter and the display of His Creation, and with the other, goes to the trouble of explaining it to us, in His manner, which is different from ours.

This study of the Bible as the work of a single author (having his vocabulary, repertory, rhetorical and stylistic methods, special attitudes, ways of development and transition), and the transporting to the edition of a series of Books through successive prophets the gestures which He used to create the world, is the story which the early Fathers carried on and one which offers the investigator a limitless and constantly renewed subject matter. Elsewhere I have treated the question of imagery and vocabulary. But if we restrict ourselves to the New Testament, it is obvious that in the Gospels (and also in the Epistles), the ideas are developed in a special way which has no analogue in any profane literature. And in this regard, how incomparable is the four-fold document composed of blatantly independent writings, each of a particular delectable style, and of a similar combination of traits! Where can be found in historical literature so convincing an *exhibit* whose slight discrepancies prove their sincerity, for nothing arouses the suspicion of a trained judge as much as the exterior uniformity of testimonials? And within the Gospels that essential flower, the quadruple story of the Passion, which precisely for our deep joy during these last days have been read to us once again, might be called views of the same landscape taken on different days and by means of different rays, such as blue or infra-red. And throughout it all, that special style of the story which, carried ahead by a continuous movement, has, however, interruptions, intervals and very curious inversions[9] (the best example is the parenthesis in Saint Matthew which opens the story of the Resurrection) and continues, not in a naively chronological sense, but, as in the rest of Holy Scripture, through a system apparently illogical in allusions, shadings and assortments, side connections, in sudden flashes, in anastomosis and splices comparable to the most delicate anatomical drawings. Suddenly the earth opens and gives us unexpectedly, gratuitously, those lilies of the field which disconcert the involved labor of exegetes.

Saint Luke, always so original, in whose accent I like to believe I hear a sweet feminine sound—virginal and Virgilian, like a pure echo of Mary's voice itself—gives us the clearest

9. These intervals of the Gospel exposition may be compared to those "squares" where all kinds of streets begin and end. *I searched for him in the squares*, says the Song of Songs, and the Apocalypse reveals to us that *the two witnesses* (the two Testaments) under their rough covering shout *on the squares* where their corpses remain exposed three days, for the greatest satisfaction of various professors, demonstrators and necrophagans.

13

picture of the Last Supper, where so many details remain obscure.[10] According to his story, the supreme meal of the Son of God with men was divided into two phases, in two periods of time, and during the interval between them would have been said most of the speeches reported by Saint John. In the first phase, the Son of Man, surrounded by His Church, consumed and absorbed in Himself under the solid and liquid species all the Creation, all the figures of the Old Testament. *I shall eat no more*, He says over the food, *this Passover*, this viaticum, this ration of the traveler which helps him to go farther, this food of desire, *until it is fulfilled in the Kingdom of God*. And above the cup: *Take it and divide it among you*, share in keeping with your own needs and with the offices of fraternal charity, the virtue of common expression which is contained in it. *As for me, I shall no longer drink from the generation of the vineyard*, I shall stop feeding myself in the temporal mode on the human vineplant, drawing from it through successive generations the support of my incarnation, *until that day*, Matthew and Mark add, *when I will drink it again in the Kingdom of God*; that is, when, through the fig-

10. For example, what meaning can one give the word *recumbere, discumbere?* It is quite impossible to imagine Christ and the Apostles indolently stretched out on beds around a table. In all the pictures of the Last Supper, no artist has ever dared or tried that. How does one eat and drink in such a position? How would Saint John's gesture and the invitation to Judas be possible? They must have been simple benches on which the Saviour and His guests were seated, and they were served from behind the table. In that case, *discumbere* would have a mystical meaning: it would mean perfect repose, an extension and peaceful relaxation of all the limbs in the presence of food, *coram mensa*. The piece of bread held out to Judas indicates that he must have been quite close to the Saviour, probably on the left, Saint John staying on the right. It would be impossible to think that for the eating of the sacramental lamb, the Son of Man would not have scrupulously conformed to the stipulations of the Law (standing, barefooted, the staff in His hand, etc.).

14

ure, I will draw reality to me.[11] In the second phase Our Lord took again the bread and wine of which, in harmony with the Church, He perfected the symbolic consummation, in order to transform them substantially into Himself and distribute them to His people after raising them to the dignity of Sacraments.

Thus rises up at last, in the center of the History of Nature, the supreme Lily, the perfect Chalice, the aspiring and breathing Flower in which the work of Creation is resumed and

11. *A vineyard I have of my own* (Song of Songs 8:12). *Bid them drink deep at thy fountain of contentment* (Ps. 35:9). *Would that thou wert my brother, nursed at my own mother's breast! Then I would meet thee in the open street and kiss thee, and earn no contemptuous looks.* (Song of Songs 8:1). Extremely interesting texts suitable for commentary here. This is the complete passage in which they are found: *Solomon had a vineyard; and when he gave the care of it to vine-dressers, each of these must pay a thousand silver pieces for the revenue of it. A vineyard I have of my own, here at my side; keep thy thousand pieces, Solomon, and let each vine-dresser have his two hundred.* The Vineyard, naturally, is the Church (constantly in Scripture likened to the Soul, to Mary and to Wisdom), which the Saviour on the cross confided to the keeping of the clergy. It is the vineyard *which has the people*, which gives them form in itself and which another text compares to an *embattled array* (S. of Songs 6:3): this is the Church Militant. It is in her that all find that peace, not *such as the world gives*, but of which He alone could authentically say: *I give you my peace*. A word which the third invocation of the *Agnus Dei* recalls before communion, and the solemn kiss at that moment (*deosuler Te*) which the Celebrants give one another. (*Accipite et dividite inter vos.*) It can then cry out: *Facta sum coram Eo quasi pacem reperiens*. The fruit of this vineyard is so precious that the amateur capable of evaluating it does not hesitate to offer a thousand pieces of silver for it. Silver is the reflection of gold, and the Book of Kings tells us that at the time of King Solomon, the first monometallurgist, it was of no value. It has the character of a divided value, and adjusted to the *thousand* needs of daily practical life. It is money. It can be assimilated to infinitely varied good works which permit us to *draw* on divine Grace. The number one thousand indicates both division and fullness.

crowned. In the course of this long story, whose progress and commentary these eight days ceremoniously depict before us, we have still to understand the transplanting, from that reserved Garden where its bulb in the ground waited for the activity of the Seventy weeks, to this complete paradise which is the world, that transplanting of the living contrivance of unification, clarification and perfume, and how, during the night, from darkened Israel to the blind Gentile world, took place the handing over of the Son of Man.

Thus Psalm 83:11 tells us that *one day spent in the courts of the Lord* capitalizes in itself thousands of years. Isaias (7:23) shows us a thousand feet of vineyard equivalent to a thousand pieces of silver, of that metal out of which was made the auspicious cup hidden in the bottom of Benjamin's sack. An amazing passage in Genesis shows us the nomad Abimelech paying a thousand silver pieces to Abraham as a ransom to free himself from Sara, wife and sister of the latter, whom he had seized without recognizing. But possibly it was she who captured him. (Gen. 20:16) *See, I am giving this brother of thine a thousand silver pieces; such amends will enable thee to look the world in the face, wherever thou goest; only, do not forget that thy pretence was discovered.* If divine Joy (*Soror mea sponsa*) uncovered her face before us, how would we find enough courage to finish our pilgrimage and complete our negotiation, when a single glance of this sister-wife suffices to pierce our heart almost mortally? (S. of Songs 4:9.) Let us then pay our ransom in works of mercy which will give us the right to complete our course in the exterminating presence of time. But may she remember that henceforth there is between us this understanding, this bargain, *and that one day we caught her in the act.* Until we see her face to face, may she wear that veil, like the one which separated the Holy from the Holiest, which is the condition of our merit, the instrument of our provisional separation and the guarantee of our security. (cf. the veil which Moses coming back from Sinai put over his face. Exod. 34:33).

As for the contribution—I was about to say 200 dollars—which belongs to the vineyard keepers, it is a figure composed of two perfect unities, exactly equivalent, like the sicle of the Sanctuary itself, spoken of in Exodus (ch. 30) and whose weight of twenty farthings we are carefully reminded of everywhere. Every Israelite

The public life of Jesus Christ began, as it ended, with a meal, the symbolic banquet of Cana where the spiritual Husband inaugurated His mystical relations with Humanity and transformed into an intoxicating wine the water of the Commandments for the purification and the restoration of souls: water drawn up from the springs of Paradise. Then began and continued for three years that period I will call emanation, when the Saviour seemed to hide His face and let His works speak for Him. It is like Good Friday when the crucifix is brought to us veiled, and when from the cloth gradually drawn aside one hand emerges, then the other, and finally the face and the entire body. From all the stirred up land of Israel, from the depths of the prophetic tradition, is made clear and gradually formulated, with a more and more general insistence, that question which the manna from heaven had placed on the tongues of the escaped from Pharao: *Man hu?* what is it? *Tu, quis es?* It is the solemn question which John the Bap-

---

must carry in his palm half of this sicle when he presents himself for the census, *as each man is added to the count* (Ex. 30:13), that is, when, a conscript of Eternity, he passes to his definitive name, to compare Eternity to the inviolable measure preserved in the Tabernacle. (*Every valuation must be made by sanctuary reckoning.* Lev. 27:25.) It is always a question of a comparison between human measurement and divine measurement applied one on the other (like the Prophet and the dead child), of which many examples are found in Scripture. Miraculously Grace comes to join with our good will. And verse 15 carefully adds that the abundance or the meagreness of our personal means have no effect on this mystical balance. Therefore when our text tells us that the *keepers of the Vineyard*, namely the priests, are made the holders of 200 pieces of silver, that means that they have received guardianship of a spiritual treasure—in other terms—of the sacraments, of a common treasure—where God and man each deposits separately and where our initial share of the required provisions provokes an equivalent effusion, but equivalent according to the *sanctuary reckoning*, which *abounds* beyond Justice and *superabounds beyond sin*. (cf. Rom. 5:20).

tist, in the name of the entire Old Testament, administered to the New-comer: *Tu, quis es?* And the Lord answered in the words of His action: *The blind see, the lame walk, the lepers are made clean, the deaf hear, the dead are raised to life.* (Matth. 11:5) And he added this amazing word: *Blessed is the man who does not lose confidence in me,* which means, who does not find in the miraculous and kind acts I perform, an occasion for scandal (and this refers to all the shadings of anger, from indignation to a dull irritation). This speech is worthy of being examined.

What seems to have shocked the Synagogue (those representatives of organized religion) in Christ's deeds? The reproach which returns on each page of the Gospel, is that He performed miracles, that God carried out His own business, on the Sabbath, the very day when, in a solemn declaration, He fixed Himself and imposed Himself, in a kind of contract or charter similar to that of His Rest. He has no right to this! the agents of the Chosen People cry out in a piercing voice. He has not the right to come and upset us! This is the Seventh Day! He deprived Himself of the right of interference. He separated Heaven and Earth. For Himself he took Heaven, and gave us the Earth. It was not easy to arrange. If now He permits Himself to intervene personally and rearrange His work, He is not keeping His word. It is a scandal, an unbearable transgression! And the sincerity of this complaint is such that since the day of the first Parousia, it has not ceased filling all Humanity. The miracle is the scandal *par excellence.*

> In the name of the King it is forbidden to God
> To perform a miracle in this place.

Malebranche is here to forbid Him formally to manifest Himself through individual wills. And when our modern apologists try all kinds of circumlocutions and precautions to ex-

cuse, veil and minimize these *coups d'état* which visibly tor-
ment them, and to make out of them insignificant miracles
which science will explain and vulgarize one day or another,
what are they doing except taking back for themselves the
troubled, discontented and irate pose of the Authorities of
Israel?[12]

Thus, in order to save those blood-shot eyes fascinated by
the spectacle of the public square (sad servants of a poisoned
heart), Christ for three years disappeared in a certain sense
under cover of the good He did. He *passed*, as Saint Peter says,
doing good. He does not only speak, He acts in similes and
parables. In remaking the body, He manifests Himself and signifies Himself to impure spirits, to the deaf, the blind, the
crippled. But when they want to seize Him, before His time
has come, when the crowd for whom He has multiplied the
bread wants to make Him King, when the Pharisees try to take
hold of Him, He escapes. *He passes through their midst.* He

---

12. We see however on many pages of Scripture the ungodly
asking for signs which God refuses. Thus in Matth. 12:39, *The
generation that asks for a sign is a wicked and unfaithful generation; the only sign that will be given it is the sign of the prophet
Jonas.* And in Luke 23:8, Herod (the adulterer) was overjoyed at
seeing Jesus sent to him, *for he had been eager to have sight of
him.* In the same way Dives at the bottom of hell asks Abraham
unsuccessfully for some sign which will serve as warning to his
sons. And elsewhere the Lord reproaches His listeners for needing
signs in order to believe (John 4:48). And yet: *If I had not done
what no one else ever did in their midst they would not have been
in fault* (John 15:24). And still elsewhere (Matth. 11:23); *Sodom
itself*, etc. Thus God refuses to allow Himself to be maneuvered
by curiosity and pride. It is not a question of amusing us, but of
piercing the rock (Ps. 77:15), of initiating the ways of the Almighty for the profit of souls over all the obstacles of habit. The
characteristic of a miracle is that it goes directly from God to man.
It is addressed to the heart by an immediately creative power. The
ray of Grace attacks us, following the latent dispositions of need,
of desire and fruit, which it alone discerns, by that fundamental,

is no longer there. *There is one standing in your midst of whom you know nothing* (John 1:26). To find Him, you have to seek Him in those matters which are His Father's (Luke 2:49). He Himself avoids answering. It is from the hearts of

---

formative part of us which precedes our faculties. Intelligence, the apparatus of analysis and taste in us, has other means of reaching truth. The miracle passes through the zone of dialectical elaboration. It is Being which directly seizes being. That is why Our Lord in the text I quoted above indicates, as the example of a miracle, the case of Jonas, namely divine action penetrating to the *heart of the earth*, and what is more the *heart of the earth* than that which beats in the side of the children of Adam? Thus in the Prophets we see Bel swallowing the Church and God obliging him to restore what was not made for him. *I will make him disgorge his treasures. You that are my own people, separate yourselves from her* (Jer. 51:44).

This does not mean that the miracle will not furnish nourishment for the intellect since it is addressed to the entire man in us of whom the intellect is an essential aspect. But it does it, so to speak, laterally and *a posteriori*. It increases the datum for the intellect. It adds to the quantity of matter on which it has to work. It furnishes it a *sign* which, duly accepted, procures for the mind, loyally used, the means of accurate and easy conclusions. This is the meaning of the answer Our Lord makes to the emissaries of Saint John: You have seen what I did. Conclude. I leave to your intelligence the ability to go from the fact to the consequence. But precisely it is this consequence which terrifies a depraved heart. It wants a sign which will amuse its curiosity and feed its machinery for arguments, but it is terrified of that hand over it which is preparing to remake it. *Ask for a sign*, says the prophet Achaz. But look out, King of Israel! It is a sign *which goes from the depths of the earth to the summit of heaven*. Thus confronted, Achaz is afraid and modestly withdraws. He understood what it was about, and preferred not to be exposed to the unknown, to that moving about in the depths which was preparing to devour him. *I do not want to tempt the Lord God.* But the day comes, despite the reluctance of that man of the world, when the new Jonas satisfies with his flesh the appetite of the freed monster, when he unites with him flesh to flesh, and when Being Itself comes to fill with Its presence that emptiness in us which is non-being.

those who question Him, it is from the Rock itself which He *pierced* (Ps. 77:15-Matth. 16:15) and on which He suddenly confers the power of *crying out* (Luke 19:40) that He elicits an answer. The Waiting of all the centuries is, during those three years, pushed to its extreme point of exasperation. All of Judea is gradually saturated with a questioning from which there is no longer an escape. The moment has come to speak clearly.[13]

Then it was that for the celebration of the last Passover, the Son of Man returned publicly, solemnly, and in a way officially, to Jerusalem where, until that time, he had made brief and almost furtive appearances.[14] Every escape blocked, the hour came to confront Israel at last, to give over to her and place in her hands the full realization of that Waiting of the entire Universe, of which, through centuries, milleniums and eons, she had been the constituted lawful expression. The necessary time and means were given her to reach an opinion. Numerous signs were furnished. Prophecies were fulfilled and the center, its two feet on the earth, was manifested, at the appointed hour, to the immense network of the converging plans. Now came the moment of supreme clarification. Until now Christ had expressed Himself to God; namely, by acts which are the distinctive specialty of God, of a Creator, and by general behavior from which He told us to draw conclusions. Now it was He attacking and calling. It was He questioning Israel directly, and bearing down, so to speak, on her with all His weight to call up the indispensable question so that it in its turn would provoke the eternal, explicit and definitive answer. Speak, speak, Israel! You are needed. There is no

13. *Now thou art speaking openly enough; this is no parable thou art uttering.* (John 16:29).

14. *He says that He is not going there, and yet He does go.* (John 7:8).

backing down now. It is up to you to utter the sacramental Yes. The hour has come. *Ecce adsum!* It is the Son of God, clothed with all the attributes of His mission, who comes Himself to refer to you, to put it, so to speak, into your mouth. Speak, speak, speak, Israel!

It began with the resurrection of Lazarus. Here it was no longer a question, as in the other two earlier cases told by the Gospel, of somewhat episodic events, realized in obscure corners of Galilee—and in a manner of speaking, incidentally, as if they were not deliberate—throughout a long career of preaching and charity. One could easily say, in more or less good faith, that Eliseus had done as much. But this time it was at the vigil of the Passover, in the presence of all of Israel convened, at the gates of Jerusalem, on the threshold of the Temple, in the presence of an eminent man, in dazzling publicity, prepared and poignant; in so insolent a proof that we can well believe it was for the human authorities standing opposite, a scandal and a defiance, that the *Fact of the prince*, that the Fact of God, was perpetrated. It could not be said that the fellow was sleeping. He had been in the tomb for three days, and besides you had only to get the smell. Moreover Jesus did not invoke the Almighty. He affirmed His union in substance with Him. He commanded and acted as if He was one with God, like one having authority over life and death. *Lazarus, come out!* (John 11:43). It was to the entire crowd listening, to Jerusalem over yonder trembling and grinding its teeth that He addressed the question which Magdalen heard first: *Credis huc? I am (Ego sum) the resurrection and the life: he who believes in me, even dead, will live. Do you believe that?* Many did believe. But the great politicians of the Sanhedrin were not so easily convinced. The dead can rise up as much as they want. That was only one further disorder, or rather it was the supreme disorder, the intolerable insult to the established Order, to nature and to that second nature called habit. It could not go on for long this way. Everything was turning about and collapsing, everything was going to fall on us. It has to come to an end. It is out of place! You can't trust the extraordinary and the exceptional! You don't know how matters stand. You can't trust the extraordinary, the inexplicable, the new! There will be a return shock and then we will be in a fine fix: *Et venient Romani. Then the Romans will come, and make an end of our city and our race* (John 11:48). The attitude of Israel, of resisting God, was definitively consolidated. *It is no!* In vain did God Himself make supplication at the foot of ancient Judea, the Almighty was not able to bend Israel. But by a surprising deviation, what He was not able to stop, He profited from. The Holy Spirit breathed on Hell, inspired Caiphas and drew from him that very word which the Universe had been waiting for and which the annual Pontiff had authority to utter: *It is best for us if one man is put to death for the sake of the people* (John 11:50). It was decided. The time had come for the prophecies to be fulfilled. *Was it not to be expected that Christ should undergo these sufferings?* (Luke 24:26.)

The resolution of the Synagogue was followed by a secret terror. They would doubtless have preferred to temporize and wait for a predicament. They would have liked to rub out silently this intruder, and gently install him in a state of non-existence. They would have liked to avoid all the chances of damage which come from any brutal public action. In the midst of Passover, with the crowd of pious people and strangers (which Josepheus has described for us), all the unknown element, and the latent destruction which this formidable Impostor was able to create in the seething dark mass—the operation was delicate; prudence, experience, common sense, everything advised abstaining. *Non in die festo*, as I have just

23

heard roared and shouted *a capella* by the Sistine Chapel choir which with formidable gusto, once again expresses the crowd, today sunken and inert around me, *non in die festo ne forte tumultus fieret in populo.*

It is true, *but the hour is at hand.* What you have to do, Israel, *fac citius,* do it now. It is Passover. It is the obligatory date indicated by the full moon. This is the Passover which for centuries your Saviour had desired to consummate with you: *longed for with a great longing.* Since you slip away from His invitation, He Himself will force the door and invite Himself, whether you like it or not, to your symbolic meal. *The oxen have been killed, and the fatlings* (Matth. 24:4). This is the day when the Lamb is to be slaughtered for good: *unless blood is shed, there can be no remission of sins* (Heb. 9:20).

The liaison officer is already at work. Through some unheard of chance, an intimate associate of the adversary brings up his collaboration. With him there is no fear of any cruel disappointments which once left us ridiculous and distressed. He is an Apostle: he has the power to deliver—*tradere*—Christ, as today a bad priest has the power to consecrate. But haste is necessary: Judas is possessed by an eloquent persuasive demon. Tomorrow it will be too late, because he has to confess, that under the nose of Simon Peter he begins to smell of something burning.

. . . What are those cries all of a sudden? What is that hurrah which just broke out, that enormous crackling noise you hear only on days of riot and revolution, when the human voice replaces all other noises? It is a kind of detailed teeming elocution, detached like a delirious commentary on a roll of thunder, on gusts of a hurricane. It flares up, stops, starts up again, grows; and suddenly the sharp cries of women are almost more than the nerves can bear. Our senators, painfully tensed and pricked in the right place, jumped onto the terraces with a mad rush which compromised the security of their phylacteries. And then what do they see? Oh, it is not the modest triumph which later a well-intentioned commentator will pretend to have surmised. It was to end like that! There is not one terrace not fringed with bodies, not one relief, not one balustrade not decorated with human garlands hanging on. And yonder from one end to the other of the valley it is the same thing, along all the roads and paths, you see only files of people running and goading their beasts from behind to make them go faster. But what is seen from the top of Sion is something which, in the pit of their dried stomachs, makes Annas and Caiphas tremble and provokes between the heart and the liver that clash which the Talmud speaks of. Before the east gate is a human mass like dough or grease, and in the midst a narrow groove which a single line is following. And behind them—it makes me want to vomit and speak out a bitter flood of oaths—over there, very small, on four legs walking, is an ass followed by another animal without a saddle and on it a white figure. We know too well who He is. We easily recognize that cursed weakness under knees when He turns towards us His awesome face.[15] So it was not enough for Him to have prosecuted us for three years, we the responsible

15. *Pueri Hebraeorum*, shouts the choir which comes again to draw from the old antiphonies the tumultuous triumphant sound of ancient buoyancy, while from one end of the church to the other all hands are armed with green branches, *comportantes ramos olivarum obviaverunt Domino clamantes et dicentes: Hosannah in excelsis!* Another antiphon answering this, speaks of clothing flung under the Saviour's feet. You hear the curses of the terrible bourgeois who see this spectacle from the top of Sion and who devour it with their terrible eyes, *terribilibus oculis*, under bristling eyebrows. The brigands! They have destroyed my olive grove! And what is that pantomime? What are they doing? They are dancing! They are clapping their hands! My word! they are undressing! They are throwing their clothes under the feet of that charlatan of woe! I hope my daughters are not at the window!

25

men of Israel, from Galilee to the Rock of the Desert! Now it is in us, in our own conscience that He comes to get us! He Himself comes to meet us! It is our own door He breaks down at the head of the mass of people moving, of a human tide about to carry everything off! It is our own beard His terrible hand seizes! There is no more time to hesitate. It is between Him or us! If He misses us, we will not miss Him!

So, how sweet and refreshing will the affirmations of Judas that night seem to us (in spite of his boasting in such bad taste)! It is so plausible, so obviously necessary a plan, that one cannot restrain a certain elation. Everything fits together smoothly, the most learned of those pundits says into his black beard, but first let us have this excitement quiet down a bit. Let us profit from the supreme truce which the last days before Passover offer us, and then we will leap on Him suddenly! After all, it is shaping up now, it is becoming possible. They will get rid of Him in a flash, in the confusion of a feast day, while the people are thinking only about their devotions.

The action has started now and will continue without respite until Maundy Thursday. Now it is Jesus attacking. He is not waiting for someone else to seek Him out or discover Him. He Himself each morning goes up to the Temple[16] and seizes by the beard, by the throat *coram populo* those living sepulchres, and inexorably rattles those soulless bones in which the petrifaction of avarice and pride preceded the decomposition of the flesh.[17] Come now, do what you have to do! *Fac citius! fac citius!* Yes, I am Jesus! Yes, I am the Messiah! Yes, I am

16. Whence he unceremoniously expels the usurers, to the great dismay of those gentlemen of the Sanhedrin! One day's sale, at the Passover, is not a slight matter, and we were counting on it to settle those payments of ours. He is really at home! You could positively say that He is at home!

17. *Son of man, he said, can life return to these bones?* (Ezech. 37:3).

the Son of God! *Before Abraham was, I was! Ego sum! It is I! It is the Principle who speaks to you!* It is God who speaks to you directly and tells you who He is! And if you do not believe Me, here is My Father who is in heaven, who speaks and confirms my affirmations in a clap of thunder. One after the other, the miracles multiply. The man born blind, the man confined to his bed in Bethseda, less obscure, less impotent, less deformed than this people tied with a triple knot, and behind them, through the centuries those tribes endlessly renewed with rheumy-eyed mandarins and false witnesses for whom Christ came as if He had not come, to whom a heart was given to feel nothing, eyes to see nothing with and a mind with which not to understand. To the plea of the Saviour who is thirsty, the human Tree answered by an immediate withering and now henceforth it is withdrawn from the temptation of fruit and is established in the function of gallows. Let it be put up over yonder, on the other side of the dishonored mountain where Jerusalem, under the rays of a sinisterly attentive sun, bears the aspect of a necropolis. Dark afternoons when the Saviour in tears, after the terrible morning struggles, climbs to the Witness stone and comes to feed His heart for the last time on that people who do not want Him!

Do not be grieved, Son of Man! The sacramental kiss which You came to bring to Mankind and which You sorrowingly reproach Simon for not having returned to You (Luke 7:45),[18] is the secret kiss which at the mass the deacon comes to receive reverently from the lips of the Celebrant to distribute then to all the Choir. They return Your visit! You willed it! In its turn, Jerusalem moves toward You! The kiss is moving through the night toward Your heart and Your mouth! It is Your apostle, Judas, who, is officially charged with it. *Judas, is it thus by a kiss that you betray* (or that you *deliver,* which

18. *Come here, my son, and kiss me.* (Gen. 27:26).

27

is the same word) the Son of Man? And how, O Lord, in any other way could he have made delivery of Your person and given it over, as he had pledged to do, to his jailers? Isn't this the meeting You Yourself called with a great desire? Isn't that red haired wretch whose insolent eyes and flat nose lit up from time to time in the light of a torch, the ambassador of someone much greater than the Solomon of the Queen of Sheba—I mean the human soul of those millions of engulfed patriarchs and future priests who cry out with the Bride of the Song: A *kiss from those lips!* And didn't You expect to encounter on our lips, Lord, something else than the taste of our unworthiness and betrayal? What other attraction was able to draw You and hold You? What other mark could be left on our sacred lips by that wretch who was the first in bewilderment to breathe in the Word at its source? Now You belong to him and You will not cease being his! You will not cease being the center now of the brutal mob of passions and drunken soldiers who mistreat You. You have given Yourself up and You have been taken.[19]

Like that terrified intellectual they showed us just now (and who since then, let us hope, rid of his shroud, found the means of recovering his shirt and his personality), we now follow the way Christ took from that first spark of fire in the

19. This is the place of the episode I explained elsewhere of those armed men who looked for Christ and fell backwards as soon as He told them who He was. And also Malchus whose ear was cut off impulsively by Simon Peter: a symbol doubtless of that tempestuous zeal which makes us attack in our listeners the very organ, the funnel and the canal of communication. Happy if the sweet intervention of the Saviour repairs the damage we have done and delicately pastes it together again and fixes it. But how many matadors among the champions of the Church offer to the public the ear of Malchus, as in Spanish bullfights the tenors of the *muleta* offer the ears of the elegantly sacrificed bull? Put your cutlass back in its sheath, brave Veuillot and valiant Léon Bloy! (not to mention P.C.!)

night of midnight, which a wrathful and exalted old woman brandished in her lantern, at the head of a troup of policemen, to the quartering, to the evidence, to the terrible showing on Calvary before the face of all time and all peoples, to the crucifixion at noon.[20]

Now we have joined up with Him again. But we can hardly see Him, despite His being so tall, through all the crowd of dwarfs beating down on Him. The flame of a torch brutally lights up from time to time that face bathed in blood and sweat and which casts in a terrifying way a reflection of the wrath of his assailants. He is like a great stag at bay, stumbling in the midst of the dogs! Right now we are crossing the river David spoke of, toward which cries the great Stag sent by God.[21] Let Him drink from this rapid stream, from these waters which rush swiftly to what is lowest![22] The moment has come when we ourselves shall drink from a surer source and when we shall possess in their principle, outside of time, those pilgrim waters which it pleased the Saviour to appraise on His way to the Cross.

They pulled Him with ropes from the bottom of the depths. He is heavy. Like one of those contentious animals you are allowed to pull out of the cistern on the Sabbath. Let us move on! To go from here to Annas' house, to Caiphas' house, only a short effort is needed. The brigade pushing and yelling, dragging with it all the night owls which an oriental city can provide the night before a holiday, is swallowed up in the judiciary cavern already half-filled. It is the tribunal of shining calabashes and ferocious eyes. It is so crowded you can hardly

20. *Where now is thy resting-place under the noon's heat?* (S. of Songs 1:6)

21. *Nephthali is like a roe-deer that goes free* (Gen. 49:21).

22. *Let him but drink of the brook by the wayside, he will lift up his head in victory* (Ps. 109:7). *So, rejoicing, you shall drink deep from the fountain of deliverance* (Is. 12:3).

29

move. This is the recruited public, a foul-smelling assize court to whom the Son of God will make His statement. They have pushed Christ into that, into such a press that He is one with the flesh of His people. All of Israel is a winepress on Him. And it is there, at the end of an insane questioning, in the inextricable medley of witnesses who condradict one another, that the terrible cry will come forth, the intolerable "Blasphemy" which will divide the world in two: *Yes. It is true. I am God. It is I.* If we could only stop up our ears!

At last! At last we drew it from Him! He said it. From His mouth we heard it! He is God. He said that He was God! *I adjure You by the living God, are You Christ, the Son of the living God? And Jesus said: I am.*

He said it! He is God! He said it! What need of testimony is there? Through all the fissures of the judgment apparatus escapes the terrified whispering which is going to fill the universe and time and unfurl like a tidal wave over quarrelling academies and fallen empires! *He said He was the Son of God! He said He was the Son of God!*

During that time we were not there. We had stayed outside to warm ourselves with the low-born. A little warming at the fire does no harm in the wet cold weather of March. It did not keep us from listening to all that was happening. There was a story going on uninterruptedly beside us which our heart did not relinquish although it does not understand such Latin, a speech divided among three voices who share the main theme. One forms—if I can say this—the horizon. It is joined to that flow of time which we became aware of outside by the wind rising and the slow rising of the full moon whose face is veiled or purified from time to time by pierced clouds. And the other comes from the accident and the circumstance around us, a worried Jerusalem which sleeps badly, its head on a stone. There are cries, sobs, a lamp yonder which we

watch obstinately and which suddenly goes out, in agreement
with that large star in the sky which an invisible hand has just
snuffed. And the third, a deep voice which two or three times
escaped from the cube of masonry! Rather than hearing it, it
would have been better for us never to have been born! But
there is no need to listen to it, and that sharp, piercing, yelp-
ing, terrified voice, overcome by the hysteria of that old rogue
of a high priest, would be enough to trace in our mind a form
we should prefer to have left void. "The boss is really in a
rage," that idiot with a hanging lip says near me with a sneer.
Insults, mad hurrahs and demonic yells come out from that
small hell. It is best to be inconspicious. But He does not have
the upper hand. It is terrible. Everyone is against Him. We
did not realize that they should hate Him that much! And
that was the very moment that ridiculous woman chose to ask
us if we knew Him! No, Madame, no, no, a hundred times no,
we do not know Him! I do not know Him, I tell you! What do
you want me to swear on? It seems to me that the three years
I spent uninterruptedly with Him give enough weight to my
statement. And if it is added to that declaration which once
in a passion of good will I remember making before the face
of the sun on the road of Cesarea of Philippi, it is, you will
agree, a confused situation in which the present moment is a
bit too upsetting for me to try to understand things clearly.
For the present, everything goes badly. The only thing to do
is to get out of the mess without losing face, and I am afraid!
There is only one thing to do—establish in some way a separation between my person and that terrible din outside, with the
heavens collapsing and the earth slipping from under me!
(No! it simply means that Tenebrae has been sung and the
clergy are going to the stipulated noise.) Too bad if the hour
has come for the Prince of this world! We will see tomorrow!
After all, it is not my fault if God has failed. How far away is

the throne of David! Poor Peter the fisherman, what have you gotten involved in? So ... at the end He lost out and Jerusalem after all was right—just as a certain rabbit's heart in me for a long time has been suggesting! I do not know that man!

And all at once, while the words were on his lips, the cock crew (Luke 22:60).

What power gives the cock its sure instinct? says old Job (38:36). Who suddenly in the heart of that frightful night of temptation, who, both counsel and paralysis, mingling with the very substance of our flesh and our mind, called forth that peremptory bird? Whence comes that sharp cry and the echo in the back of our henhouse, of that command of the first day: *let there be light!* The Holy Spirit does not always borrow the accents of the plaintive dove. Here it rises with irresistible authority, like the leader buckling on his belt.[23] Sun affirmation and trumpet of the Last Judgment, come out insolent, gratuitous, immediate, from the depths of my being in the presence of cowards and pedants!

Such is the first *delivery*, the first payment of Jesus Christ which the newly ordained group of Apostles, Judas in revolt and Peter losing interest, operates within constituted Judaism, within the official and authorized spiritual power. This time, it is not a question of a child and of that wailing promise at dawn which an indistinct virgin put into the hands of a dull old man. It is a delivery, legal and paid by arrangement, and no longer of a contestable infant, but of a Christ matured, perfect, public, certified, affirmed, tested, recognized, with full weight, all the clauses of the contract honored. And this is the verified Christ whom the Synagogue, through the authorized organ of its high priest, solemnly declares it does not want, that He does not exist for it, that He is incompatible with its possibilities. It gives Him to the universe, in species

23. *The cock* (*Loins-girt—they call him*). (Prov. 30:31).

represented by Pontius Pilate, procurator of the Roman empire.

Here is Jesus given over to the universe by Judaism. What will He do with it? Jesus is brought to Pilate. A very embarrassed man. Who are You? Where do You come from? What did You do? How do we go about taking You?

The remarkable thing in the story of the Passion is that no one wants Jesus Christ. *He came,* says Saint John, *to his own and his own did not receive him.* The Jews gave Him over to the Gentiles, and the world of the Gentiles did not know what to do with Him. A secret instinct, deep within, told this world that it would be better not to swallow the bait. *Nothing between you and this just man,* advised the wife of Pontius Pilate, who is that thing half-dreaming and sleeping called the Wisdom of Nations, *for I have suffered many things in dreams because of Him.* Pilate tried to send Him back to Herod. But Herod wanted nothing to do with Him. After examining Him, he declared that He was really not amusing. He was a disappointment. I expected something else. Nothing can be drawn out from Him. He does not answer. I beg to be excused. I am only a man of the world. All that I can be asked to furnish, is that blank certificate, in the form of the robe He wears I send Him back to you.[24] And here He is again, more dazzling than ever in my hands, and clothed with that absolution which irony gives to innocence. What if we tried to have Him taken back by those maniacs? *Take Him yourselves and judge Him according to your own law!* Excuse us! answer the Jews, but you forget that you took away from us the power of killing Him. You retained in the world all execu-

---

24. *Their poison seems to eat away the very garments I wear, clings fast about me like the collar of my coat* (Job 30:18). *Ah, but my shift, I have laid it by: how can I put it on again?* (S. of Songs 5:3.)

tive power. All we could do was to bring you Christ, duly authenticated by us. It is up to you alone to finish the business and *execute him, for we have no power to put any man to death* (John 18:31). But there is perhaps still some way of getting out of it. There is a way of putting back into their hands that power of life and death they pretend they do not possess. Right now I have in my storehouse a first class number, one Barabbas (in Hebrew, *son of the father*) who is guilty of all the crimes against social order and human law. There isn't a better example of his class. You can have him. Choose between him and Christ. If you prefer Barabbas, and if you choose Christ and draw Him from that loophole in the law I was ready to let Him profit from, it becomes very evident that you alone are responsible who condemn Him *gladio linguae* by a choice of your deliberate will and for motives foreign to human order. And the Jews, not only the notables, but all of the people, with a common voice and by a kind of plebiscite, the very ones who just now led Jesus in triumph but whose temporal hopes this man in white once again disappointed, cry out, as they stamp their feet, in a voice which still today makes the ceilings of our cathedrals shake: *Non hunc sed Barabbam!* With Barabbas at least you know whom you are dealing with. We've had enough trouble with Jesus. *Tolle! tolle!* Our nation spews Him out! Take Him away! Let us see Him no more! We can't deal with Him any more! Let Him leave us in peace! Let us rid the atmosphere of Him! It is not a question of *guilty* or *not guilty*. We simply don't want anything more to do with Him. We assume all the consequences. *Let his blood fall on our heads and on our children's!* Are you satisfied now? What more do you need?

Three times in succession Pilate came back and left. He questioned in turn Jesus and the people (that people whose

succession, under the roof of Saint Patrick's, is continued today by the mute sullen congregation), and three times in succession there was, through the intervening of Pilate, recom-
mendation of Jesus to Judaism. From neither one nor the
other did Pilate receive a direct full answer. The accused
clearly admitted He was king. That was fine, and it would
therefore be possible to construct a sentence of high treason,
but He declared immediately *that His Kingdom is not of this
world.* Elsewhere, on any act whatsoever, on any attempt
whatsoever of accomplishment, testimonies are non-existent,
the files empty. And there is no way of dragging anything from
those Asiatics except that insolent stupid affirmation: *We
would not have given him up to thee if he had not been a
malefactor* (John 18:30). Thus there is no actual direct cause,
there is nothing on which to attach a judgment, there is no
impropriety, no conflict of right or truth, no contact even
between the public activity of the character and the order I
am responsible for. Everything transpires as if we were in another sphere. And yet the facts are there. Whether it is today
or last Sunday, in one direction or another, there is a commotion in the people such as I have never seen during my two
years of proconsul. Could that crowd be right when it affirms
that in no domain can one establish a rivalry with Caesar, that
no one can call himself King without detracting from the
Prince of this world, without shrinking his importance and
diminishing his power over bodies and souls? This man just
told me that He came *to give witness to the truth.* This is puzzling. What is Truth? that truth of which He claims to be the
agent? And in that case, what are we, my Master the Emperor
and myself? Something fictional? The authority invested in
me is not so safe that it is prudent to allow any insult or re-
striction. Let matters take their course. I wash my hands of

35

them all. In this way, I fulfill for them the legal gesture whose
privilege the priests give me.[25] On the other hand I get rid of
this troublesome King by giving Him over to ignominious
death. On the other hand, shame as well as responsibility falls
on the Jews. I am going to face them with this: INRI, JESUS
OF NAZARETH KING OF THE JEWS. There it is. Look at it. It is
written. There is the Sovereign they chose for themselves. The

---

25. See in Deut. 21:19 the procedure of expiation for a murder
whose author is unknown. Murder is the image of mortal sin,
which, like it, destroys in us the image of God. The murder whose
author is unknown, is original sin whose author is deprived of the
power of reparation. *When a dead man's body is found, elders
and judges must betake themselves to the spot where he lies, and
find by measurement which of the neighboring cities is nearest at
hand.* And for the ceremonies recommended *they will choose the
one closest,* the one the most immediately at hand, the one with
the closest relationship with the victim and whose crime does the
most visible wrong to integrity. That city is the one whose divine
law makes the charter. The substituted victim is a heifer *that has
never borne yoke or ploughed furrow,* thus recalling that free animal which followed Our Lord's mount last Sunday. Our Lord
compared Himself to a hen. Other passages evoke the image of a
calf in terms of its suitability for sacrifice. The heifer, like Him, is
an innocent being, pure from any brutal domination and any ser-
vile attachment to the earth. (cf. Heb. 9:13. *The ashes of a heifer
sprinkled over men defiled, have power to hallow them.*) It is led
into some wild and rugged glen, that was never ploughed or sown,
something sterile, suitable for traps and falls, without mentioning
those stonings which circumstances do not spare us. The neck
bones of the animal are broken, those which attach the head to the
body (so intimately at times that a certain people with a hard neck
cannot turn around or be *converted*). Around the victim, the text
adds, priests will assemble, whose office is to bless, to authenticate
in the name of God everything that happens and to distinguish
the pure and the impure. *And they will wash their hands over the
heifer that lies slain, protesting, not ours the hand that shed this
blood; our eyes never witnessed the deed; be merciful, Lord, to
Israel, the people thou hast claimed for thyself; do not charge
Israel, thy own people, with guilt because it is stained with an innocent man's blood.*

36

proof they took Him seriously, the proof that they recognize a certain solidarity between themselves and Him, is the eagerness they show to get rid of Him. That is the answer to their protests of autonomy. Henceforth it is finished and we heard it from their lips: *Non habebum regem nisi Caesarem.* Their title to David's heritage is henceforth facing all peoples and attached to the cross, in Hebrew, Greek and Latin. *Jesus of Nazareth, King of the Jews.* It is useless to protest. *What I wrote, I wrote.*

The delivery now is consummated. In the name of the universe, the Roman Emperor received from the hands of the dispossessed Synagogue the Son of God. Now let us go to work on Him! Now there is among all peoples, among all human groups a common cause, a common interest, expressed at that time in the international crowd of executioners and mercenaries recruited from all the corners of the Empire, who hurl themselves in one mass on Christ! To work on the heavenly grain of wheat, we must use all the jaws which the human race has, all the instruments which human ingenuity has combined to give form and activity to its essential void! *What means this turmoil among the nations; why do the peoples cherish vain dreams? See how the kings of the earth stand in array, how its rulers make common cause, against the Lord and his Christ*[26] (Ps. 2:1,2 Acts 4:25-26). Against the eternal Word we have recourse to modern methods! Nothing happens now in the world save in some relationship with Christ. It is from Him alone that all nations together ask for the basic elements of their attitude. In relationship to Him they realize themselves. It is on Him as on an always present anvil that they strike and forge. *I bent my back to the oppressor* (Ps.

26. Ps. 34:21 and 21:5. *See how they mop and mow at me, crying out, Joy, joy that we should have lived to see this! All those who catch sight of me fall to mocking.*

128:3). It is on Him that crews of questioners through all the centuries take turns. *Sore have they beset me even from my youth* (Ps. 128:1). All matters are going to be referred to Him. It is by opposition we will oblige Christ to define His stand. Our duty will be to supply Him with darkness so that light will shine in relationship with us.

The first question to Christ is spittle. It is the first blind and instinctive reaction of the animal to divine danger. Our entire being contracts with horror and we try to eject it from us. I mean simultaneously the spoken spit which are insults and blasphemies, and real spit. We try to give Him the contact of our refusal. We affirm that He is not here for us. We pull out from ourselves something solid in order to deny Him, to eradicate Him. Our inner humility (what fills our mouth, what serves us both as dissolution and assimilation of food and speech) we hurl at His face, we spit out at Him our kiss! Speech has become excrement. The Lord once with His saliva, with His speech mingled with earth, made an ointment to cure our blindness. Let Him now receive from us in exchange this stream of mud!

The Gospel, in its description of the harsh treatment inflicted on Jesus Christ, speaks to us next of the blows and especially the slaps and violence against the Face. It is the immediate preparation, against what disturbs us, of the means which nature has placed at our disposal. Against God we use our own flesh, our limbs, our animal impact. We resist Him, we rise up against Him, we try in every practical way to get rid of that Being looking at us,[27] and destroy His identity and send Him away from us. These are the instincts, the beasts, the wild passions, the turbulent movements of a crowd crazed by smoke, throwing themselves on Christ and trying to crush Him under their weight, to bruise Him, mangle Him, disfigure

27. *He has eyes for what the Gentiles do* (Ps. 65:7).

Him. *My enemies ring me round, packed close as a herd of oxen,* says Psalm 21:13.[28] Listen to the violent slapping of that hand against the sacred flesh! Our right hand imitating the hand which created the world!

During that time they bound His hands, they reduced Him to impotency, they stripped Him of what would be anything but pure and simple presence. It is fitting that we perform at our ease, that we strike directly, that we ourselves verify this consistency He compared to *the hardest stone.* He must not try to hide His face in His hands, or dissimulate Himself in His works. This is personal business between Him and Us. *Tu loquere palam!* We are going at it in right earnest.

Such was the first wave of the enemies of Christ, the violent and the instinctive. A second wave will follow, more intelligent and dangerous. All manner of mockery and buffoonery filled the interval. In the presence of that wretched impotent God whom we rigged out in a glaring rag and armed with a broom handle, the laughter of the simple-minded broke out while hypocrisy joined with irony and relayed its learned homage. It was so comical a spectacle that it roused the dumbest minds and gave spirit (not the Holy Spirit!) to the very stupid. From Lucan to Anatole France, including Renan and Voltaire, it was a continuous fire of jokes, a general fluttering. But on the other hand, haven't we seen the censer swing in the hands of an Alexander VI, of a Cauchon and of a Talleyrand? Hasn't history sometimes seen the livery of Christ on the back of a pervert and a drunkard? Hasn't it seen the mitre and even the tiara totter over monsters who are to be compared only with badgers or drunken pigs?

Now to blind rage succeeded lucid hate. What was needed was no longer that bewildered face, it was all of Christ from

28. *Still one man my enemies single out for their onslaught* (Ps. 61:4).

head to foot, stripped of all veils and accessories. It was with Him we had to deal. It was from Him, from that body, before us, naked and trembling, that the moment had come to take our measurement. And what better measurement was there than the lash, whose point is duly balanced by the weight of our personal judgment (*flagrum*), already impatient in our hand?

I have often read that whipping is the symbolic expiation of our sins of impurity, and I do not contradict this, although to my mind a better comparison would be that of the inner wound spreading beyond the ulcer. The physical expression of concupiscence, the poison it instills into the human form, is best realized when we turn the pages of books on venereal diseases. It is leprosy in which finally the fires of Astaroth are extravasated. To my mind, the real meaning of flagellation is the work which, since the advent of Protestantism, the exegetes and those small minds formed by study, have carried on about the Word made flesh. The loaded whip which they brandish in their fists, is the serpent of Genesis who has placed himself at their disposal, and the piece of lead or the hook at its end is the image either of an extinguished dead soul (of self-centered, self-sufficient spirit concentrated on its own weight) or of a terrible rapaciousness totally directed toward destruction. Rage alone animates that device which, left alone, hangs down feebly. Hurled at full swing, the whip attaches to the victim, hisses, adheres, folds over it, enters and penetrates the most secret recesses like a ray of fire. It performs on the victim with its entire length a kind of sharp destructive act— whips, cuts, divides—and the heavy contrivance which terminates it brings back pieces of our flesh. It traced all manner of chance designs on the sacred flesh. From the base to the summit, it attacked everything which in Christ was form and outer shape. *No health anywhere, from sole to crown, nothing but wounds, and bruises* (Isaias 1:6). While leaving Christ intact, in such a way that *not one of His bones will be lacking,* they took from Him (with the help of the merchants in the rue Bonaparte) elements of his appearance and attractiveness. *Nay, here is one despised, left out of all human reckoning; bowed with misery, and no stranger to weakness . . . A leper so we thought of him, a man God had smitten and brought low; and all the while it was for our sins he was wounded* (Isaias 53:3-4). Strike, executioners, strike with your whip, as hard as you can! On His back, His sides, on His stomach and His buttocks! (Doesn't the judicial expression of Pilate, *emende, corrige,* recall the annotations and ameliorations whose critical editions encumber the Gospel texts?) And each piece of flesh is a soul taken away from Him!

In the meantime what are those amateurs busy with in the corner? No, they are real artists who are tastily carrying out a small job of superior basket-making. Those three long branches of carefully chosen briars, and the job of bending, intertwining and consolidating one with the other into the form of a perfect crown, and placing the atrocious thorns without the artists wounding themselves, but in such a way that the beneficiary will preserve all profit—all that is a manipulation we see today entrusted to more ingenious fingers than those of tough soldiers. After all, a crown is necessary for the King who has been handed over. A real crown, something woven and untearable, something solid, sown to the flesh itself, rooted in the temple and the bone of the skull. *Come,* says Humanity to her Lord in the words of the Sulamite, *You will be crowned* (Song of Songs 4:8).[29] This chain, this logic of suffering sustaining itself and reappearing, this complex, this supple adaptation of circumstances to our capacity for princely dignity and knowledge, constitute a communication with everything which, in

29. *Thy head covered,* says Ezechiel 24:17, *no veil on thy face.*

our limbs and the most delicate fibers of our individuality, introduces a notion of exterior incompatibility and banishes from our self-possession the finest of our qualities: a perfect crown. An animal suffers in an animal way, when attacked on one point or two. Man alone is invested in prodigious detail and in a fullness of psychological pleasure over that suffering which a cultivated conscience allows him to enjoy even in the most attenuated shadings. But Christ put everything at once around His head. The older law speaks to us of "the Crown's Domain," of those diverse rights and powers which "come from the Crown." Well, all suffering in us, moral or physical, comes from the Crown of thorns and, joining us with Christ, invests us with His character of expiation, authority and leadership. He is caught and attached to us. He is incorporated in our sacrifice. He is the ram caught in the thicket which Providence offered to Abraham to be substituted on the altar for his own son. This is no longer, as it was a short time ago, a rain of rapid blows, a lashing destruction. Now all around him is a hostile persistent presence. This is a more grievous, more envenomed doubt than negation. The knot—the serpent—the intertwinings around His head have become permanent. It is a circle of fire and sharp points. With each thorn which pierces the surface and strikes against the bone, Christ feels our refusal joined with our verification. And now we can no longer see Him save through that complex confused system with which our Principle is embarrassed.[30]

30. Speaking of *thorns,* we find in Psalm 57:10, the following very controversial passage: *Green stalks the whirlwind carries away, while yonder pot waits for fuel!* To understand *green stalks* for our own thorns, is what we just above called "to come from the Crown." It is to associate our own garland with the diadem. To suffer or to die, Saint Theresa said, as if she were stating an inevitable alternative. All that suffers, all that lives contributes by its intelligence and its acceptance to the *passion* of Christ and

This is man, at the first phase of expiation. This is man tormented, examined, accoutred, restored, in the eruptive plenitude of penance, which the representative of the universe exhibits from the top of Gabbatha over the rise of events and races in the contemplation of all time. *Adam, where are you? Where did you keep yourself hidden? We have found you at last. Ecce Homo!*[31]

Now begins the second part of the accomplishment, the implanting, the exaltation, the unfolding, the definitive and unshakable consolidation above us of the Son of Man. But between Gabbatha and Golgotha, and leading to that dirty knoll

---

finds iself absorbed therein. Still in reference to the briar or the bush (Rhamnus) there is in the Book of Judges (9:7-15) a fable about which it may not be amiss to place here this commentary. *There was a time when the trees went about to anoint a king who should rule over them, and said to the olive-tree, Come and be our king. What, said the olive, would you have me forgo this rich influence of mine, for the service of God and man, to win promotion among the trees? So they asked the fig-tree to be their ruler, but the fig-tree answered, What, should I cease to yield this pleasant fruit of mine, and win promotion among the trees instead? Then the trees would have the vine reign over them, but the vine said, What, would you have me cease to yield wine that both God and man delight in, to be the foremost of the trees? So at last all the trees went to the bramble, and would have the bramble reign over them. And the bramble said, If you have chosen me for your king in all honesty, why then, come and rest in my shadow. If your hearts are false, then burn bramble, and set light to all the cedars of Lebanon!* Thus the royal anointing was conferred neither on the olive in spite of its oil, nor on the fig tree in spite of its fruit, nor on the vine in spite of its wine. Either as material powers or as sacraments, they are servants of man, they are not his masters. But suffering has over him an irresistible ascendency and an unbreakable authority. It dominates and commands everything. Happy is the man who has learned how to rest under its shadow, but for the man who resists, it is a fire which devours and consumes the proud.

31. *Whereupon Adam and his wife hid themselves in the garden, among the trees* (Gen. 3:8).

in the angle of the wall,[32] outside of the enclosure on which opens the *Door of Filth, Porta Stercoris,* there is a road. It is difficult to imagine those dumping grounds outside of large cities, where each morning they push all the refuse and rubbish that has collected the preceding day, all the dirty broken bottles, the soiled pots, the crockery and jagged cans, to which the Psalmist compares the lost soul: *I am lost to memory, discarded like a broken pitcher* (Ps. 30:13). And did not Saint Paul say of Christians that they are like the waste and sweepings of the world? This is the place chosen to erect the infamous gallows. That is where we are going. Already the procession around us gets into position and starts off. Each Good Friday hereafter it will accompany us around the Church.

For the moment of expulsion has come. Christ who last Sunday entered Jerusalem in triumph along a road strewn with humanity and palms, this irresistible Christ before whom doors were pulled off their hinges, this Christ who just now, facing His people and on the stone of David confessed in words confirmed by thunder,—Juda solemnly declares that she wants nothing to do with Him and the moment had come to eliminate Him. The moment had come at last to get rid of this benediction which had been tormenting her for millenniums. Not only condemned but anathematized. He blasphemed! He can no longer stay with us. Out with Him! *Take the blasphemer,* says Leviticus 24:14, *beyond the confines of the camp.* The delivery of Jesus Christ to the universe began with this extradition.

It was this expulsion from the city of a soul, of an atoning

32. *They made their escape by way of the gate between the two walls, by the royal garden . . . They chose for their flight the road which leads to the desert* (Jer. 52:7-8). *Two irrevocable assurances, over which there could be no question of God deceiving us, were to bring firm confidence to us poor wanderers* (Hab. 6:18).

44

animal figuratively loaded with all the sins of the people which the ceremony of the *Scape Goat*, described in Leviticus (chapter 16), had represented. The goat in the Bible, for numerous and manifest reasons (stench, lubricity, super-abundance and coarseness of hair which are the characteristics of bestiality, horns which rise above the head and curve back on themselves, violence, fantasy, savage and unmanageable instinct) is the symbol of sinful nature. Everywhere it furnishes the matter of sacrifice offered *pro peccato*. It is he whom the High Priest is committed to send forth into the desert, duly cursed and anointed with the ritual imprecation, into the *outer darkness*, according to the prescribed form in verses 20 to 23: *Sanctuary, and tabernacle, and altar so cleansed, he has still to offer up the goat that is left alive. He must put both hands on its head, confessing all the sins and transgressions and faults Israel has committed, and laying the guilt of them on its head. And there will be a man standing ready to take it into the desert for him; so the goat will carry away all their sins into a land uninhabited, set at large in the desert. Then Aaron will come back to the tabernacle.*

But it is not simply with imprecatory words that the Victim chosen to be ejected outside the Holy City into the desert of the Gentile world (through the care of that *man standing ready* in the place of Caesar) appears laden before us, but with three pieces of wood, one long, a heavy rigid beam, accompanied by two chevrons, not yet the cross which will take its stature and form only on Calvary, but the substance of the cross. A legend, to which we have no reason to refuse a place, says that this beam was a part of the woods which, on Nebo, served to protect among the sacred vessels buried by Jeremias, the Fire transformed into *thick water* (II Macch. 1:20).[33]

33. The fire dissolving in water.

Some even consider the filiation going back as far as that primordial stock in the Earthly Paradise.[34] Let us consider the new Adam expelled from the City of men as his ancestor once had been expelled from the divine Plantation, laboriously carrying with Him that trunk which was going to be the instrument of expiation, as it had been the support of temptation. It is by a similar effort that Saint Peter formerly transported the huge implement from Jerusalem to Antioch, then to Rome and from there sent so many missionaries into all parts of the world that now we see each morning the cross reflower on the back of the priest mounting to the altar, in accordance with the word of Isaias (11:12): *The Lord will raise his sign toward nations.* But heavy indeed is the testimony inscribed by the centuries in the concentric fiber of this age old patriarch! Be it a mast or piling, it is by the sweat of our brow that the son of Joseph (the *son of the increase*) invites us to his carpenter's vocation—or rather one can see in it the essential piece of a winepress.[35]

34. "For the cross was not made of ordinary wood. A branch was first broken off from the tree of good and evil, then planted on the grave of the first man. This branch developed, grew with such magnificence that no tree could be compared with it. That was the predestined wood, the mysterious imperishable trunk. It was one of its branches which Noah's dove brought to the ark. Another, later on, furnished Moses with the staff with which he struck the rock. It furnished the bridge over the torrent proposed by Solomon to the Queen of Sheba and on which, through respect, she refused to set her foot when she entered Jerusalem. It was then miraculously preserved in the depths of the pool in Jerusalem until the moment of the Passion." (read somewhere)

35. The cross is perhaps the *vitulus Libani*, the *son of Lebanon* spoken of in the 28th Psalm. The divine woodcutter cut with heavy blows of the axe into the tremendous foliage in such a way as to reveal this frame at whose base stands the Church. *Revelabit condensa.* In vain does the thistle address ridiculous and insolent propositions of alliance to the cedar of Lebanon, as is said in the Book of Kings (IV Kings 14:9): *Let my son have thy daughter to*

Concerning this wood, under which we see the Son of Man
appear tottering and crushed—and which three times got the
better of Him—so many writers, more learned than I am, have
written, that there is little left for me to say. Adam ate the
tree with the apple and now he is one with this robe of wood
which associates him to the root of each of its fibers, physical
and spiritual, to the knot of its joints, to the travail of birth
and death agony, to the accomplishment of its vegetable purpose. The wood, this rough cross which had not yet achieved
perfect form, is everything to which God has under the circumstances entrusted the task of making man again in His
image, everything which in this ambiency is born to exercise
on him an action, a formative constraint. It is the framework
and the director. It is the instrument of the painful harmoni-
zation in ourselves of the inner with the outer. In this marriage of the cross and man which it is called upon to mould,
there are three things to consider: resistance, effort, transport.

First, resistance in us by weight. Something like water which
opens under the keel of a boat and transforms into an active
compensation a double inertia. Take the case of the man who
married, of the man who took on a family, the one who brutally from his youth entered into conversation with his limitations, the man who gradually took possession of an incurable
malady, the one whose heart each morning and each evening
sickened at the accomplishment of an insipid task—something entered into each of these and caused the soul to stop
yielding and to affirm it was not dead. They knew there was

---

wife. The frail sterile thistle, inconsistent in spite of its preten-
tious stature, producing only thorns and a wretched down which
the wind carries off, is the emblem itself of heresy and of those
graceless products of a single season engendered by a strong soil.
To the alliance propositions of an Auguste Comte, or Angelican
heretics, or some potentate or other, or some momentary regime,
the Church, faithful to her crucified bridegroom, remains deaf.

an end to suffering and that they were still living. On the one hand, there is a reduction of our freedom and an amputation in several directions of our possibilities. On the other hand, there is an increased awareness of ourselves, a mustering and accommodation of our forces, a tension of our resilience, a charging of our batteries, and, what is more interesting, there is from the outside and the unknown, a contribution, an indication—we might say the will of God—which is insistently applied to us, in familiarity and grief, and it falls directly on us between the neck and the shoulder, according to the expression which we find so often in Scripture: *incidit in collum*. This will is both mute (acting on us simply because of its co-existence) and immediate(but not always precise). It is intimate because it applies to the most substantial, profound and supple part of us. It is, in a manner of speaking, cut to measurement and we recognize it because precisely we want to be rid of it. And finally, it is active because it presses down on that vital point in us which would involve destruction if it did not offer, by suggestion, the urgency for a compensatory construction, even if simply provisionary and fortuitous. Deep inside us we feel something of that labor in nature from which the species issued.

That is not all, for behind that great Isaac at our head who carries His beam, we also must learn, like small ants, to transport our straw and how to hitch our collaboration to that straw on our back. At first we have to hold it tightly or it will fall. We have to put our arms around it and our hands also play their role, and certainly we wish not only that it were less heavy, but also less hard, less formless, less cutting. By a series of small experiments, of tiny movements, we have to find the place where it hurts the least and where, for a few seconds, we shall know a kind of relief and painful commodiousness from that horrible discomfort. And even in that state of awkward-

ness and dizziness, a few steps are gained. Let us answer the
suspension on our back of this dead weight by arranging an
intelligent balance. We must be especially careful not to let
it drag on the ground, because we already have enough weight
without adding the movement of pulling. Especially we must
not allow ourselves to be pulled back by the horrible power
of habit and by that which, from the depths of the out-
distanced past, happens to us without our seeing it. Neither
must it go too far ahead of us, lest some careless haste makes
us fall. We must watch our feet, for the road is full of ruts and
pebbles, not to mention the slipperiness, and we must also
watch with both eyes and both ears for what may fall on us on
our left and our right. But that, alas, will not keep us from
falling more than once, twice, three times! And if, from time
to time we meet some good Simeon recruited willingly or by
force to help us, I thank him in advance! A helping hand is
not to be refused, O father of Rufus and Alexander so oppor-
tunely met!

The one thing certain is that we will not be reproached as
the workmen of the parable were (Matth. 20:6): *How is it you
have done nothing all the day?* We received our bit of substance, cut and measured exactly, to carry from one point to
another.[36] It is an ell added to us, or if you prefer, an increase
which will help us measure everything and on which everything in its relationship to us is measured. It is that cubit
which by ourselves we would be powerless to add to our stature—but God is able to, He who raises us by surpassing us.
It is something which no longer makes us compatible with all
passages and all openings. Lord! yes, it is true! it is something
very onerous and very cumbersome, this cut tree, this large
awkward loose beam which You gave us to take away, and we

36. *A litter king Solomon will have, of Lebanon wood* (S. of
Songs 3:9).

hope that at the end You will still find in it enough greenness and sap to judge it good for a better use than to start a fire! Let us endure for a bit longer this object whose imposition on us the sun and the earth joined with one another for so long a time to prepare. For the moment, everything transpires in this operation of transport as if it were we who had to do the principal thing. But we know that we must not relinquish this piece of wood at any price and that at the end of the road we shall understand its use and usefulness. Who knows, definitively, whether it is not a bridge cut in advance to the exact measurement of that fissure we shall have to cross, just broad enough to pass from one bank to another? *All the beauty of Lebanon shall be brought to thee, fir-wood and box-wood and pine-wood mingled together to adorn this place, my sanctuary; I will have honor paid to this, the resting-place of my feet* (Isaias 60:13). *No tree in the forest but will rejoice* (Ps. 95: 12).

Christ came to the top of Golgotha and He carried out the delivery of His burden. It is for us, workmen committed to this duty, to complete the cross, for us to assemble the three pieces and to raise toward heaven this eternal supplication in the form of an open angle whose two parts both converging and diverging will be joined by the two arms of Christ.[37]

37. *He is our bond of peace; he has made the two nations one, breaking down the wall that was a barrier between us, the enmity there was between us, in his own mortal nature. He has put an end to the law with its decrees, so as to make peace, remaking the two human creatures as one in himself; both sides, united in a single body, he would reconcile to God through his cross, inflicting death, in his own person, upon the feud* (Ephesians 2:14-16).
See also what Ezechiel says (37:6) about the two pieces of wood on which are inscribed the names of Ephraim and Juda.
Two irrevocable assurances, over which there could be no question of God deceiving us (Heb. 6:18). *Whereupon Adam and his wife hid themselves in the garden, among the trees* (Genesis 3:8).

Mary is standing on Calvary and she contemplates at her feet her Son, a prey to that crew of workmen, who, directed both by demons and angels, are occupied in profiting from that material which had been given them in order to construct the crucifix, by following all the resources of art. From this man whom they gave us, from this instrument they put at our disposal, it is for us now to derive what we can. First the tree and the man must make only one, and for that not rely solely on the strong fastenings nor on the supports which we will use under his back and feet (as close and precarious as our good will of momentary penitents). Our client must not be tempted to come down and answer the invitation which those gentlemen of the Sanhedrin are about to offer Him. Between the body and the cross there must be a form of active adhesion, of bracing, attraction and integral suction. To this is doubtless due that curious disposition in the form of a "Y" which has been revealed to us in visions of Anne Catherine Emmerich and Theresa Neumann. As far as we can understand, it is a question of joists having at their base a certain mobility as they function, by diverging in the manner of levers or pump-handles.[38] In this way and by the very effort of the device, the body will be maintained and stretched automatically to the limit of resistance of tendons and joints. Christ is not only suspended on a hook, He is snapped at by

---

And that night all the fighting men made their escape by way of the gate between the two walls, by the royal garden. They chose for their flight the road which leads to the desert (Jeremias 52: 7-8).

38. The funnel had a leather bag in its upper section. Two mobile arms, similar to levers and penetrating the trunk on each side, pressed the grapes closed in the bag; and the juice trickled through the holes which had been made in the lower part of the machine. Therefore it was both a cross and a wine-press. Japhet's wine-press, described by Anne Catherine Emmerich, *Life of Our Lord Jesus Christ*, VI, 19.

a mechanism.[39] With the two thieves on the right and the left, there is no need to take all these precautions.

We must understand around what this timber-yard is established. Legally and materially, Jesus has already been withdrawn from this people to whom He belonged and with whom He was, so to speak, mingled in the horizontal sense. Now it is in the vertical sense that He is pulled above all humanity. When we look up, we must be assured always of finding Him in the same place. That is why we made Him fast at the three corners of this tightener. It is the bronze Serpent of the Book of Numbers (Num. 21:8-9) to which the Lord compared Himself (John 3:14), that serpent whose curative sight is sufficient to remedy the bite of the other inflamed reptile which attacks our feet in the sand. By which are meant those passions of a soul devoted to the earth: grovelling whips and lashes, offensive traps, forked tongues around our invisible ankles, full of fury and poison. This is the animal adapted to the narrowest and most sinuous part of our breathing and veins (and the serpent also resembles an intestine: it is an animated intestine), whose image the Lord bears and exalts, whose resemblance with the arms of His gallows He felt at His death, mingling redemption with that spurt impregnated by the sin of poison which now brings us life.[40] Henceforth we need only to look at that image, and absorb it through our wide open eyes of Faith, to be cured. What was made *to eat dust* (Gen. 3:14),[41] we see now at the summit according to

39. *Every question must be settled by the voice of two witnesses or more* (Deuter. 19:15-Matth. 18:16). The Word is placed forever as in between the two gaping jaws of Humanity.

40. Has not Our Lord elsewhere been compared to a worm? *Vermis et non homo* (Ps. 21:7). *Jacob, poor worm, poor ghost of Israel, do not be afraid, I am here, says the Lord, to help thee; I am here, says the Holy One of Israel, to ransom thee* (Isaias 41:14).

41. The text of Genesis uses in order to distinguish the serpent not the expression *animal* but *animans* not animated, but animating.

the words of the Apostle: *You must be heavenly-minded, not earthly-minded* (Col. 3:2). We are invited to draw the essential savor of what is above us: *Take good care that no poisonous shoot is allowed to spring up* (Heb. 12:15). *You must lift your thoughts above, where Christ is* (Col. 3:1).

What it was that met . . . the touch of our hands, says Saint John (I John 1:1). They are not the delicate fingers of the Blessed Virgin which raised the veil over the new-born. This is not the devouring awesome adoration of the sinner who seizes the feet of her Lord, nor is it even the aggression of that bestial fury to which He had just now given Himself. The hour has come of the technician, of the executioner who knows his trade. It is to the entire body, to the entire Christ in His bulk, in His volume and in the division of His members that those fat adroit and hateful hands are directed, in an action which resembles both the butcher and the chiropractor. We will strip Him first, before the necessity is imposed on us to use direct force and before the body cries out under the jack. We shall begin by pulling off from Him, in a burst of laughter that *many-colored cloak* with which his mother had clothed Joseph, the dreamer of dreams,[42] all that prophetic cloth of colors and designs with which divine Wisdom had wrapped the Messiah. And it is all right if the skin comes with it! See, after all, from head to foot, He is only a man on whom no illusory or foreign covering prevents our taking measurement. He is now reduced to a general type—pure man—outside of any age and circumstance,[43] and whom we are going

42. *They stripped him of his long, embroidered coat* (Gen. 37: 23). See what Exodus says concerning the veils of the Tabernacle *opere polymito.*

43. *Ah, but my shift, I have laid it by*, says The Song of Songs (5:3). *How can I put it on again?* meaning perhaps thereby the cross, that figure of the sinner, abridged, rigid and dead. *Dutiful observance was still the vesture I wore, my robe and crown integrity* (Job 29:14).

to *prepare,* as they say in a butcher's language, on that frame-work.

Behold the Word opened before us. Behold the Word un-folded before us and we can read in Him as in an open book. Behold Him consolidated before us forever, in that essential attitude in which He made Heaven and Earth.[44] All heretics can hitch themselves to His arms and legs, they will succeed in dislocating His thigh-bone, but they will not succeed in un-settling the hypostatic union, that basic articulation, that other thigh-bone on which, the Apocalypse tells, *this title is written, The King of Kings, and the Lord of Lords* (Apoc. 19: 16). This is the invitation to us of those two arms which made the world and which will remain extended all day until they have reintegrated it.[45] Here are those great outstretched wings which make of two things one. Here is God, here is Love, be-yond all modesty, opened and unveiled before us. Here are the heights that Habacuc speaks of, *the heights beckon from above,* here is Jesus crucified on a triangle and completing it with His own person, the man of vision who extends over Jerusalem the highest level (Zach. 1:16).

The task of the executioners is not over. It is not enough to have stripped Christ, it is not enough to have raised Him, it is not enough to have stretched Him, it is not enough for us to be sure of Him and to have arranged that forever He will be one with that evident unshakable cross: the moment has come, if I dare speak grossly, to put Him in a wine cask: now He must flow, for people are thirsty! The inner virtue there is in Him must gush forth, that source in Him must pour out, whether we bleed Him from His four limbs, or whether we open up a passage directly to His heart. It was not for nothing

44. *Thou art the maker of heaven and earth, so wide thy reach* (Jer. 32:17).

45. *I have stretched out my hands all day to a people that re-fuses obedience and cries out against me* (Rom. 10:21).

that He spoke to us of *that spring whose water is life* (Apoc. 21:6). Behold it leaping in big sobs, from deep openings, from a still burning heart. *There was only spring-water,* Genesis tells us (2:6), *which came up from the earth, and watered its whole surface.* And farther on (10): *The garden was watered by a river; it came out from Eden, and went on to divide into four branches.* This is the renewed cry of Moses in the desert (Num. 20:6): *Lord God, listen to the plea made by this people of thine, and open to them thy store-house of fresh water.* We know what the Lord answered, and it is our turn to apply this advice given to the Patriarch: *lay thy command upon the rock here. This water thou bringest out of the rock will suffice to give drink to the whole multitude,* and to their cattle. It is our turn to speak to the Rock!

Thus, happier than the ancient Israelites, through the repulsive covering we made our way *into the interior of the desert,* to what there was inside this Unknown God whose title the Greeks, with a hesitating hand, had inscribed on their altars, into that negative Presence, into that vacant empty being before whom the poor Moslems still today prostrate themselves. We obeyed the precept of the Gospel: *Knock and the door shall be opened to you* (Matth. 7:7). We did not simply look over this text proposed for our study, we scrutinized it, as we were advised, and dug into its root and principle; and, passing from the outside to the inside and from the visible to the soul, we put our stamp on it. These are not the chance contusions which serve only to deform and discolor. We came against the vein itself. There was no point that did not bring forth a hemorrhage, whether we were or were not its beneficiaries, according to the word of the Apostle that *as our fault was amplified, grace has been more amply bestowed than ever* (Rom. 5:20).[46]

46. PSALM 73: (4) *See what havoc thy enemies have wrought*

55

Let us now consider Christ raised "on the stocks" above the entire earth. At His feet, around a jumbled pile of wrappings and clothes, a group of crouching gnomes are playing cards and with all the noises of the Passion is mingled the din of dice in the dice-box. For it is not solely a question of "liquidating" Christ, it is a question of dividing Him up. It is a question of those gratuitous numbers which the sun in the sky when it is extinguished leaves to blind chance and to that portable hollow in the fist of a drunkard. It is a game so confused, a backgammon so complicated, between Man, Time, Justice and Providence, that it belongs solely to this parody of the chalice to utter in successive hiccups decisive and inexplicable numbers. All the agitation is the making of a number in the bottom of a goblet. No more betting. The prizes given

---

in the holy place, how their malice has raved in thy very precincts (literally, "thy solemn feast.") This solemn feast par excellence is the Jewish Passover, in the midst of which Jesus was put to death.

(5) setting up its emblems for a trophy of conquest. They themselves determined the characteristics to which they attributed the value of signs, of those signs in which they agreed to recognize the Messiah (see verse 9). They did not recognize the Messiah who was to leave Jerusalem and be elevated on Calvary.

(6) Blow after blow, like woodmen in the forest, they have plied their axes, brought it down, with pick and mallet, to the ground. This concerns divine Glory and the support where it dwells. The forest is the jungle of time, of places and circumstances, all the natural vegetation which came with Adam from the ancient Paradise, through which the redemptive Will has to make its way, as if with blows of the axe. Each passage it creates in this way is like a door opening, up to that last door which noble Samson carried off on his back. The way is long from the tree of Genesis to that supreme apple-tree to which the Bride of the Song of Songs compares her Bridegroom (2:3). An apple-tree in the wild woodland. The axe is the instrument of the woodcutter, the saw or the chisel belongs to the carpenter. Cutting down the tree is not all. You have to fashion it industriously. You have to make a cross out of it. You have to put it on the ground in order to work on it more easily.

(7) They have set fire to thy sanctuary. The Commentary tells

since the beginning of the world are given back to the masses. It is not only the interest which has to be distributed, it is the entire capital which is put up for sale by auction. Around this hook on which hangs palpitating flesh, there is great activity, intense although invisible activity, as on those days of great stock market operations, where piles of securities and large sections of ant-hills swell, collapse, divide, amalgamate, change shape, possessor, and meaning. Thus, for three hours of agony and torture on the cross, all manner of bonds are made and unmade and propagated. At the sound of the Seven Words which come down from the cross, a new world through the other is created. Full meaning is given that word of the Prodigal Son when, on the point of leaving *for a distant land*, he asks His Father *to divide His substance.*

---

us that the Machabees saw the gates of the Temple charred. The fire is either the suffering of the Passion (*Piscis assus, Christus passus*), or the figure of that devouring zeal, of that charity with which the heart of Christ is kindled. *Was it not jealousy for the honor of thy house that consumed me?* (Ps. 68:10). *It is fire I have come to spread over the earth, and what better wish can I have that it should be kindled?* (Luke 12:49). *Lord, must thy jealous anger still burn unquenched?* (Ps. 78:5). *They sullied the dwelling-place of thy glory in the dust* (Ps. 73:7).

(8) *They think to destroy us like one man, sweep away every shrine of God in the land.* We should dismiss God and tell Him to leave. He should no longer be concerned with things of the earth. He should not insinuate Himself any longer as a troublesome and worrisome element.

(9) *Our own emblems are nowhere to be seen.* The good ones, those we ourselves determined as such. *There are no prophets left now or interpreters between Him and us. None can tell how long we must endure.* He will not recognize us. The relationships are broken. *Nescio vos.*

(11) *Why dost thou withhold thy hand? That right hand of thine, must it always lie idle in thy bosom?* The *hand*, which is the left hand according to the Hebrew, and right also, are now spread out their full length. Why do you hold them so far away from your heart and your breast, unless it is for us to find passage more easily to that God thus reduced to impotence?

Part Two

The Seven Last Words

THE FIRST WORD:

> *Father, forgive them; they do not know what it is they are doing.*

For all time Jesus is implanted on Calvary, His back turned toward Jerusalem and the Jews. He can no longer see them. That is over. They can no longer see His face. His profile is no longer turned toward them. Of Him they will have nothing save this human silhouette against the sky with which He blots out the future. They will know Him *a posteriori:* in reverse order. Forever they will remain behind, like a negative counterfeit shadow. The heavy thud of the Cross sinking into its place resounded like a battering ram to the very center, to the middle of the earth, and this formed between the gate and the road an irreparable cleavage. Israel succeeded in expelling the promise which since the days of Abraham had been tormenting her. She was emptied in one moment, like Judas, of what she had inside—and she was left with nothing.

On the threshold of the journey which begins, the first word
of Christ, now raised to the very lips of the One who sent
Him, was: *Father, forgive them; they do not know what it is
they are doing* (Luke 23:34). The Jews who were the instruments of the first Sacrifice are the beneficiaries of the first
Mass.

While I write, there is someone here who often looks over
my shoulder and asks me two questions.

You remember that scene in Jules Verne's novel, *Hector
Servadac*, when the hero on the banks of a sea which is on the
verge of freezing because of a terrible cold spell, provokes the
freezing as far as the eye can reach, simply by throwing a pebble into the water. Must we believe that from one end of the
world to the other, the curse of the crowd before the praetori-
um of Pilate, *His blood be upon us, and upon our children!*
had an analogous effect on Israel already dispersed? Must we
believe that at that moment, the people of Alexandria, of
Cyrene, of Rome, of Iberia and China, who did not even know
the name of Jesus, and with them their children not yet born,
became incumbents of a curse superadded to Original Sin,
that they were in some way solidified in that negative attitude
which their official representatives felt duty bound to assume
in their name, as a closed system? Must we believe that that
formula, snatched by the demon from the heart of a community in which ferment old leaven of superimposed apos-
tasies, has had a reverse efficacy comparable to that of baptism, and that the incriminating blood of Christ henceforth
mixed like a devouring fire in her veins has raised up in Israel
a new man? When you say blood you imply plastic virtue.
Must we believe that she was called at that time to continue
on a different mode her ancient role of witness and cooperator,
that God needed that invincible indestructible refusal, as
once He needed that affirmation, something on which He

knew He could lay a foundation, that sure and confirmed darkness without which we are to infer that the light could not historically have been manifested, the *a posteriori* accompaniment of truth by negation, the modulation and development, proportioned to circumstances, of the original refusal, as of a shadow which grows with all the progressive realities which its unsubstantial blackness is called upon to contradict?

And many other questions are related to this. The blood which Israel asks to recuperate in such a way that *it will be upon her and her children* does belong to her, in truth. It is hers, and it is she who through the generations gave it to Christ. For blood according to Scripture is the vehicle of the soul. It is on those Waters that the Spirit rests, and it is at their source in the heart of the Most Blessed Virgin Mary that the hypostatic union was accomplished. That blood belonged to Israel, it was hers, but encumbered with a mission, which was to make Christ. When therefore she claimed that blood, which in truth, by nature and by rights belonged to her, it was as if she were abjuring her mission, as if she removed their meaning from those great figurative effusions which Jehovah on Sinai prescribed for her, as if she were constituted in a closed system, as if she claimed for herself all the drops of that liquid capital whose administration the Lord entrusted to her. Deuteronomy (11: 26) says: *Such is the choice I set before you this day, blessing or curse.* And Psalm 108 adds: *Cursing he loved, upon him let the curse fall; for blessing wraps him about* (which means, like a wrapping adapted to our form), *sink like water into his inmost being* (a kind of reversed baptism), *soak, like oil* (a kind of reversed consecration, a kind of lubrication of all his actions), *into the marrow of his bones! Let it be the garb he wears, cling to him like a girdle he can never take off* (namely, the will narrowly defined around her). This last image suggests the idea of that horrible circulation which constitutes an evil conscience. Israel knows, something deep within her knows for her, that this blood she received was not for her, that she had, as concerns union with God, an innate covetousness, and now, rather than exhaling it, she swallowed it and had to keep within her this incompatible guest who devours her.

This is the way my counsel *a latere* speaks and to his words my inspirer *a tergo* addresses the following remarks:

He who asks pardon for the Jews on the cross is the Second Person of the Trinity, the Son coequal and consubstantial with the Father. Therefore there can be no difference or delay between His prayer and its answer, between the word and the deed. He who declared that *He was not praying for the world*, we hear Him expressly say that He prays for the Jews. But *the Father loves His Son* (John 3:35). *The Father, instead of passing judgment on any man himself, has left all judgment to the Son* (Id. 5:22). *As the Father has within him the gift of life, so he has granted to the Son that he too should have within him the gift of life, and has also granted him power to execute judgment, since he is the Son of Man* (Id. 5:26). *My Father and I are* ONE (Id. 10:30). Hence there is no doubt concerning the efficacy of the prayer uttered by the One who created the world. Just as there is in Israel a state of malediction (solicited, chosen, desired, assumed, constituted by her), there is from the beginning, in God, a state of pardon. How can these two points be harmonized and what can one say of an immediate pardon which is not translated outwardly by any effect? For the Jews, as Saint Peter and Saint Paul admitted, crucified Christ, *not knowing what they did and even believing that they were glorifying God*. So, as Abimelech questions: *Must a nation perish that has done no wrong, except through ignorance?* (Gen. 20:4).

Once more we come face to face with the fearful problem

64

of the impotent Omnipotence, of that exclusion of God through the will and the denial of an autonomous free Creature. But the pardon from God has already intervened. Henceforth it lives in the present contemplation of that future moment for Him and His beloved when gratitude and reconciliation will come about. Therefore there is on the one hand the pardon already gained of the Almighty, and on the other the refusal of Israel, closed, walled up, cemented and cut off in her ignorance. And between the two there is that kind of conformity and pact over things which exist together: suggested by the resemblance of those words which in Latin mean *to pardon* and *to be ignorant of: ignosco* and *ignoro*. God *suspended* Israel as today one says that the bishop suspends a bad priest *a divinis*. And henceforth He does not know her, she is for Him as if she were not. She is deconsecrated, there is nothing more to say to her, she has been relieved simultaneously of the privilege of hearing and of disobeying. In one moment she exhausted all the evil she could do: having slain God, she is henceforth immobilized in an act beyond which there is no possible progress. *If he does not recognize it,* says Saint Paul (I Cor. 14:38), *he himself shall receive no recognition.* There will no longer be in her an organ and an opening through which exchange and communication may be carried on. The lack of recognition in God corresponds to the disavowal in Israel. You can hear said that a tribunal does not *know* such and such an offence. Israel suffers from a form of exterritoriality. Speech with her Creator is only in the roots of her history. Whatever she attempts with regard to Him is spoiled by a nullifying vice. She serves her time within a sentence of pardon. Their relationship, which cannot be expressed, is that of reciprocal passivity.[1] Israel lasts by enduring

1. Isaias says (34:9): *pitch they shall be henceforward, the brooks of Edom.* Pitch is that thick substance, sticky and formless, which adheres to itself and which you cannot pour.

a God she does not know, as if for her it were forever, perpetually, that overpowering atmosphere before a storm.

Yet Saint Paul assures us that *at the end,* Israel will be reconciled and that Our Lord's prayer will be realized in time. This is the meaning of two of the most important parables in the Bible: the Prodigal Son, so full of inexhaustible meanings; and the Genesis story of the Patriarch Joseph.

I realize that the Prodigal Son is usually looked upon as the image of the Gentile world, but it might also be that of Israel who asked for the dividing of the property and who claimed immediately her portion, her inheritance, what was due her, in order to profit from it temporally for her own personal advantage. That departure *to a far country* where her father's name was never heard, might be the deepest instinct of that nomad whose vocation from the beginning was *wandering.* Unable to reach any place, she whose land had the position of a corridor between the north and south, the east and west, preferred her precarious tent, her portable rags to *Sion walls* (Ps. 86:2). And when we read today the sermons of a famous rabbi, we see that the prophecy of Scripture has been realized and that Israel literally disputes her spiritual food with swine. For how can one fall lower than below the heretics? Israel now feeds on those humanitarian platitudes ground by the feet of animals, the foulest slops from the stable of science and comfort, the nameless beakful brought to it by the sinister crows of Baptists and Methodists! This is the poverty to which the descendant of Solomon has been reduced! The prophecy of Jeremias has been carried out to the letter (Lamentations 4: 5): *Ever they fare daintily, and now their fingers clutch at the dung-hill.*[2] That is the degree of filth and debasement her pros-

2. Does not the term *dung* apply precisely to that repulsive humanism which perpetually consumes the product of its own digestion?

titutions under every *leafy bough* (that is, under every earthly expansion) have led the daughter of Jerusalem. But already the bullock spoken of in Psalm 50, has reached its growth in the farm of the Father of the family.[3] *Let us eat, and make merry; for my son here was dead, and has come to life again, was lost, and is found.*

In good Joseph who aroused the hatred of his brothers because of the sheaves and the stars he saw prostrating themselves before him, the Fathers always took delight in seeing a figure of Our Lord. Nothing is more striking than the parallelism between his Passion and that of the Gospel. The terrible hatred of his brothers whose crimes stand out in the light of his innocence, the stripping of his clothes, the immersion in the bottom of the well, the bargaining over twenty pieces of silver with the Madianites, the robe stained with blood placed before the eyes of his father, are transparent elements. Joseph went down into Misraim or Egypt,[4] which is interpreted as *darkness*, by which is meant the darkness of paganism. There he made increase and prodigiously prosper all that was entrusted to him. And the Lord *gave him large revenues of stock and store* (Gen. 39:5), which means that he derived from all creatures who until then had remained simple and sterile an infinite number of meanings and words for the glory of God—as the sun reveals and puts together and multiplies one by the other all those things which were hidden. After a trial when his understanding of substances showed in diverse ways the sacramental efficacy of the species of bread and wine, namely the elements of restoration and sacrifice, with

3. The Gospel uses the expression *saginatum* (*fattened*) which means in a way, *stuffed*, whose form adjusts to the most various and opulent content.

4. *No man has ever gone up into heaven; but there is one who has come down from heaven* (John 3:13).

their relationship to the cross,[5] he was constituted the master of all the land of Egypt. Pharao invested him with the ring, the linen robe and a gold chain, as if they were the concentric zones and divisions of his power throughout the Oecumenical land. He made him mount on the chariot which is appropriate for processions of the Second Person (Gen. 41:43) and said to him: *No one in all Egypt shall be free to move hand or foot without my permission* (Gen. 41:44) *and he gave him a new name, calling him in Egyptian Saviour of the world.*

5. I urge here my travelling companion who, I am sure, as he reads me, takes the precaution to keep a Bible constantly opened on his knees, to refer to the dream of the imprisoned cup-bearer and pastry-cook, in chapter 40 of Genesis. The first saw a vine with three shoots which gradually grew into buds, flowers and grapes, from the juice of which he filled the cup in Pharao's hand. The second saw himself carrying three baskets of loaves on his head, and the top basket contained pastry of every kind, but the birds came and ate it. Who can hear of bread and wine in the Bible without thinking immediately of the two parts of communion? Wine is the secret juice which slowly feeds the long vine until finally, reaching its maturity, it swells a generous heart and over-flows as an intoxicating effusion into the royal cup. *Until I drink it with you, new wine, in the kingdom of my Father* (Matth. 26: 29). It is the image of sacrifice. They are the flowerings of the soul which intertwine on the divine vinestock and take from it fecund-ity and virtue. The loaves are the bodily substance, as wine is the fuel of the spirit. They represent the clay of our substance, taken from the soil itself. They are tangible, a gift like the manna whose prescribed ration the Israelites each morning collected in baskets. As the latter *had all tastes—omne delectamentum in se habentem* —all food rests in the top basket on our head which is Christ, *so that the birds ate it,* and they were doubtless the angels. For is not the Eucharist called the *bread of angels,* that *cibus invisibilis* they use? For the glorified cup bearer as for the sacrificed pastry cook, the Hebrew text uses the same expression (verses 13 and 19): *Pharao will restore thee to thy old office,* and adds, concerning the second, as an additional light, *and so hang thee on a gibbet.* Thus the pastry cook as well as the cup bearer is Christ seen in different phases of His ministry.

The figure *three* doubtless means as in Daniel and the Apoca-lypse *the time, the times* and *half of the time.*

In that country where he established himself, Scripture shows us Joseph as administrator during years of abundance and famine. It is the parable of the seven sleek cattle which devour the seven gaunt cattle and the seven plump ears of corn *growing from a single stalk* (Gen. 41:5). The figure *seven* indicates a musical period, a phrase which modulates and resolves in time, whether it is a question of completing an experience of prosperity, spiritual or physical, or, on the contrary, one of decline and poverty. The history of Humanity and that of the Church are full of wandering curves which follow one another like those barometrical sinuosities on the graphs of the weather bureau. *Everything must be done by turns,* says Ecclesiastes (ch. 3), *no activity here beneath the heavens, but has its allotted time for beginning and coming to an end. Now we take life, now we save it; now we are destroying, now building.* Thus we see so many celebrated places of which there remains only names and ruins. Of the ancient pulpits of Saint John Chrysostom and Saint Basil, there remains only a mutilated column reflected in a stagnant pool. The entire Greek Church has slowly dried up as it separated from the Apostolic root. Now it is only dead wood. And how often did the communities themselves of the west feel the inconveniences of abundance and wealth! A *people so well loved!* says Deuteronomy 32:15. *And now, pampered, they would throw off the yoke. Pampered, full-fed, swollen with pride, they forsook that divine creator, revolted against their deliverer.* Consider the number of religious orders, and the moral and scientific disciplines from which life imperceptibly has withdrawn! You might say that suddenly they bored the Almighty and that He became unmindful of them. Thus the Sorbonne continues to reverberate with the cawing of disputes, while two divine sparks fall, one into the heart of a Lorraine virgin, and the other into the heart of a Dutch monk. The Bible tells us that while Joseph directed Pharao's economy through abundance and penury, he gave to the world two sons, one called Manasses (Oblivion) and the second Ephraim (Fruitful).

Oblivion is only an appearance. Joseph forgot the straw which is good only for making fire and manure, but he did not forget the grain, food and seed, which filled his bags with his purified gold. This was true of the wise steward, praised by the Gospel, *who knows how to bring both new and old things out of his treasure-house* (Matth. 13:52), and who made everything he touched benefit from his infinite power of recreation and refreshment, for *Behold*, says the Apocalypse (21:5), *I make all things new*. Thus in our time we have seen scholasticism recover its honor and mysticism its interest. And who knows whether soon Scripture and the Fathers, today so sadly abandoned, will not resume on the tables of the religious the place occupied by fairly sickening historical and scientific apologetics? And yet Israel in the midst of her devastated fields and dried up wells gnaws the leather of her sandals and continues in a promised land, once flowing with milk and honey, but of which today the Dead Sea constitutes the principal curiosity, her harsh wintering. She might be saying the words of Job (17:13,15): *Among the shadows I must make my bed at last. What hope is this? Wait I patiently or impatiently, who cares?* Like the prophet's hostess, she does not even have a handful of flour and a drop of oil. All her meagre reserves are consumed. And precisely comes that *hunger* over all the earth predicted by the prophet Amos (8:11). *Man cannot live by bread alone, there is life for him in all the words that proceed from the mouth of God* (Deuter. 8:3). Men have become like dogs prowling about the city and foraging in garbage for a forgotten crust (Ps. 58:7,15). Then the man famished remembers former feastings. What he refused as a son, he thinks he can solicit as a mercenary. He heard that in Egypt where the famine is not less, there are strange things happening and there is a group of well-fed men in the midst of general distress: *beggars, that bring riches to many; disinherited, and the world is ours* (II Cor. 6:10). Why not levy taxes there to see what happens. We'll take money with us. It is not money that is lacking. Inflation has taken care of that.

Thus it is that between Joseph and his brothers contact was reestablished at the end. For centuries they were able to carry on as if this contact had not existed. Now they need it! *Quare negligitis?* They come back to him with bags and money for purely materialistic economic reasons. They speak to him because there is no way to avoid it. We only plan to ask him for *just* (the *just* being expressed by a given number of pieces of silver) what is necessary for our own independent existence. Thus it is that today all theologies, moralities and traditions are silent. Around the Christian City there remains only a scattered group of Bedouins who live off our leavings, our pieces pecked at and bartered and in exchange for which the Church receives one chance, a pass marked with the face of Caesar, an abstract power of acquisition. But these chance fragments are consumed almost immediately by usage. We needed less than a generation to see the end of Kantism and lay morality, and Israel returns famished to her unknown and inexhaustible brother. We see their bargainings. "Your intentions are not honest," said Joseph. "You plan to enter here as spies, *exploratores*, to explore in Pharao's land what is weakest and ill-defended, to carry out the role of destructive critics to which you have been so well adapted." To which the Jews find nothing to answer save a reference to their origins and their past— since the present is doubtless an insufficient guarantee. "Well!" says Joseph, "I give in! I will lengthen the rope! I grant you the measure of subsistence you need to persevere in your own way a few years or a few centuries. In the meantime you will permit me to keep as hostage Simeon, appropriately bound. But I ask you for Benjamin, whom your father Israel keeps close to him."

Who is Benjamin? Benjamin means the Son of the Right Hand.[6] There is only one Son of the Right Hand, the one about who is said in Psalm 109: *Sit here at my right hand.* Therefore when Joseph called for Benjamin, it was Jesus asking for Jesus, it was Jesus of Egypt, Jesus of the Humiliation asking for Jesus of the parousia, the last, *novissimus,* the one of whom He solemnly announced to Caiphas: *you will see the Son of Man again, when he is seated at the right hand of God's power, and comes on the clouds of heaven* (Matth. 26:64). And from whom does Joseph claim him? He claims Him from Israel in whose power He was mysteriously placed, because we know from Saint Paul that the conversion of Israel is the ante-

6. Benjamin and Joseph are both sons of Rachel, which means in Hebrew, *Ewe.* The son of the ewe is the *Lamb.*

This lamb, in the testament benediction of Jacob is compared to a wolf, *a ravening wolf, that must devour his own prey in the morning, and have plunder still to divide at nightfall* (Gen. 49: 27). But Isaias says: *Wolf and lamb shall feed together* (Is. 65: 25). The wolf is the unjust marauding animal to which the Lord allowed Himself to be compared, like a *thief,* when they said to Him: *Lord, knowing thee for a hard man, that reaps where he did not sow, and gathers in from fields he never planted* (Matth. 25: 24). The morning of His apparition *He will devour the prey,* namely all the nations given to Him as tribute according to the promise of Psalm 2:8: *Ask thy will of me, and thou shalt have the nations for thy patrimony.* Hence the words: *Slay then, and eat* (Deuter. 12:15). Transform the figures into substance. *Now, they shall rejoice in thy presence, as men rejoice when the harvest is in, and booty taken* (Is. 9:3). In the evening of the Last Judgment *You will divide the plunder,* the bodies with which we shall be again clothed, some for light and others for fire.

It is to be noted that Saint Paul belonged to the tribe of Benjamin (Phil. 3:5). He compares himself to a prematurely-born child: *And last of all, I too saw him, like the last child, that comes to birth unexpectedly* (I Cor. 15:8).

cedent of and the condition for the definitive Revelation. For Israel, through her incredulity, holds the χατεχον of the Apocalypse. It is she about whom it is said in Psalm 88:39: *Now thou hast only loathing and scorn for us; heavy thy hand falls on him thou hast anointed* (the three phases of Israel's attitude).

All this Joseph understood, although they did not suspect it (he always spoke to them through an interpreter). (Gen. 42: 23).

And the tribe returned to its Author, the blind patriarch Jacob, who did not agree to leave Chanaan. But the situation was not long in becoming again the same. The food brought from Egypt disappeared almost as quickly as that manna which melted in the rays of the sun. But once already the Eleven, without knowing it, went to Jesus through Joseph, and conversed with the One who is *the Way and the Life.* They even knew the conditions of final salvation. They have to take back with them their brother, the youngest, *minimus.*

And here the Gospel texts occur to me in great numbers. Jesus always identified Himself with small children. *Whoever welcomes such a child as this in my name, welcomes me* (Mark 9:36). *Unless you become like little children again, you shall not enter the kingdom of heaven* (Matth. 18:3). *The kingdom of God is like a grain of mustard seed; when this is sown in the earth, no seed on earth is so little* (Mark 4:31). *Father, thou hast hidden all this from the wise and the prudent, and revealed it to little children* (Matth. 11:25 and Luke 10:21). It is therefore useless for them to return to the Son of the ewe unless they take, as ambassador and guarantee, the smallest among them, *minimus.* Elsewhere it was said to them: *This man we told thee of warned us with a solemn oath he would not give us audience* (Gen. 43:3).[7] There is only one

7. cf. *They have angels of their own in heaven, that behold the face of my heavenly Father continually* (Matth. 18:10).

way to me which is that of humility and simplicity of attention.[8]

Then Juda, from whom all Jews today have taken their name, assumed full responsibility. *Give me the child. Never forgive me if I do not bring him back and restore him to thee. Let him go with me. If there had not been this delay, we might have been back again by now.* (Gen. 43:9-10).

So, in company with Benjamin, they left again, laden with presents, wild honey which Saint John the Baptist fed on, mastic which is used to glue together what has broken, myrrh, and almonds which in their shells resemble the dead wrapped in white in their caskets and waiting for the resurrection. They also brought *a double amount of money*. Silver *seven times refined* is the word of God which the Psalmist (11:7) says is *true*; that is, not prostituted to human use. The sum it makes is *double*, because the literal meaning has now received its accomplishment with the Messiah (cf. the two horns of the Lamb in the Apocalypse). The primitive sum which represents earthly values is now repeated in those cash transactions over the Atlantic which we know today.

From the top of his tower, Joseph saw the caravan approaching, the file of small trotting donkeys, the nine impressive Rabbis on their backs and their last brothers with them. And then he said to his servants these words which seem borrowed from the parable of the Prodigal Son and the Banquet: *Take these men home, and kill victims, and make a feast; they will eat with me at noon.*

Noon is the hour of full light, without shadows, the hour when the Bride of the Song of Songs takes hold of her spouse.

In the ante-chamber of their host, the Israelites did not feel

8. This direction upwards toward what is smallest, is the meaning, according to Father Athanasius Kirchner, of the Iota (jot), the letter i, the raised finger indicating the smallest point, the sign which the Lord Himself says will not disappear (Matth. 5: 18). The vertical *Iota* is the symbol of unity.

particularly reassured. Their money was refused, and they remained therefore in the position of debtors, having nothing to offer for the new credit against an asset which had no currency. This procedure of the Egyptians was puzzling and of a nature to worry heavy consciences: harshness, defiance and insulting language on one side; and on the other, in their bags, the free clandestine wheat. Now that we have fulfilled the required conditions, and that our reprieve is over, are we to be put into irons like Simeon? Like chosen victims of calumny, are you going *to hold us here in pawn, and our beasts along with us?*

Our beasts along with us! What are those gaping donkeys they want so much to save? In that time of famine when humans were half dead, the wretched donkeys must have been in a sad state. Wouldn't they do better to exchange each one of them for a sheep, in accord with the Counsel of Exodus (13: 13)?[9] Did they see in that animal which is both recalcitrant and docile solely the means of moving away and the guarantee of their independence? No. The ass, *Brother Ass*, as Saint Francis says, is our close associate, our caricature mount, our wretched body, made, as Ecclesiasticus (33:25) tells us, for *fodder, the whip and a pack to bear*. And yet the harps which the ancient Israelites hung from the willows of exile, the lament of the Israelites today before Solomon's rock, do not equal the terrible sob which that humiliated creature is capable of emitting from the depths of his nostalgia. Often his body alone is wiser than the proud intoxicated spirit, like that of the prophet Balaam, and refuses to take the road which a demented perverse will imposes on him (Num. 22:23).[10] Then it is that the ass crushes our foot (unless it is gout), as it

9. *When an ass has its first foal, thou shalt offer a sheep in payment of its ransom; if not, it must be killed.*

10. *The angel stood in a narrow entry, between two vineyard walls; and at the right of him the ass cowered close against one of the walls.* Calvary comes to mind.

cowers against the wall. And if we continue to berate it with bad treatment and wish we could kill it, it of itself bends its knee. Let us not fear, as the animal man does, the servitude they want to impose on *our beasts along with us.* Did not the Apostle say (I Cor. 9:27): *I buffet my own body, and make it my slave?* Rather than listening to this example of evil will, let us accept the advice which a bit farther on we hear Jacob give to Juda (Gen. 49:11): *To what tree will he tie the ass he rides on? The vine for him, the vineyard for him!* May its tendrils twist about the halter!

Then it was that Joseph in his majesty advanced toward his distressed brothers and invited them to take their places at his table. Verse 43:31 tells us that he *washed his face* of all the spit, doubtless, and blood, insults and impurities which were still on it from the time of their last interview. Everything transpired as in a dream, a dream of *deep sleep* from which they tell us old Jacob was going soon to awaken. The ancient order was reestablished, which is that of primogeniture. The Egyptians were in their place and Israel in hers, which was the first. But what is the feast composed of? What is the food they are invited to consume? Is it perhaps the unrecognized blessings whose inner meaning the time has come now to assimilate? It was a meal like that of Emmaus when the Lord, risen among His brothers, after revealing the prophecies to them, was recognized by them *in fractione panis.*

After the meal, according to the Oriental custom (still practiced in Japan), Joseph gave to each of his brothers a portion of the food, but the text tells us that Benjamin's portion was five times that of the others. It was therefore 6 to 1. Six is the number for Friday, the day of the week when all work is completed.[11]

11. And here another memory perhaps is not completely out of place. We should recall the story of Saul in search of strayed

Once more the Israelites set out on their asses with their sacks filled with wheat and the money for the purchase replaced for each one in the mouths of the sacks. If silver is the word of God, should we see in this symbol of the consecration formula pronounced over the unleavened bread[12] by which the physical cereal is transformed into a supernatural bread? But in the bottom of Benjamin's sack, there is also the silver cup which is the emblem of sacrifice and alliance and in which recognition and reconciliation will be consummated.

Thus we see that it is possible to interpret, without an ex-

---

asses, which are, in the service of man, the means of transport, investigation, commerce. They disappeared and their owner did not know what had happened to them. Following the advice of the virgins who went to get water, he decided to consult the Seer; and as he had no bread, he gave him half of the half of the shekel reserved in the sanctuary (*Media pars sicli Domino.*) which was in his servant's hand: all that remained in his possession of God's word. Samuel, who was giving a banquet that day, recognized him instantly, and taking him to the place of honor, said: *Eat thy fill; it was put aside for thee on purpose, when I invited my company. And here is all the best that Israel has to give, waiting for whom? For thee, and for thy father's kin.* And Saul answered: *For me, a man of Benjamin, the smallest of Israel's tribes?* Saul was then anointed, and as a sign of his mission there came to him three messengers bearing sacramental species (*) who *question him about peace,* and after them a company of prophets in whom those of the Old Testament can be seen. After which he was recognized as King (the King of the Jews!) and Samuel spoke to Israel this solemn warning: *You see how great is the wrong you have done; but now follow close where the Lord leads you, and serve him with all your hearts* (I King 9 and 12).

* *Then thou wilt reach the oak of Thabor* (the Thabor where the Apostles later will want to erect three tents), *and fall in with three men on pilgrimage to Bethel; one with three goats, one with three loaves of bread, one with a flagon of wine.* All emblems of the Trinity, which has been denied for so long a time by the Talmud.

12. *The tradition which I received from the Lord,* says Saint Paul (I Cor. 11:23), *and handed on to you.*

77

cess of subtlety, the entire story of Joseph and his brothers as that of the relationship continued in a clandestine way, *a tergo,* by a person or figure interposed between the Messiah and His people, when in the middle of the week, which is the entire duration of the universe, *offering and burnt sacrifice shall be none and desolation,* more terrible than the famine which once devastated Chanaan, *shall continue.* (Dan. 9:27). Between the moment when Joseph was thrown into the well and sold to the Gentiles for a few pieces of silver, and the moment when after many comings and goings, puzzling gifts, hidden propositions and fostered mistakes, the cup was found in Benjamin's bag, many centuries will have had time to pass. *But I am,* as is said in Isaias and the Apocalypse, *the First and the Last.* It is the application of the parable of briars (in Latin *zizanie.* Matth. 13). The double harvest, of wheat and sin, must both reach maturity, the first to be transformed into nourishing bread and the second to burn in the fires of love. *The wrong-doer,* says the Apocalypse (22:11), *must persist in his deeds of wrong, the corrupt in his corruption.* Meanwhile, not one particle of the compassion on the cross is lost for Israel. Joseph capitalized on it in his granaries. For what the ingratitude of the favorite child cost the heart of a father and a brother, you have only to refer to the story of David and Absalom in the Book of Kings. Absalom! my son Absalom! And in the story of Joseph we constantly see the unknown and unrecognized brother turn aside to weep, without seeing in him ignorance and hardness. Until the moment came, when, in the words of Genesis 45:1, *Joseph could contain himself no longer.*

So he gave orders that all these should leave his presence; there must be no strangers to see it, when he made himself known. But when he spoke, he burst into such a fit of weeping that these Egyptians, and all Pharao's household, could not but hear it. I am Joseph, said he to his brethren; is my father yet alive? But his brethren were so overcome with fear that they could not answer him, and he must needs use gentleness; Come closer, he said, and then, when they had drawn close to him, I am Joseph, that brother of yours whom you sent away to be sold as a slave in Egypt. And now, do not take it to heart; waste no regrets over the bargain that brought me here; if I came to Egypt first, it was on God's errand, to be your protector. It is two years now since famine came to these parts, and there will be no ploughing, no reaping harvests, for five years more; so God would have me here in readiness to preserve your race, by giving you food to live on. It was not your design, then, it was God's will that sent me here; he it is that has put Pharao himself under my tutelage, made me regent of all his domain, with the whole of Egypt under my care. Make haste, go back to my father and give him this message from his son Joseph. Tell my father of all these honors I enjoy, and of all you saw in Egypt. Then Joseph kissed all his brethren in turn, and wept over them, till at last they found courage to speak to him.—Bring your father here, and all your family, to share the blessings of Egypt with me, and live on the best the land can give. Leave none of your farm stock behind you; all the wealth of Egypt awaits you. He also had two new garments brought out for each, and gave Benjamin three hundred silver pieces and five new garments of the choicest sort. Thus he sent his brethren home, and his last word, as they set out, was Be sure there is no quarreling on the way. When they reached their father Jacob in Chanaan, they gave him their news, Thy son Joseph is still alive, and it is he that rules the whole land of Egypt. Jacob heard it, with the look of one just awoken from a heavy sleep, but at first he would not believe them, and they must tell him the whole story from first to last. Then, when he had seen for himself the waggons

79

and all the gifts, he could breathe again. If my son Joseph, he said, is still alive, that is all I ask; I will go with you, and have sight of him again before I die.

What can we add to this pathetic story except a few secondary difficulties in our role of stammering amateur exegete? If the conversion of the Jews is to be put off until the end of time, why does our text say that we are only in the second year and there will be five years of famine during which we will neither sow nor reap? We might say that according to our text the definitive return of Israel seems to take place at two times. Joseph told them who he was without provoking in their hearts anything save terror. It was only when *he had wept over them in turn (ad singulos)* that their tongues were loosed and they dared to speak to him. It would therefore seem that the general moving of Israel's flocks to green pastures is to be preceded by a series of individual conversions. Israel must herself be in Israel the interpreter and the ambassador of that brother once given over to the nations. That will take time, for Jacob is no longer in one place. He is enlarged to the size of Chanaan. We are no longer at the time of the Ghetto. The Jews have answered the invitation to come near. Christian life, customs, books and ideas envelope and penetrate them from all directions. Their desperate poverty and the Catholic superabundance at the heart of that Delta watered by all the rivers of Paradise, coexist and cohabit. Several commentators esteem that the Thousand Years of Triumph of Christ in the Apocalypse are contemporary and coextensive with the Reign of the Beast. Perhaps this applies to the Seven Years Famine and Plenty. It is by His Presence that Jesus Christ created Absence. It is by Bread that He created the need for Bread. It is by Revelation He gave its meaning to blindness. It is by light He constituted darkness. He sent Fire, and the prophet Amos tells us He also sent Hunger. The coarse bread watered with tears which natural religion permitted man to harvest from difficult perilous furrows has disappeared. All that is left to feed humanity are those synthetic products, copiously wrapped in three or four charlatan advertisement envelopes which M. Homais keeps in his drug-store jar. Outside of the Church, there is no longer the means of sowing or harvesting anything whatsoever, and she is the source of whatever is able to send forth some shoot. *You have been yoking my heifer to your plough*, says the prophet (Judges 14:18), *or my riddle would be unanswered still*. Accept boldly, Israel, this alimony which through a happy fault the brother not outcast but merely sent on ahead drew up for your profit. At these words, Genesis tells us, Jacob became like a man *just awoken from a heavy sleep*, but he did not want to believe yet. He had to be shown those chariots ready for his moving, for the transport of what legitimately belonged to him, from the realm of the letter to that of the spirit. That famished man who forgot the taste of bread has to relax his jaws closed tightly in a convulsive refusal, for is it not of him that is written: *Drained of strength, like grass the sun scorches, I leave my food untasted, forgotten* (Ps. 101:5).

THE SECOND WORD

Woman, this is thy son. This is thy mother.

THE first word of Christ on the cross concerned the people, the city He had behind Him, *a tergo*, back of Him. The second is addressed with a final testament authority to the group standing at His feet: to Mary and John. The word of God is an act and does what it says. When the mouth which created the world said to Mary, in designating to her under

81

the name of *disciple* all who, with regard to the teaching of Christ, are capable of listening and following: *Woman, this is thy son*, it was in effect and efficaciously a mother who was given to us, a maternal relationship in the most complete sense of the word which was established between her and us; that is to say, someone with us in relationship to that seed of Christ which placed in us does not stop engendering and nourishing.[1] Let us examine this idea more closely.

God is both outside of us and within us. And the work of the soul in prayer, sustained and penetrated by Grace in the most intimate of its habits, is to bring One to the Other according to this word of the Song of Songs (8:1,2): *Would that thou wert my brother, nursed at my own mother's breast! Then I could meet thee in the open street and kiss thee, and earn no contemptuous looks. To my mother's house I will lead thee, my captive; there thou shalt teach me my lessons, and I will give thee spiced wine to drink, fresh brewed from my pomegranates. The brother,* just born, *nursing at our mother's breast,* may well be the Child Jesus, whom Christian art in our churches has represented in all centuries in the arms of the Madonna. And the Mother who feeds Him is Mary, associated at the most imperceptible beginning with what in us is the apparition, the forming and the growth of her Son, and who furnishes him counsel, cooperation and matter *(materia)* for she is supremely the *Mother of Good Counsel.* It is she who says to us in essence: *Do all that He says.*[2] When her Son seems to rebuff us, she is not deceived and she encourages with a swift pressing of her hand. *Do whatever He tells you.* And

1. *Blessed is the womb that bore thee, the breast which thou has sucked . . . Blessed are those who hear the word of God, and keep it* (Luke 11:27-28).

2. At that moment Jesus has just said to His Mother: *My time has not come yet* (John 2:4). But it is by her it will come. *They have no wine left,* she said (remember the passage of the Song of

already she is prepared to furnish us explanation, advice and strength. It is she who in occult fashion secretly furnishes us below with the funds destined to satisfy that credit with whose everlasting demand the Spirit through the Son makes on us, from on high. These funds may be called milk, substance, sap, materials of our house, or of our body. It is because of her that we can give to God what the Proverbs (31:31) call *Work such as hers:* works which in reality belong to her and which, reaching their maturity, glorify, when they appear at the threshold, the mother who engendered them. Her understanding moves in every direction. She knows the propitious moments, like those piercing eyes of a woman always attentive to the circumstance. She encourages by telling us softly, like Rebecca, that, after all, we have to deal with a blind father, always on the point of being deceived, and that she is strong when needed. Moreover she has with Him a relationship which goes way back, farther back than the camels of Eleazar could go. For the Epistle of the Immaculate Conception informs us that, occupying the principal place in the plan of the Creation, *she was ordained for all eternity before the earth was,* and that when God was composing all things, she was there playing in a hundred reflections. This is precisely what Ecclesiastes (3:11) tells us that *the curse of the Mother uproots the foundation* of our nature and that the Fifth Commandment on the theological record tells us *to honor the Father and the Mother.*

But Scripture, in the words of King Solomon, invites us to consider with more detail this operation of Woman and this

---

Songs we just quoted and the other one (2:4): *Into his own banqueting hall the king has brought me, shewn me the blazon of his love.* And Jesus pretends to reprimand her impatience: *Nay, woman, why dost thou trouble me with that?* She knows very well what she can trouble Him with!

arrangement of resources which we leave at her disposal with more or less avarice. Listen to the words of King Solomon and the vision by which his mother taught him. This could not concern poor Bethsabee. It is the famous text of the Strong Woman, whose name recalls the Strongly-armed one in the Gospel, and who begins with a cry of love, a deep and almost animal-like accent of the loving woman: *My beloved! The beloved of my womb! The beloved of my prayers!* As at the marriage of Cana, it was no longer the time of water, but of wine, and the instructions at the beginning of time of this experienced ancestor echoed in advance the words with which the public life of Our Lord began: *They have no wine left.* But for whom is to be poured the wine of the Spirit whose effusion on the day of Pentecost caused the Apostles to appear like men drunk? Not for those whom our text calls *the Kings* (that is, the elevated faculties of the soul, the established authorities, the intelligence and the imagination), for fear lest they totter and grow confused and indiscreetly reveal that mystery which is the seal of love. *Do not disclose hastily what thy eyes have witnessed,* says the Book of Proverbs (25:9), and Isaias (24:16): *Heart, keep thy secret; heart, keep thy secret!* The place of the secret is in the depths of our being, as the place of the wine is in the cellar, according to the Song of Songs (2:4): *Into his own banqueting hall the king has brought me, shewn me the blazon of his love.* The chalice is reserved for humble and penitent hearts, according to these words of verse 6, and the words of Psalm 59:5: *Heavy the burden thou didst lay on us; such a draught thou didst brew for us as made our senses reel.* The effect of wine, of that liquid fire in us, is to open and liberate what was closed and to dilate what was confined. *Give thy voice for dumb pleader and for doomed prisoner* (Prov. 31:8). He is a prisoner, in truth, who receives birth from us in our image, and those acts which

84

create habits and those habits which gradually constitute in him a second nature, and make a new being. Happy is the man who recognizes himself with glory in those works, in those legitimate sons issued from a deeper bond than flesh and blood, and which Scripture (Prov. 17:6) compares to a *crown. Her children are the first to call her blessed* (Prov. 31:28). On the contrary, much to be pitied are those who by weakness, disorder and perversity nourish and let grow in them *alien foes* from whom, in the prayer of the Psalm (143:11), we ask that God deliver us. They do not recognize themselves in these foes, their own works cause them surprise and horror. *The alien born,* says another psalm (17:46), *come slinking out of their strongholds to cringe before me.* And the Song of Songs (1:5): *My own brothers had a grudge against me.* Genesis (21:10) speaks of them in an image: *Rid thyself of this slave woman and her son.* For (Gal. 4:31) *we are sons of the free woman, not of the slave.* It is for us, by means of inner attentiveness, to have an eye on what transpires within us, to scrutinize the mass, to discern and encourage those sentiments —poor, timid, transitory, fugitive sentiments—which an unbearable pressure prevents reaching us, and to invite them to come in and tell us what they have to say.

That is where the support of the *strong Woman* is necessary for our infirmity. It is in the name of that uncertain stammering image of her Son within us that we appeal to her maternity. She shares all the secrets of the Sacred Heart. Is it not she who cries out in Psalm 118:162: *Victors rejoice not more over rich spoils, than I in thy promises,* and Psalm 67:13: *Routed the kings, routed their armies; they have left their spoils for house wives to carry away. She comes, the princess, all fair to see,* Psalm 44:14 tells us. It is by a certain decorum mysteriously shared that Grace exercises its multiform attraction on our hearts, won over by admiration. *Foes so violent,* says

Isaias 53:12, *baulked of their spoil! Such is his due, that gave himself up to death.* In this sharing, she will have her part.

Does she not busy herself with wool and threads. These are the most supple and solid material products in the animal and vegetable realms. *Plying her hands with ready skill* (Prov. 31:13), with her ingenious multiple hands she crossed the thread with the woof (like a pianist whose right hand either listens to the left hand or pretends to ignore it). *Who held the winds in the hollow of his hand?* another text says to us (Prov. 30:4).

Ever she steers her course like some merchant ship, bringing provision from far away (Prov. 31:14). This word admirably suits the Virgin Mary whose role is to be intermediary and negotiator between two worlds *(procul et de ultimis finibus)*, and who brought us the eucharistic bread which she can rightfully call *hers.* There is a long course navigation and a coasting navigation.

From early dawn she is up, assigning food to the household so that each waiting-woman has her share (Prov. 31:15). It is she in secret, like nature, and within our consciousness, while we sleep, who begins to work and takes care to strengthen our spiritual forces, *to suggest all things to us,* as it is said of that Spirit which *she holds in her hands.*

Ground must be examined, and bought, and planted out as a vineyard, with the earnings of her toil (Prov. 31:16). This ground she looked at is the Church, and it is also our soul to which she furnished redemption and about which it is said that it was bought at a high price.[3] The vineyard she planted from that fruit we see in her hands, is the cross.

3. *Do not be afraid, I have bought thee for myself, and given thee the name thou bearest: thou belongest to me* (Isaias 43:1). *Out on the rebellious city, the defiled city, so full of wrong!* (Sophonias 3:1).

How briskly she girds herself to the task, how tireless are her arms! (Prov. 31:17). She is strong both in resistance and operation: both a tower and an irresistible and diligent arm.

Industry, she knows, is well rewarded, and all night long her lamp does not go out (Prov. 31:18). In turn she enjoys God and enjoys our soul transformed by Grace. As the steward at the marriage of Cana tasted the water transformed into wine (John 2:9), she applauds the result of her transactions. *How gracious the Lord is! Taste and prove it* (Prov. 33:9). She is, in the dark night, around us, the lamp of vision and faith, which does not lack oil.

Jealously she sets her hands to work, her fingers clutch the spindle (Prov. 31:19). The hard things are the great enterprises of penance and apostleship. The spindle turning, while her fingers detach from the tow a loose thread, is the continuation of the Church, the pure unbroken tradition, like unto itself, of hierarchy and doctrine, which is disengaged from the confused whirl of circumstances.

Kindly is her welcome to the poor, her purse ever open to those in need (Prov. 31:20). Not only does she give to the poor, but she seeks them out, she offers her hand to them, she establishes a contact and a bond with them.

Let the snow lie cold if it will, she has no fears for her household; no servant of hers but is warmly clad (Prov. 31:21). Mary was not afraid of the cold of the snow at Bethlehem, when embracing her new-born child against her heart, she made for Him with her arms a love nest. Thus every Christian home over which she presides like an honored queen has nothing to fear from the outside inclemencies, from that hard season of contraction and avarice when water rather than spreading and bringing life, is congealed into a geometric figure and when the entire earth seems to us an empty desert, monotonous and desolate. Her servants are armed against the harshness and hostility of the atmosphere. They are in truth a party to that privilege of the First-born to whom, according to Deuteronomy 21:17, *a double share of all his goods belongs,* which means both in reality and figuratively. For Ecclesiasticus (42:25) tells us: *All things he has made in pairs, balanced against one another; never a fault of symmetry.* And elsewhere: *Consider the works of the Almighty: two and two and one against one.* Thus everything in Creation is contrast, opposition, composition, complement, reflection. Everything has a right and a wrong side, and in everything within or without we discover the blessing of the Creator.

Made by her own hands was the coverlet on her bed, the clothes of lawn and purple that she wears (Prov. 31:22). We think of those varied and embroidered figures, *opus plumarii,* which, according to Exodus, covered the veils of the tabernacle. One stitch beside another stitch, a chainstitch as seamstresses say, and from all those lines and colors are born all kinds of forms, shades and suggestions. Is she not the one who, as our book says, *plays in the presence of the Almighty,* the Ark of the Covenant in sight of His face which transforms light into color? Psalm 44:15 tells us that she wears *a robe of rich embroidery.* Such are the endless marvels which the Communion of Saints offers us. *Clothes of lawn and purple that she wears.* Lawn is what we are able to furnish ourselves. The whiteness is an ability to receive divine impressions, while the purple, which is our glory and the insignia of our royal priesthood (I Peter 2:9), is the blood of Jesus Christ.[4]

None so honored at the city gate as that husband of hers, when he sits in council with the elders of the land (Prov. 31:23). *The husband,* spoken of here, is supreme Man, the Son of Man. Rightfully the Virgin Mary in speaking of Him applies the possessive: *that husband of hers.* He does belong to

4. *Esther put on her royal robes* (Esther 5:1).

her completely, both juridically by the consent they exchanged, and materially by the flesh and blood she gave to Him. Of all the roles by which a woman can envelope a man and prevent him from being elsewhere, wife, mother, daughter, sister, none here is lacking. It is certainly of her that the prophet Jeremias spoke when he uttered the oracle (31:22): *weak woman is to be the protectress of man's strength.* She surrounds him completely, furnishes him with everything which contains the word in the voice, with everything that is necessary to its form. Through an unimaginable miracle, the finite captured the infinite and contained it, gave it stature, expression and means. *I might span the sky's vault,* says Ecclesiasticus (24:8), *pierce the depth of the abyss, walk on the sea's waves.* I participated in the effusions of the inexhaustible source, and they served me as road. *I was there,* says the Book of Proverbs (8:27), *when he levelled the fountain springs of the deep.* And as she fashioned Christ in her own womb, so she fashions the Christian in the image of the One she loves, until the moment comes for him to leave. That is why the sacred texts represent her especially as presiding over gates. *At the city's approach,* says the Book of Proverbs (8:3), *close beside the gates. Blessed are they,* says verse 34, *who listen to me, keep vigil, day by day, at my threshold, watching till I open my doors.* This refers to the two commandments. *Our God,* says Psalm 67:21, *is a God of deliverance; the Lord is our Master, that saves men from peril of death.* It is the *peril* in the eternal *sunrise,* mentioned in Psalm 64 and to which leads the *Eastern Gate. When he sits with the counsellors of the earth,* who are the *elders* of the Apocalypse. The elders represent what is oldest in humanity, old age, that time when the primordial and unalterable element in us has the upper hand, when, from the principle having reached its full maturity, man has taken possession of his domain and realized around him all there was to do. *The innocent*, says Psalm 91:15, *will flourish in a green old age* (and Wisdom 4:9); *ripe of age*, a stainless life, a life not sullied by the insult of mud and the skin eruption of sin, the whiteness which is the fruit of age as it is the flower of innocence.

She made a shroud and sold it, and furnished a sash to the man of Canaan (Prov. 31:24). The covering is all that clothes us on the outside, all that Grace adds to nature, according to the word of Saint Paul: *It is not because we would be stripped of something; rather, we would clothe ourselves afresh* (II Cor. 5:4). It is both a luminous colored emanation of our personality and a separation from the exterior. It is the priest's robe. It is the habit or the veil of the religious. (Of a nun you say that she is taking the veil.) It is the finery of the bride. And it is also the shroud of the dead. *Cloak of divine protection thrown about thee*, says Baruch 5:2. *And she sold it.* We think of that one pearl, which, to procure, it is recommended not to hesitate to see all that we have, and it is suggested on each page of the Gospel, as a counsel of perfection, to sell all in order to follow our master. To sell is to transform what we have belonging to us, adapted to an immediate pleasure, into something abstract, general, future, eventual and portable. It is to transform our possession of something into a right over everything. *But perhaps*, says Deuteronomy 14:24-25, *the journey will be too long, the place which he has chosen too far distant. Why then, sell all this tithe of thine?* Everything is transformed for us into that round Yes, into that piece of money which we have only to open our hand to give up, so that what is destitution for man will correspond to what is gratuity for God, and that with Nothing we buy Everything. *She furnished a sash to the man of Canaan.* The Canaanite was the inhabitant of the Promised Land before the people of God had colonized it. He is the Pagan in us, the natural man. It is not enough to furnish him with a new covering and to clothe him with it. The clothing must suit him, cling to the body and make one with him rather than float about him vaguely and ridiculously, impeding his gait. That is the function of the sash, exact in its measurement, which goes around the body and represents the precise commandments—general and particular—within which we have to form our habits. *Love of right shall be the baldric he wears,* says Isaias 11:5. *Faithfulness the strength that girds him.* (Just now it was lawn and purple.) You might almost say his equipment, like the *armor of light* (Rom. 13:12) with which Saint Paul clothes the Christian knight.

And she will laugh at the last day, or, in Hebrew, *she will laugh at the future* (Prov. 31:25). Laughter is that joy which opens up the countenance—a burst which mounts to the eyes and face and makes it blossom like a rose—when eternal hope in us surmounts the momentary obstacle and is amused at the victory which it offers, at that contrast between what is going to be soon and what already no longer quite exists.

Thus Mary is depicted for us in Scripture, and also the Catholic Church of which she is the figure. To both can apply the sublime praise which I have just now respectfully let pass between my fingers. The Church is in truth something quite different from the abstract definition of a collective fact. It has a life, a conscience, an activity, a figure, a personality, a leader, and an intelligence dominating an instinct quite clearly perceived in a purpose; it has a capacity for appraisal infinitely attentive, patient and delicate, with regard to inner and outer decorum; a decisive force of elimination with regard to harmful foreign elements; a common vocation served by an infinitely complex detailed organization—a government and administration by itself—and above all that, a name, and above the name, a crown. In certain traits the Church resembles human Societies. But human Societies are all formed in view of a particular advantage, permanent or temporary. They are the result, and even nations are, of a pact which, practically speaking, requires only a feeble part of our activities, and from which the individual is always able to escape. They are at the service of the individual and for his advantage, and it is solely through an abuse that they pretend today to grant the primacy to the state and animate that idol. The family itself is only an arrangement of limited proprieties. But there is another type of society: animal or physiological colonies of which not one element could subsist outside of the whole. In the beehive, in the coral reef, in those cellular complexes (which Dr. Alexis Carrel has carefully studied and which seem to know in advance what they have to do—a tremendous labor of invention and construction), it is the society which does the essential, and the individual is only the integrating element which, if separated, would perish. And it is with this second type of society that the human individual himself, with all that he unites in his own body, is the best example, and with which the Church represents the closest resemblance. I mean that it is both infinitely multiple and intensely one. As the soul uses the body in order to realize itself in relationship with the exterior and furnish all that is needed for its operation and impression on the circumstance, so this obligation to the expression, to the praise and to the beauty which calls forth and maintains this bride of Christ, is also the profound reason for the appearance of each of us and the development of each of our roles. In like manner, the dove and the fish provide for their feathers and scales. *Speciosa mea, columba mea.* Our tribes, harmonically and organically necessary one for the other in the bond of love, are completed and joined as in the shadings on the breast of the turtle-dove. We do not dispose solely our strength for loving, understanding and serving God, but of everything at once, from the Blessed Virgin at the summit of all the heavens to that poor African leper who, a bell in his hand, uses a mouth half rotted away to breathe out the responses of the mass. All creation visible and invisible, all history, all the past, all the present and all the future, all nature, all the treasure of the saints multiplied by Grace—all that is at our disposal, all that is our prolongation and our prodigious equipment. All the saints and all the angels are ours. We can use the intelligence of Saint Thomas, the arm of Saint Michael, the heart of Joan of Arc and of Catherine of Siena. We have only to touch all the latent resources in us to see them rise up. All that is good and important and beautiful from one end of the earth to the other, all that creates holiness in the world, is, in a sense, our work. We participate in the heroism of missionaries, in the inspiration of doctors, in the generosity of martyrs, in the genius of artists, in the burning prayer of the nuns of Saint Clare and the Carmelites. From the north to the south, from alpha to omega, from the east to the west, all is one with us, we are clothed with it, we instigate it, we are both revealed and humbled in this orchestral operation. Food, breathing, circulation, elimination, appetite, perfect balance of debt and possession, whatever in the undivided body is entrusted to the monks singing in their monasteries, is found in the immense encompassing of Christianity. All that is in us almost without our knowing it, and the Church translates it in general lines and depicts it outside of us on a scale of magnificence. Our brief blind impulses are wedded, revived, interpreted and developed in immense stellar movements. Outside of us, at astronomical distances, we decipher the text microscopically inscribed in the bottom of our hearts.

This is the person whom Christ at His death ordered to go to meet us like a *cherished* mother, so that she would establish herself in a *cherished* people (Ecclesiasticus 15:2 and 24:16). It is she who possesses the beginning of all things and in whom we know our care has been entrusted. It is with her in the most comprehensive part of our nature that we reached an understanding. *What am I*, asks the Church (Prov. 8), *the wisdom that speaks to you? Good counsel is mine. Through me kings learn how to reign, lawgivers how to lay down just decrees. Love me, and thou shalt earn my love; wait early at my doors, and thou shalt gain access to me.* Consoling words for those who have the habit of daily mass and for whom it is written a bit farther on (v. 34): *Blessed are they who listen to me, keep vigil, day by day, at my threshold, watching till I open my doors.* This means the heart, the thought and the eyes are directed toward the Tabernacle. *The gifts I bring with me are riches and honor, princely state and the divine favor . . . failing never to enrich the souls that love me with abundant store* (v. 18, 21). And then begins the famous text which I have commented on so many times: *The Lord made me his when first he went about his work, at the birth of time, before his creation began* (Prov. 8:22). He considered this creature both passing and eternal, made of a head and members, which furnished Him His residence and allowed the Creator to possess His creature in a close conjunction. It is for her and through her that all things have been made. It is for her, says verse 28, that *he fixed the sky overhead*, Heaven whose keys He gave her, with the power to bind and loose. It is she who provides Him, so to speak, with a contact, a support, a separation justified by love, a consolidation in difference, a basis, a deep enough abyss to absorb this sublimity. She disposes of all His treasures, she has been made their dispenser; she has put Him into her cupboard. *When he enclosed the sea within its confines* (Prov. 8:29): these are the dogmas, the canon, the theological definitions, the disciplinary moral prescriptions, *forbidding the waters*—thereby miraculously associating gratuity with the condition of things, *to transgress their assigned limits,* for it is said in the Book of Wisdom (7:24): *nothing can penetrate this way and that, ethereal as she.* She penetrates with that intimate virtue which allows her to communicate in everything with the essence, with the most essential, with the last end. *When he poised the foundations of the world,* that is, on the attraction of height he suspended a corresponding weight. When he *levelled the fountain springs of the deep,* that is, when prayer, effort, study, sacrifice and holy works in us answer the invitations of love, when He proportions His mercy to our needs: *See where the Lord comes . . . in all the glory of his majesty; take refuge, now, in some rock-cavern* (Is. 2:10). And Job tells us (26:8): *cloud-bound he holds the rain,* that is, the obscurities of faith, *that else would spill on earth all at once.* And that is really, as verse 27 tells us, the law by which *he fenced in the waters with a vault inviolable,* for what vault is deeper than the heart of man?

This is the Mother in whom by baptism we have received a second birth.

THE THIRD WORD

This day thou shalt be with me in Paradise.

THE Jews are behind Jesus on the cross. At His feet, there is Mary who is the Church. Let us mount higher, up to Him. On His level, at His right and at His left, sharing the same fate, raised, spread out, exposed, proposed, in the same attitude, forming with Him one group, a single garland, there are two thieves, carrying out the prophecy of Isaias (53:12): *He*

95

would be counted among the wrong-doers. These three crosses together, equipped in this way, form Calvary. These are the two companions whom He chose for Himself from all of mankind for His final stopping-place.

In early eras, among primitive peoples, the thief was exposed to general reprobation, and carried the very object of his theft, the exhibit: on his head the jar which he had stolen, around his neck the purse which he had cut off with a razor blade from its legitimate owner. To rob is to seize what does not belong to us, to claim for ourselves what existed for another. I ask you, what is less suitable for a being than nothing, for the Infinite than the finite, for the divine than a man relative, weak, mortal, animal? When God took possession of the human form, when He assumed it for His use, when He entered it, and was hypostasized therein, He committed an intolerable misdemeanor, a crime, equally opposed to justice, common sense, propriety, which scholars will rant and rave about until the end of time. There are some things which are not admissible. Let us plant then on this gibbet in view of all the heavens and for the edification of all the centuries this transgressor caught in the act of recovering goods which we had every reason to consider our exclusive privilege. In procuring from us the means of dying, He stole that right to the Void which, since Original Sin, constitutes the clearest part of our assets. He embezzled our capital for His profit. He suddenly claimed for His Father all that fortune, all that money for exploitation which we considered subject for loan and for an avariciously discussed contract. That is why He deserved the title of *Thief*, which officially He ascribed to Himself.[1] Is it not said (John 10:1) that the man who *instead of entering by the door*, where the devil keeps guard, *comes to steal and*

1. *Behold, I come as a thief comes* (Apoc. 16:15). *The day of the Lord will come like a thief in the night* (I Thessalonians 5:2).

plunder? Because of the Virgin's complicity, a secret theft has been perpetrated on our nature. And the damage is permanent. Our wall henceforth bears a cleft, which despite our labor, we will never be able to repair. *In my God's strength,* says Psalm 17:30, *I shall leap over all their defences.* We are no longer safe in our own house.

But then, you will say to me, why is it written in Psalm 68:5, *Should I make amends to them, I, that never robbed them?* It is true, Jesus Christ did steal something. He contracted a debt by fraud. He took possession of a fortune—human nature—which is mortgaged. He accepted full responsibility for it. This is explained in the two hands of Our Lord, extended on each side and those co-representatives whom Humanity hoisted up to them on His right and on His left. God in His definitive manifestation had to appear in His legal place which is the middle, according to these words of the Gospel (John 1:26): *There is one standing in your midst of whom you know nothing,* and of Proverbs (8:2): *Wisdom stands, on some high vantage-point by the public way, where the roads meet.*

With all the vision we have, let us consider on the summit of Calvary this triple sign-post, and, on either side, the beginnings of that double chain, continued in endless links, which is attached to the median pike. In the first of His words Jesus put the Jews behind Him; in the second, He constituted a Church at His feet; in the third He established in relationship to Himself a right and a left. He elected and therefore rejected. He caused a separation. It was like this on the days of Creation. He appeared as God immersed and almost disappearing in His operation, in full humanity, on the cross itself, in full sin. Around Him there is only sin, according to the word of David: *None can lay hands on the king whom the Lord has anointed but he incurs guilt* (I Kings 26:9). For if there had not been any sin, there would not have been any redemption, nor any penalty. There would not have been any appeal of air, that monstrous rising up to Him of blasphemy and need. The left hand of the Good Thief asks Him to be there, the right hand of the Bad Thief desperately asks Him not to exist. Each of these two hands seems separated from its other by an impassable hiatus. And God remains in the middle, His arms extended, as on the days of Creation, according to the word of the prophet (Jer. 27:5): *My strength it was, the exertion of my power, that made earth.* And it is in the same extreme attitude that He continues to be present in the activity of His redemption (Deuter. 5:25).

Our arm is a lateral, direct, jointed and rotary member attached to our shoulder, an appendage which serves for practicing exterior swinging and action feats, and for moving, with regard to the outside, from the general to the particular. The microscope shows us in the most rudimentary being, in the ameba which is a semi-fluid capsule, the faculty to grow and create at will all kinds of ambulatory, tactile or prehensile antennae, adapted to the humble task it pursues, and to be in a state of preparedness with regard to whatever surrounds it. The arm, solidly attached by the clavicle on man's shoulder and on the triangular plate of the shoulder-blade, is a universal instrument—a powerful supple assemblage of levers, pulleys and ligaments—a mechanical reduction of all the possibilities of our person, which prolongs our intelligence and our sensibility and permits it domination and enterprise over matter. This powerful member at our disposal is like an attribute of divinity. *Let us see thee shew strength like the strength of God* (Job 40:4). It is the right hand which works and the left hand which serves as support, reserve, auxiliary. *Your right hand, Lord,* says Exodus, *has been magnified in strength.* And in Isaias (42:13): *Like a giant the Lord shall go out to battle, like a warrior that stirs up his own rage.* It is this same right hand now which He stretches out to His work to take it back and draw it to Him: *To the work of your hands,* says Job, *you will stretch out your right hand.* He took the initiative, with this generous open hand which the decisive nail forever keeps from closing. *His own right hand brought him victory,* says Psalm 97:1, and also (Ps. 17:36): *thy right hand supports me.* We have only to take it in order to make it ours, in order to be one with it. For if there is a virtue, as the Gospel says, in the hem of the garment, there is surely more virtue in the five fingers so delicately prehensile at the end of the hand, in that sensibility for detail which is inserted and insinuated in our hand, as strong and living, as skillful and calculating and subtle as language is. In daily life our hand is busy with endless tasks, but when we are on the cross, it is closely joined with the hand of God.

But the left hand on the side of the Bad Thief is extended the same length. What does that mean? We have said that the action of the left hand is that of support and supplying. By nature it is in the service of the right hand. That is why Our Lord tells us, in the extreme and paradoxical form He often uses: *thou shalt not so much as let thy left hand know what thy right hand is doing* (Matth. 6:3). The right intention alone is important. It does not consider our left hand which has only to provide what is commanded of it, without which there would be only disorder and clumsiness. Its role is not to judge, but to guess, to serve, as under the action of a reflex, without delay or ill-will. The right hand alone brings something new: its function is to do and to give. On the contrary, the role of the left hand is to take, not by chance, but in consideration of the advantage and usefulness it has for the work accomplished by the right hand. It furnishes and at times it proposes. But the artisan does not know it as an end—*nescit*

99

vos—he uses it simply as a means. This is what happens in the case of evil, which, unable—because of its deviation—to receive the seal of Grace, can however be useful and necessary to a work which continues toward the right, in furnishing it an opportunity and shape; and a provocation to light.[2] Whence comes the general consensus that the left, the sinister declension, is considered the side of reprobation, toward which no kind intention is directed. To go to the left is to give to the position of the means the end position, namely to sin. That is why Ecclesiastes tells us (10:2): *The fool's wits are astray; the wise man's right is to him left.* And Proverbs (4:27): *To the right lie such ways as win the Lord's favor.* God extends His arm and metes out His justice according to this word of the Apostle (II Cor. 6:7): *To right and to left we must be armed with innocence.* He is present not merely from the fact of the natural support He furnishes each of His creatures (without which the creature would fall into the void), and which causes the Psalmist to say (138:8): *if I sink down to the world beneath, thou art present still.* He is still present, efficaciously, truly, administratively, in such a way that no one development or episode or result of Revelation will not have its repercussion in the Infernal City, and add one trait, one organ to that monstrous body which is like the wrong side and the negation of the Church, for evil is not creative and all the art of Satan is the shaping of an absence by means of a refusal. The work of time in regard to Satan is to replace general blasphemy by a detailed organized refusal. It is this contact with the Christ of the entire world of sin which is provided by the extended arm of the Bad Thief, maintained by

2. Thus it is that the left hand of the pianist has as a role not only to listen, support, ask, prepare and meditate, but to create from the exterior a kind of barrage and enclosure within which the song of the right hand can develop all its power.

rope and nail, hitched to the corresponding instrument of his Creator. On the day of his uprooting, Satan, when hurled down, was at least able to hide in the bottom of hell. Now he is again hoisted in full light in the person of his tool, he is attached by force for eternity to that hand from which he is separated by a space opened to justice and which mercy cannot cross.

It is this mystery of the Infernal Constitution, of the communion and the solidarity of evil, of the organization and explicitness of sin which are revealed to us in descriptions, on the pages of chapters 40 and 41 of Job, of Behemoth and Leviathan, where limited exegetes were determined to see only incongruous portraits of the elephant and the whale, or even the rhinoceros and the crocodile, or the sperm whale and other monsters from the bestiary. We should notice first that these two proper nouns are collective expressions. *Behemoth* is a feminine plural, such as *The Beast of Beasts*; and *Leviathan* is formed on two words, one of which means *to copulate* and the other *serpent*. The gloss tells us: *Draco copulans sibi aut aliis copulatus.*[3] *Here is Behemoth, my creature as thou art. None of God's works can vie with him,* since beside Christ who is the one way, He invented this variant, this fork (gibbet) which is evil. (Remember the word of the Serpent in Genesis: *you yourselves will be like gods, knowing good and evil.) He will apply His sword,* which means He will be both the instrument and the object of His justice, of that sword which pierces, kills and separates. Behemoth seems to personify the spirit of evil, especially in its massive, impenetrable quality. It is a heavy enough block for its weight to solidify the enormous fall in its permanent condition. Nothing shakes this mass, nothing penetrates this compact tenacious granite.

3. cf. the frontispiece of the first edition of *The Leviathan* of Hobbes which represents a beast made out of a multitude.

Now, Lucifer who drank fire from the cup of Dawn, has become an eater of hay. He asks for food from what is lowest, from the grass born out of mud. His habitation is mountains which designate pride, or on the contrary the low places, congested and boggy, where the spongy earth softly gives way under the body and offers to laziness and will power the filthy complicity of a rotted sodden ground. Therein dreams the friend of darkness, sheltered by a precarious unhealthful vegetation, by today's reeds, by the willows on the edge of the torrent which seem a prey to eternal flight. It is therein that he ruminates his memories and simmers his plans. All the instincts of the flesh play around him. He feels his belly large enough to swallow all the unsealed rivers of benediction and grace, the inexhaustible baptism up above which is prepared for the entire earth. We are reminded of the Assyrian bull whose face looks at the sun, but whose lower part has become bestial and quadruped. Such is the base in the center of matter on which Satan builds his Church.

Leviathan, on the contrary, is the monster broken loose, the army in campaign, the corruption of the cause, the intelligent attack against us which marries the elements, which is incorporated into natural forces, so that Paul could say (Eph. 2:2): *that was when you followed the fashion of this world, when you owned a prince whose domain is in the lower air, that spirit whose influence is still at work among the unbelievers.* And farther on (Eph. 6:12): *It is not against flesh and blood that we enter the lists; we have to do with princedoms and with those who have mastery of the world in these dark days, with malign influences in an order higher than ours.*[4] We

---

4. *Canopied with black rain-storm and deep mist* (Ps. 17:12). *The smoke rising from the shaft darkened both the sun and the air* (Apoc. 9:2). *And the seventh angel poured out his cup over the air* (Apoc. 16:17).

were warned not to play with the monster, not to be seduced by his specious words, like foolish Eve long ago, not to imagine ourselves more clever than the devil, able to make arrangements with him from which we would derive personal profit. And we were warned that there is in what he tells us, things to use and not to use, all kinds of curious useful things, all kinds of samples to cut and interesting material for delicate but fruitful transactions. We naively think that his skin will go better than gray fox on the shoulders of our girl friends, and better than python skin on their pretty feet. His head will be the pride of our scientific collections unless it serves as bait for catching crayfish. Alas, we have not yet understood the pilgrim we are dealing with, nor the developments which the necessities of hate forced on the hideous worm which Saint Michael on the day of its apostasy swept from the threshold of Eternity. To each new arrow of truth, he responded by growing an appropriate scale, and now he is covered with an armor-plate as supple and impenetrable as steel. *The body of him is like shields of cast metal, scale pressing on scale, so close to one another as to leave no vent between; so well joined that nothing will part them* (Job 41:6-8). Thus Renan helps Voltaire, and the biologist comes to the aid of the interrupted philologist. *Firmset are the folds of his flesh, unyielding though a thunder-bolt should strike them* (Job 41:14). He has neither head nor tail. But that is of no matter! The pieces are strong and capable of causing harm. Every bolt of lightning can be parried by an old experienced serpent in opposing it with a suitable degree of obliqueness. But by comparison with this noose, with this cable which ominously sews the leaves of our door *(serpens vectis)*, the anatomy of Behemoth shows us a center of resistance and iniquity still more secret and compact, and it is at the very attachment of life—at the navel, at the genitals—that the hand of the sacred beast-fighter seizes him to make a demonstration for us. *What strength in his loins, what lustihood in the navel of his belly* (Job 40:11).[5] *Close-knit (perplexi sunt) the sinews of his groin (testicles). Testis, testiculus.* The Latin provides an ambiguity between these two words from which the commentator would be wrong not to profit. The testicles are the two glands grafted on us which are, outside of us, the guarantee of our identity, of our conformity with the species, and which give us the right to bring action, to print our sign in authentic form. It is the legal apparatus which allows us to draw upon our origin in order to become cause in our turn. So, when our text says to us that *the sinews of his groin (testicles) are close-knit,* it means that they reinforce one another, that they borrow from one another the means of their solidity, that they constitute in joining with one another an image of resistance in which each prevents the other from moving. They represent a knot (whose extremities are concealed) and the coiled serpent of original sin. It is an organ rooted in itself and finding in itself origin and energy, and consequently worthy to serve as a figure on the belly for the intertwining of instincts, interests and reasonings by which the individual, conscious of his own inadequacy, is convinced that *there is no God* (Ps. 13:1). This is the monster who raises his arms toward the Crucified to receive from Him the complement of his form, according to the word of Habacuc: *the heights beckon from above* (Hab. 3:10).

Thus Our Lord on the cross between the Good and the Bad Thief, between good and evil, is fixed as an intermediary, a balance *(statera facta corporis)*, as a center of valuation, compensation and distribution. He administers the darkness and has put it at the service of his elect. He caught Behemoth on that perfect *hook* (Job 40:19) which is the cross. *Who can*

5. In African mythology the seat of the demon is the navel.

penetrate into the cavern of his mouth, forcing the gates that guard it, the terrors of his teeth? (41:5). He profited from those eyes that see only the surface, which in their pride *look only at sublime things,* in order to seize the depths. The cross is the hook and now Satan himself serves Him as bait! We will never swallow Satan so far that we will not swallow at the same time that hook which is sunk into him. *He who rose is also the one who descended* and we firmly hold in ours that hand whose correspondent hand powerfully and skillfully rules hell.

But enough for the left side, because on the right something has just taken place. After that solemn second of deliberation which many other hearts have since known, something opened and yielded. Under the imperceptible stroke of a chisel, a soul was split from top to bottom. And we suddenly hear the Good Thief cry out pitifully: *Lord, remember me when thou comest into thy kingdom* (Luke 23:42). In the meantime the occupant of the left perseveres in a virile way with the energy which wins for him the esteem of the "strong hearts." It does not matter! For on the other side, like a gaping vase which suddenly overflows, that courtier of the void and of death, the shameless profiteer, the one hooked up on the right is filled with this prodigious promise: *this day thou shalt be with me in Paradise.*

This day! Suddenly, not only is he absolved, but he is sanctified! Grace in one instant, over this disgusting carcass, profited from all the deficiencies of virtue. On this infamous gibbet, it is not just a scoundrel who is expiating, it is a martyr in the function of a host ignited. The assassin, lewd and thieving, the convict, the professional bandit, became a saint. Only this fundamental acceptance was necessary. An imperceptible displacement, a delicate crevice in the hermetic recipient of our pride. Just one glance between the red eyelids was needed to release in the right-hand guest this penitential cataclysm, this resurrection mingled with death—this irresistible explosion of Eternity.

This day thou shalt be with me in Paradise. It is accomplished. The prophecy that *the publicans will precede us into the kingdom of heaven* was fulfilled to the letter. For the moment, in that vast locality he is the only one. He is completely alone. So far only he has come. In the presence of the Holy Trinity and numberless angels who light up before his eyes one after the other, like stars in a June evening, he is there, bewildered, engulfed, imperceptible. The throne of the Immaculate One is still empty. Peter, John, Paul, Gregory, Benedict, Francis, Dominic, Thomas, Ignatius, Teresa have not yet been admitted. The legions of the Ancient Law have just now awakened in the Sheol where John the Baptist is teaching catechism to the Holy Innocents. Jesus Himself, his Jesus is not there in the flesh. He is busy in hell, a place which holds no mystery for our Dismas. We might even ascribe to him sentiments of someone who came too early. Just imagine the son of a very minor civil servant, invited by a friend to a magnificent castle. There he is, overwhelmed, in the midst of large pieces of furniture, of an incomprehensible luxury, of waxed floors spreading out in all directions like a limitless sea. And in the distance strange colored lights, palms which until now he had seen only on graduation day! Why isn't his friend here? What is he doing? If he doesn't soon hear some noise at the end of that terrifying succession of rooms, what can he expect, especially in his inappropriate clothes, and bewildered in his feeling of poverty and insignificance? May the angels look attentively at what has just come in. From the enormous labor of redemption which for eons has been furrowing the depths of creation and whose announcement determined the fall of Lucifer, he is here, Dismas, still scented

106

with alcohol and natural produce, the first fruit. For this the blood of a God has served. He is like someone alone in the midst of a cathedral. The clergy and the faithful are busy yonder forming a procession and you hear their singing which reaches you in swells. The candles are lighted, the altar decorated with beautiful plants and flowers, the steps of the sanctuary are covered with a rich carpet, a gold silk canopy rises gracefully over the cardinal's throne, all is ready, the aisles and side-aisles have been sprinkled with sand and water. But around me, these rows and this endless population of chairs and prayer-stools are empty. When suddenly above me, in the bell-tower, over the choir, the great bell thunders forth a formidable sound!

But we should fully realize that our text says not only *in Paradise*, but *with me*. At that moment, Jesus has not yet risen and His soul enhances the low places where the weight of original sin and additional sin holds generations captive. Dismas, to reach them again, has not a long itinerary to cover, he has only to consider his own heart. Jesus brings heaven to opaque hell, but Dismas brings with him to heaven something infernal to volatilize. He is going to explode in this very different place, like a piece of sodium in an oxygen balloon. For after all, this guest does not consider Jesus absent. He is at home. You will understand me if I evoke the room where a beloved person has suffered and prayed for a long time and which he has, so to speak, impregnated with his martyrdom. Although the duties of Holy Saturday call Him elsewhere, He is really there, for Dismas, in an appropriated presence, in the heart of the paradise which this presence creates by itself. How else can we understand the expression *with me* and what is the bond which can exist between a life completely shaped by crime and one of infinite purity? If the circumstances of our past life have a relationship with this attitude—with this intimate structure in which our second nature is finally consolidated—what shelter furnished the constant orientation toward evil, the habit of violence and injustice in the new child whom Grace secretly with the predestined assistance of the cross, prepared for the eternal love of the Father? To understand it, we shall borrow a comparison from music. We have heard in the work of great masters, or in works retained in our memory, a series of weakened, changed and sad chords, with which the right hand, when it meets the sound, seeks the essential number which the left hand secretly mixes and kneads, and which soon for its delight and torture it proposes and suggests to the right hand, even if it is only through silence or through a faint sketch, but which, before a clear-cut attack, it does not cease holding, putting off, eluding at times tenderly and at times with a strange irony and at other times as if it pretended to speak of something else. It is not at all easy! The right hand must search, confront and read in every corner of the sonata (even in the first bars) with passion and anguish, the traits, phrases and chance drawings it has placed, and which now it must call up, articulate, meditate, ruminate on, and make sharp. It must fully assimilate the savor and meaning in an atrocious juxtaposition with truth, which has been mercifully put off, but whose place, necessity and terrible incompatibility with what we bring are revealed to us by our faults. This entire repertory must be taken up again, elaborated, expressed and fully exploited. An insatiable ear in the orchestra needs our blood. It is a ladder of sobs so high that it finally reaches the soul and expels it from us in the paroxysm of a horrible clot! This is how Dismas acquires his lesson of eternity and learns to be forever with Jesus in paradise. The imitation he practiced of the redemptive gesture for three hours by means of his criminal body taught him everything. Sin, punishment and salvation are only one for him.

THE FOURTH WORD

Sitio, I am thirsty.

THE Seven Words of Christ on the cross seem to follow the reversed order of the Seven requests which are taught us in the Lord's prayer. These begin with God, universal Father-hood, heaven, and by degrees descend to the earth, to evil and the devil. The Seven Words, on the contrary, begin with evil for which Jesus asks pardon, invoking the excuse of ignorance, and whence they pass to the earthly militant Church, and then to the generations already withdrawn from time and a prey to justice and grace, and then to punishment and expia-tion. And the Fourth Word, before the last three continue toward divine Will, marks a middle place, a sorrowful pause. Between heaven and earth, Jesus, deprived of both, deprived below of the love and confidence of those men He had come to save, deprived above of cohabitation with His Father, ut-tered the call, the unusual moan: *I am thirsty!* God is thirsty! In the midst of this world which He made, of this creation which received from Him all the existence it has, and whose end and reason for being He constituted, He looked out and ascertained, not from any general philosophical consideration, but from the most painful pressure of immediate and urgent necessity that there was nothing for Him. He had created the world and the world refused Him a drop of water. Incredulous or impotent humanity refused its Author and its Saviour a bit of water, the one thing in the world that is free, and which you would not refuse a wounded animal or a sick dog.

Let us imagine Jesus overcome by that abominable thirst, His mouth open, His tongue swollen between His teeth. *I am thirsty!* If Voltaire or Renan asks us: *Where is your God?* this is what we have to show. *David set out the same day, to find refuge from Saul's pursuit, and betook himself to Achis, king of Geth. And at the sight of him, Achis' men said to their master, Why, is not this David, a king in his own land? Was it not in his honour their dancers used to sing, By Saul's hand a thousand, by David's ten thousand fell? . . . So David changed his mien when they were by, swooning in their hands and clinging to the doorposts and letting the spittle fall on his beard, till Achis told his men, Why, this is a madman you have found; why must you bring him into my presence? Have we not fools enough, that you bring this fellow in to let me watch his antics? Is this the man you would have me take into my house?* (I Kings 21:10-15). Thus spoke Achis the Philistine. And all we can answer is to plead drunkenness and madness. That is the degree to which love reduced the Second Person of the Trinity. That is the thirst He took with Him and which nothing can quench. And that is the bed His mother prepared for Him. That is the feast which He wanted, with so great a desire, to consume with us.

Pagan morality rests on the suppression of desire. Aristotle, Zeno, Epicurus, the Academy, India, the Chinese, all teach us that the condition for happiness is a certain middle position, a certain state of equilibrium and proportion between the demands of our imagination and our senses, and the satisfactions which a just measure makes suitable and circumstance possible—unless we act in the manner of the fakirs and extinguish all desire for the outside world. But Jesus on the cross gives a very different lesson. And in that setting, at that noontime, we see Him torn by a double aspiration: the desire for the entire creation whose love and acknowledgment He claims, and desire for the coeternal Father with whom He has received the vocation to join His humanity. This is the double profundity to which the extended body serves as bond, this is the double traction which is exerted over heaven and earth by this Heart which joins them in the last breathing of death's agony. And it is through this desire alone, through this assumption and not through a repudiation of the cross that the saints have never ceased conforming, and never will cease conforming to the Son of God.

Let us look more closely at the nature of this double thirst. God is thirsty for God. The Son of God desires His Father. Man, representative of all creatures, thirsts only after His Maker. But below Him, God throughout the entire creation thirsts for what comes from Him, for what is for Him, for what is destined to Him. When we see the saints radiant and consumed with the desire for souls, when they try with gigantic efforts to draw water from stone, to give back to God what belongs to Him and secure for themselves the rudimentary acclamation which forms the basis of their being (that supplement of meaning and help which God has concealed for them in the hearts of so many difficult and rebellious brothers round about), they are merely repeating that lament of the Creator on the cross that He is thirsty, and that plea of Jesus to the woman of Samaria: *Give me some to drink* (John 4:7). He was seated near the well, within access of the deep water, but He needed the charity of that heedless sinful woman to bring the water to His lips. And in the same way, the yearning for knowledge, the compassion which, in the hearts of so many noble women, educators and missionaries, has become a passion, the need for order, meaning, purity and response around us; that form of intimate knowing of the sinner in order to transform him, that desire for knowledge and light which inflames so many students—all that is part of this sacred thirst of the Saviour which He has communicated to His Church: *Where is my room, in which I am to eat the paschal meal with my disciples?* (Mark 14:14).

Thirst is for something liquid. We say of something that it is *liquid* when it is without form, resistance, construction, when all it has is its weight and when its complete substance is evenly penetrated on the surface by the same aptitude, when, composed of disparate elements, it has become *sensitive*, immediately obedient to attraction or a pressing back or an impression in a given sense. In Latin, when you say of a thing that it is perfectly clear, you use the word *liquet*. In French, *une fortune liquide, une situation liquide* is something adapted to an immediate use.

In order to understand this desire in all things for what is drinkable in them (that is, appropriated for our immediate internal use), and how it applies to the traction of God on the soul, we have to consider the different modes of its appeal to the physical world. For this, let us open once again the inexhaustible album of pictures called the Book of Job. Chapter 28 of that sublime poem describes for us under a triple heading the inquest and petition of the spirit on matter. It compares it with fire, with water itself and finally with light.

When it is not purely and simply to destroy and efface the form, the role of fire is to dilate, open, melt, dissociate, surmount form by the complicity of weight and the violence of the spirit, to purify by suppression or separation of all that is foreign or useless. That is why God prefers to compare Himself with that subtle and powerful force. *The Lord thy God,* says Deuteronomy (4:24), *is a fire that burns all before it.* And Exodus (24:17): *This glory of the Lord wore the semblance of a fire.* Leviticus (6:13): *Never must the altar be empty of this perpetual fire. His throne all of flame,* says Daniel (7:10). The Holy Spirit in Acts (2:3) is compared to *tongues of fire. How small a spark it takes to set fire to a vast forest,* says Saint James (3:5). *The Lord's voice,* Psalm 28:7 tells us, *kindles flashing fire.* It is this fire, Saint Peter tells us, which will judge the world by decomposing it, *heaven and earth ready to feed the fire on the day when the godless will be judged, and perish* (II Peter 3:7), and which, from this time forth—for discernment—is applied to the very texture of our soul and our works. *Fire will test,* says Saint Paul (I Cor. 3:13), *the quality of each man's workmanship.* Fire acts to obtain what it demands, either by means of heat or fervor; that is to say, of advice and persuasion, of prolonged presence. Thus it is said in the Book of Esdras (II Esd. 7:3): *the gates of Jerusalem should never be opened till the sun was up.* Or by the means of maturing (to which is related all that we read in the Bible concerning the vineyard) the grape which the sun calls forth from the earth and which its kindly ray leads from the flower to the fruit, to the harvest and to the cup.[1] And finally it attacks what is hardest, to reduce and liquefy it.[2] *See how man has done away with darkness,* says Job to whom we have now come. The Lord placed in the darkness a capacity for transformation and *has pierced into the very heart of things* the destined ending of each thing, and *into caves under ground* all that is hard, compact and rebellious to vision *and black as death's shadow,* night and the absense of appearance, and a sign which imitates the void. He has in Himself the power to dissolve a stone and change it into metal. He calculates the exact degree which, within the matrix, iron will give and all that in silver and gold is *the principle of the vein. Where, then, does wisdom lie? Easy to trace, where the veins of silver run, where gold-ore is refined* ... (Job 28 *passim.*) Thus it is that fire dwells within the hard dark center of the heart (an avaricious container, a contracted tightened ego-

1. Among the first needs of man's life Ecclesiasticus (39:31) places: *water, fire, iron, salt, milk, wheat-meal, honey, the grape-cluster, oil and clothing.*
2. *God bids the waters flow again in plenty* (Job 37:10).

ism), and which it is able to melt as if it were an ingot of ice.

A further image of thirst or desire or attraction from the out-side excercised on the body and the soul, is water itself: there is a thirst for giving and taking, as well as thirst for receiving. See how it spreads, envelops, embraces, measures, furnishes, divides and reassembles and adapts its course to all movements; how it succeeds in entering through the smallest fissure and opening, and then, alive and elastic, how it dilates, fills, invades, reaches, soaks, probes, corrupts, softens, sucks, possesses, relaxes, releases, and inserts suspension everywhere within the weight. That is why it pleased God to take water as the sacramental matter for that baptism which not only washes us, but which in us is a principle of intimate transformation. It is the transparent invisible vehicle of that Wisdom of which it is written (Job 28:12): *But wisdom, tell me where to search for wisdom; tell me in what cache discernment lies?* It is that secret sustenance in search of all the elements which are able to construct into a single body the child of God. It makes for itself passages and ways which are known only to Him. *Here are passages no bird discovers in its flight* (Job 28: 7). By *bird* could be meant the thousand dispersed thoughts which peck on the surface of our conscience. *The roving merchant* does not pass there. By this could be meant the movements, speculations, labors and exchanges of self-seeking commerce. No *vulture* and no *lioness* are there. These would designate the spirit of violence, lust and rapine, either with the rending of flesh or with the spiritual robbery practiced by clairvoyant and stupid masters of the air and of human knowledge. Sheltered from all eyes, the idea administered by water proceeds to the construction of the Christian and of Christianity, like those artist insects, makers of themselves, whose prodigious industry has been described by observers. *Narrowly he scans,* our text continues, *the river's depths, and brings to light all they hide.* He explored cellars, galleries and reservoirs. He touched and pressed with the delicacy of an expert the glands of altitude. Following all cadences, He joined with the course of that fluid, and over all the contours of the earth possessed and caressed, He extended the net of passage and time.[3] The water circulates and rushes through

3. Concerning this invitatory and provocative virtue of water, we should read a magnificent story in the Book of Kings (III Kings 18) in which water goes to meet fire, and fire in its turn unseals, in the words of Job, the *treasures* of water, of which it is said (Deuter. 33:19): *The wealth of the sea shall foster them, the treasures that lie hidden in the sands.* There was a great drought in Israel and King Achab sent his steward Abdias to see what water and vegetation remained in the land. Elias who had been in hiding for three years went to meet this emissary and asked him to announce his visit to Achab. But Abdias refused. I know, he said, that my lord is looking for you and will move heaven and earth in order to find you. But the trouble is, I am not sure of you. You have had dangerous dealings. Confess that the intervention of God's spirit in human affairs, the spirit of which you are one of the elect, is disconcerting. The characteristic of a prophet is to escape. You want to charge me with a commission for the authorities and then, when they need you, who assures me that you will not have disappeared according to your custom into an unknown place and left me in trouble? Elias went then himself to Achab and proposed to him a kind of duel with the false gods. The plan was to assemble all the pagan prophets of the land of Israel. There were more than 450, as many as there are clairvoyants and palm readers in a large city neighborhood. Then on the top of Carmel he ordered set up two piles of fire-wood: on each pile a bull cut up into pieces (this would be a sample of creation over which man has exerted his power of exploration and divisioning, which he opened and dissected according to all the rules of slaughter and everything that is suitable to the preparation of a victim: it was there gaping, disjointed, a solemn offering of our impotence), but no fire. Heaven was to provide that. Let those clowns invoke their gods (there are 450 of them, just like the heretical sects), and I will invoke mine, and the fire will judge between us. Thus it took place. The two rival altars were erected and the mob of false prophets engaged in frenzied invocations, resembling a negro voodoo scene or a revival meeting. Their voices were not enough,

this vast body, it goes and comes, it is distilled in the converter, and through it the Author of all matter secures a palatable knowledge. It is the common center which unites everything, which impregnates and inspires all beings simultaneously.—But at that universal contact, at that rumbling action below which prepares and helps the summons of the event (as in an orchestra that particular pattern, that peripeteia of a phrase which suddenly releases and rouses from silence the section of brasses and drums), rebellious elements

---

and they began to dance, *on the altar*, the text says, which is not difficult, for rather than an altar it was a chest of drawers, a table of the gods which their followers habitually treated without respect. One tried to jump higher than the other. They say that in one of his famous leaps, Nijinsky could perform ten *entrechats*, not to mention all kinds of brilliant *pirouettes*. They have no mercy on themselves. Now they are slashing their limbs and faces with all kinds of lancets and small knives. They mean business. It is obvious that they are dead serious and more than serious. If it is true, as we are taught by our philosophy professors, that we can count only on ourselves, what is more natural than to provoke, by a few good slashes and punctures in the right place, our noumenon and the god immanent in those big hemorrhages which our moral cultivation seems to need? (See in the work of a mediocre poet of the last century that ridiculous character who believes he is answering the prayer of a brother by the shedding of his own blood.) But no sound came from heaven. Then Elias in his turn began. He poured a large amount of water over the combustible altar so that it was drenched. There is no point in insisting on the symbolism of the four buckets, the triple watering and the double trench destined not only to bring the water but to maintain it around the wood so that it would soak in it. And then, at the call of the prophet, *the divine fire fell, consuming victim and wood and stones and dust, and swallowing up the very water in the trench.* Then, while with swords they took care of the evacuation of the false prophets, and the king obeyed the order given to him: *Go back, eat and drink!,* Elias at the top of Mount Carmel listened to the gigantic rainfall which was moving toward him from the depths of the sea. And the final verses show him naked running up to the chariot of Achab who was hastily returning to Samaria, in the light of the first flashes.

arise. I have just used the image of the retort, and now verse 4 seems to suggest that of the filter. *Where yonder ravine cuts off from the shepherd-folk* (Job 28:4), who having crossed the Red Sea, are walking toward the Promised Land, *lost to all track, far from the haunts of men,* those whom it is useless to solicit and who discourage the feet of the eternal poor and the insatiable beggar. They are there and do not allow themselves to be hurried along. *For I was hungry, and you never gave me food, I was thirsty, and you never gave me drink* (Matth. 25:42).

And finally, God's third statement of nature and the soul is light. Chapter 28 of Job shows it to us in action in a triple way: elucidation, brilliance and coloring. The first two divine statements I described resulted in substituting a state of liquidity for a state of permanence. The latter substitutes, without essentially changing the subject, a state of evidence for a state of obscurity, a state of clear response for a state of stammering or muteness, a state of radiation for a state of sleep, a state of color for a state of possibility. *Glorify me!* is the entreaty which forms the supreme prayer of Christ. This is the expression coming from an impression, it is solidity in light, it is the illumination of the indestructible in the midst of the transitory.[4] To manifest the first idea (elucidation), the text uses comparisons of *crystal* and *sapphire*. Crystal is the perfect state of purity and transparency. Sapphire is transparency qualified by a kind of affectionate resistance and in light mingles joyously with our dissolved darkness. Verse 6 seems to distinguish in the human body the rocks or the bones which it compares with sapphire and *clay*,[5] or flesh which it compares with gold. *Heaven* and *earth* are still joined as a

4. *He will make the justice of thy cause bright as the sun at noon* (Ps. 36:6).

5. *That earth, from whose surface our bread comes to us, must be probed by fire beneath, till the rocks yield sapphires, and the clods gold* (Job 28:5-6).

couple in the first verse of *Beresith*. The bones represent the hidden support and the inner permanence, and the flesh represents the clothing, the nourishing respiratory efflorescence. The sapphire, or the first azure of fixed sky, the immobile water, the fixed light, polarized by transparency, is always associated in the Bible with the idea of foundation. *And now I looked up at the vault over the cherubim, and there was the hue of sapphire* (Ezechiel 10:1), and the earlier passage (1: 26): *sapphire blue towered up into the form of a throne. Thy foundation*, says Isaias (54:11) *shall be of sapphire*. It is the color of purity, but there is another transparency beside it which shines with a complementary fire, *the topaze from Ethiopia*, mentioned in Job 28:19, yellow which is complement of blue. It is the flash redeemed and restored by penitence, the sun making its way through darkness and smoke. The second figure of light incorporated is the mirror: either the flat mirror which sends back a perfect image, or the concave mirror which concentrates rays in a burning center, or metals, and gold the first, which condense and solidify properties. Verse 5 suggests the comparison of gold with that glorified clay which each summer spreads over the earth for our harvests. This is what happens, after the Judgment, to our flesh, with its value increased by grace, *this light and momentary affliction brings with it a reward multiplied every way, loading us with everlasting glory* (II Cor. 4:17), the five-fold talent above our capital of pure gold—the gold tested by fire, which is the explanation given by Pliny of the term *obrizum* —the gold which, in Daniel and the Apocalypse, serves as a garment for the Angels confirmed by their refusal of evil.[6] And finally light solicits and possesses matter and the soul according to a third mode which is a permanent impregnation or coloring, which completely changes the appearance of the

6. *His mercy like a cloak enfolding me* (Isaias 61:10).

object and its reaction to rays. *Tincturae mundissimae,* the text says, and elsewhere, *the colors of India. The very pure tinting* makes us think of the intimate subtle work of grace on the soul previously scraped and cleaned, something unctuous like oil and corrosive like acid. As for *the colors of India,* we think of the time when our ancestors discovered both the colors of the East and West, and of that sumptuous cloth (*stragulatam vestem*) which the sun folds in the morning and evening after drenching it in the deep vats of the ocean, where a sulphur bordered with green spreads and trembles in vast glazings of rose and bronze. That is the *robe of honor* spoken of by Ecclesiasticus (6:32), the royal pontifical fabric in which Aaron and Solomon walked, the brilliant variegated coat which Joseph received from his father and with which Saint Paul (II Cor. 5:4) tells us we should want to *clothe ourselves afresh.* That is the subject of the variations which eternal Wisdom displays on the veils and covers of the tabernacle. Hyacinth, purple, scarlet twice applied, painting on painting. And what is the method save an effusion on a substance which has no other merit than receiving the redemptive blood which Our Lord offered on the cross, something more brilliant than snow and lightning, in which we ourselves appear for transfiguration. *Blessed are those who wash their garments in the blood of the lamb* (Apocalypse 22:14). And Genesis (49:11): *When he washes his garments, it shall be in wine.*

Such is the thirst of the Crucified which pulls Him toward the earth, but there is another desire still more devouring which draws Him toward heaven and incorporates Him, so to speak, in the two arms of that pump to which He is attached. According to the words of Saint Paul (Col. 3:1,2): *Risen, then, you must lift your thoughts above!* and of the Saviour Himself (Matth. 5:6): *Blessed are those who hunger and thirst for holiness; they shall have their fill!* That is why Solo-

119

mon, of whom it is written that he had with great attention considered the nature of all trees, cried out when he saw rise up on Golgotha that new species: *Blessed be that tree by which justice is made!* It is the compendium of all creation, the blessed intersection of nature and grace. It takes its roots from the deepest of the arid land and the spiritual branching which is grafted on this atrociously shortened trunk extends in all directions, refreshment and life. *There must be a sharp reckoning first,* says Isaias (10:22), *before we are restored, abundantly, to his favor.* And elsewhere: *May he, the Saviour, spring from the closed womb of earth, and with him let right order take its being* (Isaias 45:8). And also (48:18): *Then had a flowing stream of peace been with thee, a full tide of the Lord's favor.* It is the bed on which the Beloved of the Song of Songs is reclining and where all creation is united with Him in the act of redemption. For He tells us in the words of Osee (2:9): *I will betroth thee to myself, favor and redress and mercy of mine thy dowry.* With Christ, the entire creation is thirsty *(parturit, ingemiscit)* and labors and achieves. *He transferred us to the kingdom of the beloved Son. In the Son of God, in his blood, we find the redemption that sets us free from our sins. He is the true likeness of the God we cannot see; his is that first birth which precedes every act of creation. Yes, in him all created things took their being, heavenly and earthly, visible and invisible. . . . They were all created through him and in him; he takes precedency of all, and in him all subsist. He too is that head whose body is the Church; it begins with him, since his was the first birth out of death; thus in every way the primacy was to become his. It was God's good pleasure to let all completeness dwell in him, and through him to win back all things, whether on earth or in heaven* (Col. 1, Epistle from the Mass of Christ the King).

The peace which I will give you is mine to give, said Christ at the last supper (John 14:27), *I do not give peace as the world gives it.* Such peace does not exist without the continuous intervention of the peacemaker. And He ceases at no moment being the author and instrument of a peace which has no other foundation than the cross. *He is our bond of peace,* says Saint Paul (Eph. 2:14); *he has made the two nations one.* It is not essentially an enjoyment, it is an action, for *the kingdom of God is not a matter of eating or drinking this or that; it means rightness of heart, finding our peace and our joy in the Holy Spirit* (Rom. 14:17). It is the realization in us of the condition, our confrontation with Christ in the beseeching attitude expected of us. There is no peace without desire, as the Angel said to Daniel (10:19): *Fears are not for thee, so well beloved, never harm befall thee!* Peace was not obtained for us once and for all, it entails an appeal to God in the midst of ceaselessly renewed circumstances. That is why the cross is represented to us as a tree planted *near the course of waters.* In this inexhaustible temporal wave, it inexhaustibly draws up thirst for eternity. It is toward the source that after drinking from the torrent (Ps. 109:7) man does not stop raising his head. *What fountain is this that comes out from the Lord's temple, and waters the dry valley of Setim?* (Joel 3:18). The sacrifice of the Mass at which we are present each morning is the reprisal, the reparation, the restoration of the daily event in the sense of the salutary meaning and capacity which were included in it. That is the fraction which the priest places on the paten, the drop he pours into the chalice, and which are returned to us transformed into a divine restoring, into a solution adapted to the functioning of our heart. *Give us today our daily bread,* says the sixth request of the *Our Father,* in which are summarized all those which Our Lord taught us on the mountain and He explains to us that

that food must be, as His own was, *to do the will of him who sent me* (John 4:34) and that it be done *on earth as in heaven,* which means in a total conformity of our earthly will to the divine plan. *His name* must in all things be sanctified, which means that each thing must be authenticated, confirmed by the impression of its divine character and that the work must clearly declare the workman. Thus it is that the entire creation, that torrent which carries us with all the rest toward the definitive disposition, is set up again, raised again, brought back to its Author, so that everything is returned to the Father in the person of the Son. Jesus thirsts after this justice which the Psalmist described when he said to us: *for thee my soul thirsts like a land parched with drought* (Ps. 142:6). And also: *My whole soul thirsts for God, the living God* (Ps. 41:3). And: *body athirst and soul longing for thee, like some parched wilderness, where stream is none!* (Ps. 62:2). This is the text which the deserts of Juda and Scete and Sahara continually maintained before the eyes of Saint Jerome, of the hermits of the Thebaid and Father Foucauld.

THE FIFTH WORD

Eli, Eli, Lamma Sabachthani

MENTION of the last words of Christ is divided among the four Gospels, according to the special accent appropriate to the story of each author, in such a way that we cannot join the documents at our disposal except by intrinsic logic. We have just heard Him cry out: *I am thirsty!* And immediately one of those present understood that the moment had come to wet with vinegar the lips of the sufferer. This was the supreme answer which the chosen vineyard was reserving for its planter. This was the taste that He bore on His tongue, a bitter gross savor of *turned* wine. *Vinea mea electa, quomodo versa es mihi in amaritudinem?* It is said in the Improperia. All is over now as far as man is concerned. Jesus raises His head toward God. Life which is beginning to leave the icy limbs takes refuge in the heart and in the dimmed eyes which look up toward the sun, only to see a black body covered with bloody hair,[1] and in this monstrous tempestuous night, the Vanquished sees shining at a great distance the indifferent stars. It is noon, the hour of evidence according to the Song of Songs.[2] But the Lord's voice which was heard in Paradise (Gen. 3:8) *after noon*, was silent.[3] It is noon and there is nothing, there is no one. *My God, my God, why hast thou forsaken me?* (Ps. 21:1). God the Father in heaven whose voice sounded like a clap of thunder at the moment of baptism and at the hand-to-hand fighting with the Pharisees, is silent. You might say that willfully He hides and withdraws and will not see and veils His face. This moment of absence is the moment of supreme manifestation. Adam, long ago, hid from God under the trees of Paradise. It is now God's turn to hide. And the Just Man, in the operation joined with the death agony which begins with that terrifying metaphysical decollating, hears at His feet the ecstatic banter, the burst of good humor, the triumphant declaration which for centuries has not ceased nourishing the superiority of all the Sorbonnes and all the Sanhedrins.

«So there he is, who had faith in God! Look at him! Yes, gentlemen, let us look squarely at him! Let us feast our eyes on

1. *The sun grew dark as sack cloth* (Apoc. 6:12). *Sun and moon linger in their dwelling place* (Habacuc 3:11). It is the eclipse: for a few moments the moon inhabited the sun's disc.

2. *Tell me, my true love, where is now thy pasture-ground, where now is thy resting-place under the noon's heat?* (S. of Songs 1:6).

3. *Shelter us, like the shadow, dark as night, that gives shelter at noon-day* (Is. 16:3). *We stumble at noon-day as though benighted* (id. 49:10).

this spectacle! Not every day can we have such a lesson. Every school should be allowed to come here. Shout, my good man! Twist and turn as much as you can! Try with all your might to get away from matter and death and the natural laws we have determined once for all, and which we, with the master's cap on our head and the epitoge with three rows of ermine on our shoulders, teach to young pupils, in conformity with the license we received from the state. The cross is solid, the nails are solid. You have been put in your place, worker of miracles and rider of an ass—good Lord of children and women! Is the temple still standing, yes or no? It seems to me that the old university is still strong whose doctrine you claimed you would undermine by introducing elements foreign to experimental verification and rational discussion and pedagogical security, as well as unquestionable rights. You will need more than three days to succeed. We've got the better of you, comrade! We've got the upper hand by legitimate means. It seems that you like the cross. Well, we've given it to you. Try to come down from it if you can. It is time for that God you talked about so much, to appear. It seems to me that we are giving him an opportunity. Come down from your cross. Tell him to help you. What? What is he saying? ... *Eli* ... *Eli* ... Did you hear what he just said? No, but did you hear it? Allow me, gentlemen and dear colleagues, to call your attention to the decisive confession which the inexorable torture of scientific investigation has just snatched from ignorance and superstition and imposture. *Eli, Eli, lamma sabachthani.* I call upon the great learning of our colleagues the Orientalists. They will have no trouble in translating for us that poor Aramaic. Let us first put aside the appealing hypothesis, eliminated by the unexceptionable laws of hermeneutics that it concerns a borrowing from the Psalms or an allusion to that famous Nabatean which flourished, according to some unauthenticated texts, at the time of the probably fictional kings of Israel. Today there is a tendency to see in it a kind of spontaneous outcrop of superstitions which raged at the time of the Maccabean decadence. But I am sure that the root *El* we find on Sumerian inscriptions and Arabic tombs will intrigue the old campaigners of Semitic philology. Whether you see in it a Mesopotamian totem, or a Hittite allusion, or a Moon lover, it is undeniable in any case that in this syllable which has so curiously reached our ears you find the origin of that *Elohim* which in opposition to *Jahveh*, has generously stained in blue the pages of our polychrome Bible. There we track down the supreme conclusion of an interesting tradition. I consider the form *Sabachthani* doubtful and even shocking, and I am almost ready to agree with delightful Professor Pumpernickel who finds in it a Galilean deformation. *Eli, Eli* or *Eloi* (another form of the vocative), *why have you abandoned me?* Why did he abandon our attractive subject? I see, gentlemen and dear colleagues, and you, ladies who grace this meeting, by the smiles on your faces, I see that no one of you would be embarrassed to answer this naive question. We all know that there were peremptory reasons for *El* or *Eli*. Peremptory, yes indeed!»

... Daily I must listen to the taunt, Where is thy God now? (Ps. 41:4).

I heard of a religious in France or Spain—I can't remember which—who was left alone to guard his monastery at one of the times when persecution was raging. After all, it seems to me that he was not a religious or even an oblate, but rather one of those natural spontaneous Christians you could call a layman, if you give to the term not a negative meaning, but a value of obscure attachment to an indefinite congregation whose rule and vows escape formulation and, like the ancient bezoar, result simply from a certain spontaneous disposition of the will in the depth of a humble, silent, attentive heart. A seed come from nowhere, which thrived outside of any care in an unlikely place. Something that grew between two stones, like plantain in the courtyard of a dyeworks. Our fellow was never more happy. High walls separate him pleasantly and forever from men and women, and, as the crowning security, within the ramparts whose circumference his professional duty obliges him from time to time to verify, there is no one. He alone is the entire monastery. A Robinson Crusoe of the liturgy, He alone has been charged, through some whim of Providence, to fulfil the *opus Dei*. He alone is the abbot now that the enclosure, whose levels and passages once resounded with the monastic herd, is henceforth given over to vacancy. The mailman will have to pull on the bell a long time to make him come. The whole library is at his disposal. From time to time he dips into a page or a paragraph in a book picked up by chance. And he is sure no man is more contented than he, when at noon, at the sound of the distant siren which confirms the outside continuity of all those things which today he is fortunately rid of, he cooks on his Primus stove his meal, composed of an egg and milk soup. He realizes that circumstances, as well as an absolute incompetence, confirmed by the most humiliating experiences, have freed him from all his obligations toward his neighbor. All he has left, in the bottom of this hole in the midst of the world of which he is the grateful beneficiary, is an existence completely absorbed by his duties of a sexton's sedulousness, who lives at the feet of that God as much abandoned as he is. And he has chosen this very abandonment for his tent, his home and his land. He chose that minute of total abandonment on the cross to expand it to the frontiers of his earthly destiny and to distill from it drop by drop its teaching into his heart like an elixir of sweetness and bitterness.

126

Of all the months of the year, November is his favorite. No other month obscures more the interest of the outside and associates us more inwardly by slow powerful sentiments of penance and compunction with the mourning and the despoiling of a land which accepts the plough and refuses consolation. If I raise my head to that vague gray light which is my ceiling, I know it will be that way for the whole day, for the whole week, for weeks on end perhaps. Winter has only begun! This isn't a simple April shower or a March downpour—similar to the biting remarks of a fretful elder. It isn't the fall of hail, or the desperate collapse of the end of summer, administered with thunderclaps by the dark giants of a whirlwind. It is not boredom and dull disgust and rain as it rains when up there it can't keep from raining. What is taking place is a function of nature, the monsoon of the south-west, the water-main connecting the uncontrollable reservoirs of the equator, the hydraulic rake over all of France in the hands of the most conscientious of gardeners. Like those gay yellow and red lanterns which once embroidered the dress of spring, long ago the pale autumn colchicums, in the field with the fallen fruit, announced the end of the time we had less and less reason to oppose. It is the month when, in the past, inside a gloomy boarding school, a poor child tasted and cried over an apple which had ripened during vacation and which his mother had just sent him. In circular fashion all this formed around our fellow a picture with which he was perfectly satisfied. And when in the morning, at noon and at evening, in order to ring the angelus he went to that rope which today constitutes his principal means of communication with other men, he fervently listened to himself in the sound of the divine salutation reverberating in all suffering humble souls.

If the day is full of charm for him, night however forms his preferred habitat and at the heart of night those immobile

hours when at the foot of the great gallows lighted by the re-
mainder of a candle, he keeps company with Christ in the
midst of an ocean of terror and majesty.

The end of a candle is not very much, but it illuminates
that dead man before whom I am told I have nothing else to
do in the world save remain indefinitely on sentry-duty. I am
alone with Christ and there is nothing left in the world to
compete with Him. My mind is at ease. I have still plenty of
time before morning whitens the long windows. Only I am
alive in the universe. All the noises of the earth are silenced
and there is nothing to compete with the accent of God in
my soul. What poverty is comparable to the absence of everything? There is no need even to think. I have only to exist
with all my soul, I have only to burn meagerly and faithfully
like that sharp trembling flame at the feet of my Lord.

Like the fifteen candles on the taper-hearse at the Office of
Tenebrae which are extinguished one after the other, so the
psalms of matins, one by one, are effaced under my fingers,
and now I am left to myself and I hear another psalm beginning in my heart. Like liaison agents who come in the middle
of the night and in low voices wake up the army, they begin
with the leaders—and suddenly the entire company, in silence, stand up and look for their guns.

And like those engraved oxydized inscriptions which the
patient wise investigator gradually sees coming to light under
successive baths, the prophetic texts, exposed for a long time
to the inner eye, deeply seize the intelligence and the heart of
this man at his station. He understands those *songs in the
night* Job speaks of, when the murmur in him gradually becomes a word and a sentence and when the word in its turn
is reabsorbed into music, music into silence and silence into
virtuality. It is this reciprocal exposition, this blackness which
under the action of occult rays is condensed in front of us as

into letters, as if we ourselves, cleansed of all colors of our own, were dedicated to the exclusive study of this opacity which perhaps the Psalmist intended to insinuate when he said (18:3): *each night passes on to the next its revelation of knowledge.* For, as Amos says (5:20): *And for you, that day brings darkness, not the light you craved for; no radiance haunts about it, only gloom. Wilt thou read my heart,* says Psalm 16:3, *drawing near in the darkness to test me.* At that unusual hour, our visitor sighs, You can be found at home, we can talk with You without witnesses, there is the chance You will let me speak. But You know, O Jesus, that even at that moment, like that of sleep or death, when my inner darkness will join the outer darkness, *all through the night my soul has yearned for thee* (Isaias 26:9).

When the hour of midnight is passed, that summit of time in the center of the sidereal fullness, and when turning on its axis, the double index of duration begins to bend and descend toward that nadir which is daybreak—six in the morning—the watcher becomes conscious in himself of an operation which was destined morally to have sleep as its only witness. He perceives that, still simple, he is a compound. His eyes are opened to that most secret part of himself which is the crux of his hypostasis, and there he feels the suffering of traction. Someone is dying on every side of him and the supreme eructation of the dying mingles with the crying of the new-born. In the immense earth sown with wheat, the destinies of human grain advance in a series of imperceptible interlockings. He would not compare the Exterminating Angel whose work over sleeping Egypt, Exodus shows us, with one of those fast runners, but rather with the relentless advance, over the circular enamel field, of that double scythe which the clockmaker has controlled for our passage and which pursues us from vestige to vestige to the stipulated place of obliteration:

the small hand marking time in heaven and its attentive servant, the large hand, in an angular relationship with the other endlessly renewed and continued, which tells time on the earth. Everywhere there is, over the buried universe, the secret metaphor of a pulse and a watch.

A *bitter parting is this of death,* Agag says in the Book of Kings (I Kings 15:32). There must be something disconnected, some equilibrium in us which is failing. Like lovers in the midst of a long affair who begin to consider parting, due less to precise grievances than to the reciprocal constitution in them of antagonistic centers of gravity, so the human being, between his principle, I mean his idea and his vocation, and his temporal condition, feels an incompatibility developing and deepening. This is the nourishment from that hour of solemn clairvoyance and mortal calm when King Ezechias cries out: *Bitter, bitter the discipline that brings me peace!* (Is. 38:17), when Rachel *refuses to be consoled,* and when the dying man finally takes possession of an horizon reaching to the cave of that inner desert over which he knows at least that the stranger has no right.[4] Under the severe examination of the intelligence, he made an estimation, a census, an inventory, an evaluation of our perspectives and possibilities. Perhaps the moment is not far off when Jacob and Laban, after a long communal life, will have to disentangle and separate their flocks. This fearful moment in the history of society has arrived when the relationship between the parts results less from a basic organic necessity than from habit which is no longer protected from criticism.

That is why we raise our eyes toward our divine preceptor and avidly fix our gaze on that heart which we see beating more and more slowly under the ribs the Psalmist counts out.

4. *Heart's bitterness none may know but the heart that feels it; no prying stranger can tell when it finds relief* (Prov. 14:10).

He who learned how to be born, who learned from us how to suffer, now we have to learn from Him how to die.

It is a Man-God we have been given to look at. A God who is preparing to die before our eyes. What makes the body is the soul. It is God who drew into the womb of the Blessed Virgin Mary the body and the soul, all of man, even the unity of hypostasis. Let us now look at what in front of us quivers, struggles and dies. Let us leave Magdalen at the foot of the cross, blazing in the realization of the holocaust, let us allow that crater of perfume loudly to emit the despair and love under the blood which rains on her drop by drop; and let us leave to their sorrow today with that humble sinner who sobs deeply, all those who are humiliated and offended, all those defiled and beaten children who see their one friend pierced on the horrible stake. The seer in order to see uses his eyes, the blind his hands, and he who has a heart uses his heart. But that is not enough for the contemplative who, within a solemn deep peace, calling on all he knows, tries to appreciate and understand all the elements of the event developing before his eyes. He resembles the bourgeois of Jerusalem who, if we can believe Anne-Catherine Emmerich, threw stones into the opening which was made in the rock of Golgotha in order to test its depths. And in truth, we have reached the summit of supreme tension—the tightest tension. The sun is no longer in the sky to distract us. We are fully occupied in being witnesses. Everything is cracking. The veil of the temple is torn. The soul of the centurion is split in two by a flash of lightning, the earth opens, the prison door falls down, something is collapsing in the caves of the priests, the hard frame of hell itself bursts and lets out a wave of dead and half-rotted corpses. And up there, over us, in the heart of Christ, the supreme debate has begun.

It is the conflict of the two natures and the two wills united

131

in the closed space of the redemptive-vocation. It is the fulfillment of the promise signed long ago by Job, the assignation honored on this day which was granted the desperate summons of that human residue on his dung heap: *Ah! if I could but find my way to God! . . . Will he match his strength with mine, use all his majestic power to crush me? The justice of my cause once made known to him, I should triumph at last. But no; travel I east or west, I find no trace of him, turn I north or south, I have no skill to catch sight of him. And he, all the while, keeps watch over my doings* (Job 23). God answered these questions with claps of thunder and, to stifle the piercing cry, he had to shake the columns of the firmament. But the litigation remained open. There was only a postponement, and God, at the appointed time, was faithful to the rendezvous. Look now, Idumean, and tell us if you are satisfied! That elusive God you complained of not seeing, of finding nowhere, well, there He is and He will not budge, He will not escape. He is there forever attached with four nails to the cross. Now and for eternity you can easily feed on that God who said of Himself that He had come not to dissolve but fulfill, not to disperse the cross, but to put Himself on it. *I have heard thy voice now; nay, more, I have had sight of thee* (Job 42:5).

While our sentinel of the abyss, tightening around him the folds of his cloak, watches on the end of that piece of wax the spasm and the fight of the flame which casts over the feet of the Crucified a glistening appearance, he hears rising from the depths of his soul—or does the noise come from those last padlocks and from whatever out of the night emanations, steals through the closed door?—a mingling of contradictory voices: *My God, my God, why hast thou forsaken me?* O You who are thus fastened before me on that expander, You are God and that is how this watch is spent when You recommended us for one hour! *He shall wait on in the ranks of the dead* (Job 21:32). That is what You have been reduced to and that is the extremity to which Your mercy has been brought by Your justice! The Angels have not been able to hold You, nor the arms of Your Father, nor the bosom of the Trinity! On the very heart of the Act by which everything exists, He was not able to defend Himself from the arrow of Love. *That is why thou art left benighted when thou thoughtest to see day, overwhelmed by the unexpected flood* (Job 22:11). What do You say now? Speak, speak so we can hear you! *In what strength should I hold out? . . . Have I the endurance of flint? Is my flesh brass?* (Job 6:11,12). Nothing in this world of the flesh is able to bring Me support and the one thing he found to raise to My lips was that sponge dripping with infamous vinegar. My food is not of this world. *Would you have me lick my lips over the taste that brings death?* (Job 6:6).

The moment of the definitive test has come. This exploit of love, this union in a single Jesus, of God and man, of Being and Nothing, of the Finite and the Infinite, of the Eternal and of Time, of the absolute and the relative, of the Creator and the creature, of holiness and sin, of life and death, we are going to pull from both sides and see once and for all if it is strong, if it holds together. *The rope for me!* says Job (7:15). The two terms of the antinomy which Job and his interlocutors repeatedly tried to join without success, here they are, by an unheard of miracle, beyond any *a priori* probability or possibility, joined in this perpendicular sign in front of us. Outside of me, *there can be no arbiter between us, to claim jurisdiction over both* (Job 9:33). An inexorable justice, concerned even with the very roots of nature, is going to test the quality of obedience or resistance of which those elements are capable, and from which Jesus, in the womb of the Blessed Virgin, derived the power to say "I." In the name of the entire

133

creation, hear Him utter that cry which all converts will repeat, all the proud who are dismayed: *Help in myself is none*
(Job 6:13). This is the specifically crucial moment when
Being makes immediate contact with the void and realizes in
its soul and flesh the agony of destruction. O God, it is true
then! I have to suffer this lance! I will have to be divided and
this flesh is going to be snatched from Me more cruelly than
was this robe, by the hand of the executioners, which was
pressed against My body.

*What has innocence to do with lawlessness? What is there
in common between light and darkness?* (II Cor. 6:14). *No
need to teach me that; how should a man win his suit,
matched against God?* (Job 9:2). And the prophet answers in
vain: *Will he confine them all in a little space, there is no
gainsaying him* (Job 11:10).

My God, my God, why hast thou forsaken me? It is not a
question of an absence, but of a separation. It is not awareness
of a schism, but the active vision of a retreat. Of all the bonds
which united the Creator with the creature, first the meaning
gave way, next the intelligence gave over in the full vision of
the radical incompatibility between the two contradictory
terms, and all that remained was pure Faith. The Second Person of the Trinity considers in His nudity the ending of this
adventure in which He was engaged and proclaims, exhibits
and unfolds as on a banner its fundamental absurdity. Traction above toward God of what belongs to God who is irresistible. And on the other end, weight, a total giving over, equally
invincible, of those satisfactions which are due Justice. *Nay,
but God's terrors overwhelmed, his majesty overbore me* (Job
31:23). God is disengaged from man. You might say He wants
nothing more to do with him. He has had enough. The human
in Him is like something obliterated which disappears. *Head
high in air he made the onslaught* (Job 15:27). Everything

collapses under His feet, everything is dissolved, everything fails, everything returns to that corruption of which Job said it was his mother and his sisters.

Faith pure and naked remains.

I charge thee, earth, to leave my blood unburied, never to muffle the echoes of my protest (Job 16:19).

THE SIXTH WORD

It is achieved.

Thus at the Sixth Hour, God on the cross consolidated and fulfilled that word He spoke on the Sixth Day when, looking over the creation completed and brought to perfection with man, *He saw all that he had made, and found it very good* (Gen. 1:31). Yet in this creation there was a defect. The creation was on one side and God was on the other. A separation existed. There were relationships but there was no oath. That is why He came on that later Friday to answer the call of creation.[1] It was the day of the second intervention, the imposition of the definitive seal over the work of the Sabbath. For *the seventh day must be kept set apart as a day that is all repose* (Levit. 23:3). Thus Plato in the *Timaeus* states that the soul of the world, prior to the world's body, was closely applied to it forming the letter X, which is the cross and the initial of Christ. This cross, this clamp placed on the world, this claw on the four points of the compass which snaps and the intermingling of this quadruple tenon, is not simply an inactive figure, it is a force at work, it is the center of the work on the periphery which gives to every point its meaning and

1. *The Lord reigns as king . . . He it was that founded the solid earth, to abide immovable* (Ps. 92:1).

135

its proportion, and which, when it existed, made everything coexist, live in a state of coexistence in relationship to the principle and in relationship to the field of action. That is why John, joining the idea of need and thirst to the idea of consummation, says to us: *And now Jesus knew well that all was achieved which the scripture demanded for its accomplishment; and he said, I am thirsty* (John 19:28). This thirst, which is given us for the consummation of Scripture, is love of the Creator for His work and also the desire which everything, having been born, has for its end. That is why Jesus tells us: *Yes, if only I am lifted up from the earth, I will attract all men to myself* (John 12:31).

There is not much more time to have Christ in this way with us. Let us profit from these last minutes of exposition to look at Him breathing. Let us watch the God-Man function. When He breathes, He attracts the entire creation to Him. *Rises ever a sigh from my lips,* says Psalm 113:131, *as I long after thy covenant.* For, Genesis tells us (6:3): *It is this God has forbidden us to eat or even to touch, on pain of death.* But the flesh itself follows the soul to which it is attached by very strong and complex bonds. *Body athirst,* says Psalm 72:2, *and soul longing for thee.* And Psalm 64:3: *to thee let the vow be paid, hearer of prayer. Still all mankind shall come to bow down before me,* the Lord says (Isaias 66:23). *And all mankind shall know that I, the Lord, have delivered thee* (Isaias 49:26). Sacrifice was made to Him once in the opaque smoke of ancient holocausts, in the enormous ritualistic grill, in massacre and butchery, with the priests, reddened in a spattering of excrement and blood, and whose arms were plunged into viscera, in suffocating mounds of decomposed matter which rose up on the altar while beside it resounded the cry of animals being skinned and of those being dismembered with chopping knives. God breathed into His lungs that odor of

sweetness, that sputtering of grease and salt mixed with aro-
matic burnings. For centuries He fed on that. He breathed
that sensation in His face. And it was that, in the beating of
wings, that He gave back to the Apostles on the day of Pentecost. It is that breath which the new priest—the newly
Anointed—receives from the bishop on the day of his ordina-
tion, with this word in his nostrils which long ago created
Adam: *Accipe Spiritum Sanctum.*

A *blessing on the wood,* says the Book of Wisdom (14:17),
that can so procure salvation!

But it is not only on wood that the Redeemer is stretched
out and crucified, it is on the universe of which He forms the
node, the center, the *raison d'être,* the heart, the pivot, the
essential vital piece: that organ with which it breathes and
communicates to all its parts. It is the entire world He draws
to Him with each breath, implants in the deepest part of His
substance by the ramifications of His feet and hands, and
which He restores to His Father in that breath which is a word.
The cross is that Act in the center of the world through which
everything is consummated in the Word. The word *consummated* unites, calls together two ideas.

The first idea is that of a point, of a summit: God furnishes
to the world its end in this visible man made of flesh and a
soul in which He was hypostasized. It is the flame for which all
matter is food and which attracts it even to that tongue, to
that eloquent luminous manifestation. God needs everyone,
all the words of that vast vocabulary He constituted to make
Himself fully explicit to the Father and to tell Him that He
loves Him. *Sure knowledge,* says Solomon (Wisdom 7:18),
*he has imparted to me of how the months have their begin-
ning, their middle, and their ending.* And Isaias 10:22: *Only a
remnant of it will return,* namely the cross, those two lines
which erase one another and are multiplied one by the other.

137

It will superabound and mount up. *I have achieved the task which thou gavest me to do*, says Saint John (17:4). And again Isaias: *The Lord God of hosts is my witness, he means to make a short and sharp reckoning with the whole earth* (28: 22). *Look where I may*, says Psalm 118:96, *only thy law is wide beyond measure*. For has it not been said to us (Matth. 28:20): *And behold I am with you all through the days that are coming, until the consummation of the world*. Of this image is that narrow window on the ark of our salvation, whose dimensions God furnished to Noah, and added: *The ark is to have a course of windows, which thou wilt make a cubit in height* (Gen. 6:16).

And the second idea concerns not only a coexistence but a cooperation with everything for a same purpose and in a same desire. They are not only flocks of oxen and sheep one behind the other which are being guided from all points of the compass toward the ancient bush of Moria. The entire universe has received summons. It is perpetual fire claiming fuel and contribution, for *the Lord thy God is a fire that burns all before it* (Deuter. 4:24). *The fire on the altar*, says Leviticus (6:12,13), *must burn continually. . . . Never must the altar be empty of this perpetual fire*. And its nature has not changed, since the cross in its geometrical clarity replaced the bush of confused figures. Everything leads to this ascent, to the exhalation of this vertical breath, from below and from the sides everything is a vein and oil. For love, everything is combustible. It is the central sacrifice which has not ceased since Calvary and which each morning the priest renews on the consecrated stone. He disengages each time from the universal figure around him the special syllable of confession, reparation and adoration with which it was impregnated and invites it by this subtraction and enriching to a new order. Thus it is that the Good Shepherd united everything in a single body, which is His, and went forth to gather everything that was scattered and put it on His shoulders. Not only the Church proper, but the entire creation which is the work and the temple of the spirit. *Through the Gospel preaching,* says the Epistle to the Ephesians (3:6), *the Gentiles are to win the same inheritance, to be made part of the same body.* And the First Epistle to the Corinthians (12:12): *A man's body is all one, though he has a number of different organs; and all this multitude of organs goes to make up one body; so it is with Christ. We too, all of us, have been baptized into a single body.* And again the Epistle to the Ephesians (4:15,16): *We are so to grow up, in everything, into a due proportion with Christ, who is our head. On him all the body depends; it is organized and unified by each contact with the source which supplies it; and thus, each limb receiving the active power it needs, it achieves its natural growth, building itself up through charity.* From hell to the highest heaven and to the farthest horizon, nothing is absent from the enumerations of thanksgiving, everything combines with the holocaust, everything is incorporated with the Word made flesh and the very figure of circumscribing matter is the work of that central fire which burns. He has officially been clothed with the world like the High Priest formerly with all those ornaments and coverings of mingled varied colors.[2] It is all that which He

2.   *Vestments of the High Priest*

Some attention might suitably be paid here to the description given in chapter 28 of Exodus. When we read for example that the High Priest has to wear above his head and hanging over his brow a plate of very pure gold attached by a blue cord, and on which is engraved the inscription *qadesh la Jahvé—Sanctus Jehovae,* one thinks of the royal title in three languages which shines above the crown of thorns and that bond of flesh which connects the divine diadem with man. Thus Job (31:35,36): *that he, the Almighty, would grant my request, that he, my judge, would write my record down; how proudly I would bear it with me, shoulder-*

high, wear it as a crown! And the rider of the Apocalypse (19:12):
*on his brow were many royal diadems; the name written there is
one that only he knows.*

But it is not only the head, it is the shoulders, and the entire
body over which is unfolded the consecration in the form of the
ephod or humeral vestment. It is consecrated by those two *stones
of onyx* doubtless borrowed from the mysterious region of Hevilath where according to Genesis (2:12) their seed flourishes beside gold and crystal. Something following the vow of Job (19:24)
is engraved on that solidification of unalterable light. They are the
names of the twelve tribes of Israel, which, according to the Apocalypse, are not only those of the sons of Jacob, but of all the just
who have deserved the praise of the Son of God (John 1:47):
Here comes one who belongs to the true Israel. For (Rom. 9:6):
Not all those who are sprung from Israel are truly Israelites. This
is full obedience, represented by the twelve stars worshipping their
youngest brother (Gen. 37:9), by the labourers of the parable
(Matth. 20) and by the twelve categories of servants over which
on thrones in heaven each of the twelve Apostles will preside. This
is the fraternal charge assumed by Him who was used to bearing
the yoke from His adolescence, *for my yoke is easy* (Matth. 11:
30). *Yield foot of thine to wisdom's fetters,* says Ecclesiasticus
(6:26), *shoulder of thine to her yoke.* And Isaias (9:6): *to our
race a son is given, whose shoulder will bear the sceptre of princely
power.* The *Ephod,* according to certain texts, in clothing the High
Priest, seems to have invested him with an oracular power. On top
there are two openings which, when joined, make only one, so as
to let the head pass, who is Christ, through the assumed cloth,
where the text tells us, *the whole of its embroidered texture shall be
of gold, blue, purple, scarlet, twice-dyed, and twisted linen thread*
(that is, the promise reanimated by redemption and *the twisted
thread,* Exodus 28:8). These colors, this cloth, these stones which
speak, are the profuse wave of tribes, languages and voices who
represent, according to the Apocalypse, the theme of the chosen
people. *Dutiful observance was still the vesture I wore,* says Job
(29:14). *Glory and beauty are thy clothing,* says Psalm (103:1).

The second vestment of the High Priest is the *Pectoral* on
which are inscribed the words *urim* and *thummim,* which mean
doctrine and truth, illumination and perfection. It is a square of
double cloth attached by gold chains to the humeral with which
it makes one piece. It is a kind of intellectual pleura enveloping
the breathing spirit. The name of pectoral in Greek is λογεῖον,

suggesting that central fundamental reason equal on all sides and like to itself, which is the seat of the Word. It is seated on the square, on the corner stone and on the intersection of the quadruple Gospel. On it the mass is eternally said. The square is also the emblem and the means of multiplication: all that is introduced is judged by the fruit it brings to its own root. That is why this square of a palm on the heart of Aaron deserves the name of *Rational of Judgment*, since it is there every conference ends in a conclusion and every figure conceals this mathematical *reason*, this sign by which it is designated. Twelve stones, divided into four orders are inlaid, twelve names, twelve distinct lights each of which is assigned to one tribe of Israel. Is it not written in effect (Wisdom 3:7-8) *they will shine out, these just souls, unconquerable as the sparks that break out* through combustible matter? *Theirs to sit in judgment on nations.* Such are the saints each of whom illustrates, elucidates by a special refraction, by a characteristic spectrum, the ray he received from divine mercy. They are like balls on the eternal abacus according to this word of Wisdom (15:2): *Sin we not, of this, too, we have proof, that thou wilt count us for thy own.*

Exodus then speaks to us of that long blue tunic which the High Priest wears and which is nothing but the clothing of flesh which the Word assumed in the womb of the Virgin Mary. The opening for the head is reinforced with a border to prevent tearing. It reaches to the feet, and this skirt is bordered with pomegranates of mixed colors and small golden bells. The bell is an ear adapted to a tongue. It is a chalice which is also a mirror and whose capacity is both to receive sound and exhale it, something suspended in the service of emotion. At each step which Christ takes, the soul attentive in its substance vibrates to its depths with what is pure in itself, to the attachment in its center with this sonorous pistil. We hear it staying: *thou hast given me an ear ready to listen* (Ps. 39: 7). Magdalen did this once at the feet of her Saviour. This stammering fringe on the robe of the High Priest, this wake of gold, this noise made by the feet of Christ as He passes in the midst of human souls, we can still hear its echo each morning. It is the tiny bell at mass which brings to their knees the faithful at the moment of the elevation. *In this Aaron,* says verse 35, *shall ever be clothed when he performs his priestly office; with the ringing of bells he must announce his comings and goings in the sanctuary, in the Lord's presence, on pain of death.* This faint knocking on the open soul is God's sign in the ear that His priest is there raises in the elevation of His hands, it is all that He uses—as formerly did His homonym on the field of battle of Gabaon to stop the sun.[3] But today it is not for the *space of a day* only, it is for all centuries that the new Josue holds back over the horizon the *Sun of Justice* and keeps it from setting until He has repaired the ancient prevarication and drawn satisfaction from His enemies. Thus is justified the vision of Deuteronomy: *He rides in heaven to deliver thee . . . there, on high, is his dwelling, and yet the eternal arms reach down to uphold thee.* And how better could I end this paragraph than by this *cul-de-lampe*: Moses in prayer, his arms extended, while Josue fights Amalec and as soon as he weakens, Josue also weakens (Exodus 17:12): *They found him a stone to sit on and bade him be seated on it; then, one on each side, Aaron and Hur kept his hands lifted up. In this way, the strength of his arms held out until set of sun.*

Everything on the cross is consummated, not in the constitution of an inert figure, but in desire, in cooperation and in a uniting organic activity. What was broken is restored. Communication is reestablished with God, something beats under the seventh rib of the new Adam by which we are adapted to Him, the entire world through the lips of Jesus Christ aspires to the lips of the Father, the Spirit and He speak through the Word.

---

and is asking audience. *Deprecatio pauperis ad aures ejus perveniet.*

3. *Sun, that art setting over Gabaon, moon, that art rising in Aialon valley, stand stricken with awe. Sun and moon stood awestruck, while the people took vengeance on its enemies . . . The sun stood in mid-heaven, and for a whole day long did not haste to its setting. Never was so long a day before or since, as that day when the Lord listened to a human prayer, and fought openly on the side of Israel* (Josue 10:13-14). *Light there shall be none that day, all shall be frost and cold* (Zacharias 14:6).

Thus everything, even the Serpent himself, that living in-
sidious root entwined on all cordages and all the vessels of
our soul and our anatomy, the lowest, eating dust for food, is
exalted as on the end of a pike,[4] within the divine plan.[5] Thus
is planted above all human vicissitudes the immutable standard, to which is opposed false human wisdom, ridiculously
hoisted as on a bar stool or on a parrot perch. *Out upon her
silly clamor*, says the Book of Proverbs (9:13), *the woman
that is so crafty, yet knowledge has none! At her door she sits,
her chair commanding the city's height, and cries aloud to
such as pass by on their lawful errands. . . . Stolen waters are
sweetest, and bread is better eating when there is none to see.*
How different is that temple which Wisdom built for eternity,
not on Mount Moriah or on Mount Garizim, but in spirit and
truth in the person of the son of God, and about which He
said, *Destroy this temple, and in three days I will raise it up
again* (John 2:19). *See, where wisdom*, says the Book of Proverbs (9:1), *has built herself a house, carved out for herself
those seven pillars of hers!* It is this temple Saint Paul speaks of

4. *Peg of the tent's rope* (Zacharias 10:4).
5. This concerns the bronze serpent which God, in the Book of
Numbers (21:8) orders Moses to make and whose sight cures
those wounded by burning serpents in the sand. Commentators
see in it a figure of Christ in accord with this passage of Saint John
(3:14): *And this Son of Man must be lifted up, as the serpent
was lifted up by Moses in the wilderness.* This seems very strange
because throughout Scripture we see the serpent as the instrument
of sin and the devil. And the bronze serpent itself we see in the
Book of Kings (IV Kings 18:4), where he had become an object
of idolatry and where pious King Ezechias broke it into pieces
with the exclamation *Nohestan*, meaning *their metal!* Might it
not be more accurate to see in it an image of original sin, the
serpent closely allied with our clay and which in the person of the
Redeemer between the fault and salvation furnished a stronger
bond than the *blue strip.* Here it is inserted in the mud, pierced,
exposed to all eyes at the end of this salutiferous wood. In the
same curative look we see our sin and absorb our Saviour.

143

when he says: *Do you not understand that you are God's temple, and that God's spirit has his dwelling in you?* (I Cor. 3:16). What are those seven columns, those seven supports for a person? Four of them are appointed to exterior works: they are the two hands and the two feet; and three are inside and essential to all our organic life: the heart, the brain and the lungs. I do not speak of that enfolded mass in us of squares and streets which serve for the passage and digestion of food, and which recall the plan of fortified towns pressed close together within their walls. The heart, the brain and the lungs are also our root, intelligence and spirit. In Jesus everything is a temple. This does not refer to architecture, but to a function, to an activity working on a substance: *We have the fire here,* said Isaac (Gen. 22:7); *where is the lamb we need for a victim?* And Exodus (12:27) answers: *This is the victim that marked the Lord's passing-by;* namely, all that the presence of the Lord as perpetual victim henceforth furnishes as means of passage. This is the consummation accomplished each morning on the altar of each of our churches. This is the convocation which the bells tirelessly announce to cities and the countryside, *this way and that her maidens are dispatched, to city heep and city wall* (Prov. 9:3). This is the appeal felt by so many priests and religious and holy women everywhere. Like diligent ants picking up from the ground the smallest grain of wheat, they go to the half eaten-away leper, to the child who can hardly breathe, and who miraculously touch the curative point in the center of a soul in putrefaction. Come, eat, drink, walk, give up childhood, learn to use your legs and profit from the road. You yourself contribute to the victim the *sacrifice of thanksgiving,* spoken of in a psalm. For does not Saint Paul say (Rom. 21:1) that you should *offer up your bodies as a living sacrifice?* The table is placed where God prepares to mingle His blood with yours,

His flesh with your flesh and His spirit with your spirit (Prov. 9:2).

It is remarkable that the word *consummate* has the meaning of *destroy* as well as the meaning of *achieve*. In the same way the word *end* means both the goal to reach and the disappearance of the movement which helps one to reach it. As if every perfection consisted of some destruction. Of which the symbol and the instrument is fire which transforms every form into light, heat, smell and weight. The consummated being has achieved his goal. He furnished all the stipulated competition, and is now invited to cease offering resistance to the initiatives behind him which his intervention released. He confesses there is nothing in him which belongs to him alone and whose destiny he consummates definitively by his own existence. He knows that his duty is to give himself up, to give over with his soul that *fat* of accumulated works which Leviticus (3:16) says: *All that is fat shall belong to the Lord.* This is the invitation to cease being, which love continues to speak to the soul and which the weak creature knows it will not always be able to resist. Is straw able to resist fire? The creature has to do with an ingenious, profound patient lover who knows how to employ caresses, force, wile, who knows the means of attracting her attention elsewhere while in secret he pillages her property, and if once she commits the imprudence of releasing the piece of gold which is her entire fortune, she will never recover the same hold on that secretly substituted drachma. In vain does she propose pacts for a while to this enemy that he will pretend to accept and during the lapse, protected by a deceptive security, he will continue to practice imperceptible ravages. All those victims she tries to substitute are not wanted—she herself is needed, who is called to furnish the subject for the holocaust. It is from this happy creature that love for eternity asks for that inviolable confession that she does not exist and that He is everything for her. He is there to ask everything of her and, in secret, behind her back, to offer her everything.

THE SEVENTH AND LAST WORD

Father, into thy hands I commend my spirit.

THESE are the last words which Saint Luke ascribes to the Saviour *et haec dicens expiravit.* They are literally borrowed from Psalm 30:6, whose title is *In finem pro extasi.* It is one more example of that fulfillment which the Word on the cross was bent upon giving the words of the prophets. Greek uses the expression πα ρα θυσμαι, I shall put down, I shall place near.

It is the formula of the New Testament. It summarizes, in a supreme exhaling of breath, the prayer which just previously, with His eyes raised to heaven, and surrounded by His apostles, Jesus uttered at the Last Supper. *Father, the time has come; give glory now to thy Son, that thy Son may give glory to thee. Thou hast put him in authority over all mankind, to bring eternal life to all those thou hast entrusted to him. Eternal Life is knowing thee, who are the only true God, and Jesus Christ; whom thou hast sent. I have exalted thy glory on earth, by achieving the task which thou gavest me to do; now, Father, do thou exalt me at thy side, in that glory which I had with thee before the world began. I have made thy name known to the men whom thou hast entrusted to me, chosen out of the world. They belonged to thee, and have become mine through thy gift, and they have kept true to thy word. Now they have learned to recognize all the gifts thou gavest me as coming from thee; I have given them the message which thou gavest to me, and they, receiving it, recognized it for truth that I came from thee, and found faith to believe that it was thou who didst send me . . . I am remaining in the world no longer, but they remain in the world, while I am on my way to thee. Holy Father, keep them true to thy name, thy gift to me, that they may be one, as we are one. As long as I was with them, it was for me to keep them true to thy name. . . . But now I am coming to thee. . . . I pray for those who are to find faith in me through their word; that they may all be one; that they too may be one in us, as thou Father, art in me, and I in thee. . . . And I have given them the privilege which thou gavest to me, that they should all be one, as we are one. . . . So let the world know that it is thou who hast sent me, and that thou hast bestowed thy love upon them, as thou hast bestowed it upon me. This, Father, is my desire, that all those whom thou hast entrusted to me may be with me where I am, so as to see my glory, thy gift made to me, in that love which thou didst bestow upon me before the foundation of the world* (John 17, passim.).

The moment has therefore come when He who had been sent had to return and give back what had been given to Him. It is the application of all the parables which portray the steward who is asked for the accounts, the son of the family whom the distant employer sends to the recalcitrant workmen, the fugitive himself who for a while preferred to his father the company of sinners and lowest animals. Now, what was sent was the spirit, that same spirit which once Elohim breathed into the nostrils of Adam and from whom He came in the presence of His Servant to receive from the mouth of Peter and all those who *born by spiritual birth are things of spirit* (John 3:6). The work of filiation, to which end He was sent, is completed. And in a supreme exhalation the *spirit of adoption* takes to the Father all of humanity and all of creation. Our names, in as much as we are Christians, are henceforth included in His. *Remember*, says Psalm 58:51, *how a world's taunts assail thy people, whom I have absorbed in Me.* The hyperbole, like a cry of impotence and despair which once Moses raised to God (Num. 11), is realized to the letter: *Lord why dost thou treat me thus? How is it that I have fallen out of favor with thee? Must I carry a whole people like a weight on my back? I did not bring this multitude of men into the world; I did not beget them; and thou wouldst have me nurse them in my bosom like a child, till they reach the land promised to their race. Where am I to find meat for such a host as this? And that is the complaint they bring me; they would have meat for their food. I cannot bear, alone, the charge of so many; it is too great a burden for me.* Now this breath we received from the Creator, the Son, in our name and in His assumed capacity of mandatary of all the human race, returns *into the hands* of His Father. Why into the hands? Because of their triple function. They are the organ of touch; they are the organ of apprehension, comprehension and conservation; and finally, they serve to give and make, in being multiple, careful, keen and supple. To fall back on them is to fall back on what created us, according to the word of Job (10:8 and also Psalm 118:73): *It was thy hand that made me, no part of me but is thy fashioning.* And even as the Word was corporeally given over into the hands of men, so that Saint John (I, 1:1) speaks of *what it was that met the touch of our hands* (I would freely translate: *What they were able to seize*), so does He bring, for a more intimate and more complete contact than vision itself, with the new smell of the earth which He submitted to His agriculture, to a Father who in a way is only hands, a person who is only a face. He is, under His ten fingers—namely under His ten commandments—a beautiful perfect instrument. *Wake*, says

Psalm 56:9 and 107:3: *wake, my heart, echoes of harp and viol*. And the text adds an allusion to the morning of the resurrection: *dawn shall find me watching*. Thus the spirit gives itself over to the hands which are able to administer it. That is why we see in the Book of Numbers (3:3) that the hands of the former sacrificers had to be *enriched*, by their official function, *and consecrated*—and still today the hands of the priests being ordained are anointed. From the first days of the Church, from the day when Christ risen, breathing on the apostles (John 20:22), said to them: *Receive the Holy Spirit*, the consecrating of priests has been accomplished by the laying on of hands and the handing over of the Spirit. This is not the Septuagint which God asked Moses to admit in order to answer the prayer I copied above: it is the immense Church drawing inexhaustibly, abundantly and with its entire capital, from the heart of the Father, that Spirit, that administrative power which the Word made flesh placed at its disposal on the cross.

The man who loses his life for my sake, it is said in Matthew 10:39, *that will secure it*. To lose one's life (soul) takes place when the soul consents not only to find elsewhere than in itself its interests and its motives, but also to lean on something other than itself and speaking to God, to make its end Infinity. By losing itself thus, it will recover itself since it will acquire a simple vision both of its characteristic which is nothingness and of its *raison d'être* which is the call of God. That is why Christ says to us (John 10:17): *This my Father loves in me, that I am laying down my life, to take it up again afterwards*, which is to say that I give and receive, that I expire and aspire. *Nobody can rob me of it; I lay it down of my own accord. I am free to lay it down, free to take it up again; that is the charge which my Father has given me*. Those who by this example, having given their lives, take them back and one can say according to the Apostle, *their birth came, not from human stock, not from nature's will of man's, but from God* (John 1:13).

Because Christ is *the first birth out of death* (Col. 1:18), because He is the head of that body of which we are the members and because *there where I am, there you will be with me,* it is not irrelevant to seek the meaning and the consequence for us of that supreme and total remission of the Son of Man to His transmitter. Just as the perfect act of obedience of the Blessed Virgin, when she replied to the proposition of the Trinity that she was *the handmaid of the Lord,* was the condition for the Incarnation which permitted God to be born with the world, so the perfect act of obedience of Jesus Christ, when He put Himself on the cross in the hands of His Father, was the condition whose accomplishment permitted the *many brethren* Saint Paul speaks of (Rom. 8:29) to be born in God with their eldest born.

Jesus on the cross gives His soul back, not only in a general way to God, but *into the hands of God,* that is to say, to God especially considered in His active operative aspect. He *places* it. Henceforth there will be no word of God—no act of divine will with regard to a particular—to which we will not be bound in the past, present and future and in eternity, through a kind of basic intelligence and congenital intimate solidarity. We shall understand by means of our very principle how God goes about creating all things and maintaining them. We shall be associated with each of His creative acts and we shall feel their effect on our very substance. We shall be interested in each of those initiatives, in each *sunrise* that Psalm 64:9 speaks of. With all our senses we shall contemplate the first cause. With an intelligence so clear and informed that it will become as immediate as sensation is in us, with a fidelity of all our being, with a will as prompt and subtle as the flame of a fire, we shall espouse all divine behavior and we shall be the cause of all that is caused by it. To use an imperfect image: powerful music seizes us and carries us off. It transports us and imposes its appearance, rhythm and melody and makes us contribute to that ocean of sonorous realization which it provokes and dissolves ceaselessly around us. Our spiritual destiny is a perfect communion of our will with divine activity, an affiliation with the supreme counsel, with that conversation outside of time carried on by the Three Persons. We shall be at the source, our ear—like Saint John's—will be on the divine Heart, on that spot which Lucifer left unoccupied and which the prophet lets us hear when he speaks to us of the throne which the King of Tyr once occupied *in corde maris*. And in truth we shall be in the center, at the heart of that immense movement, of advance and retreat, of the universal tides of desire and grace. We shall be with Love which calls all things to Him and then only shall we understand fully the Saviour's word: *Yes, if only I am lifted up from the earth, I will attract all men to me* (John 12:32).

Christians, we should immediately answer this invitation, and try in our writing, to rise above those light flakes which, on the day of His Ascension, were enough to rob us of the sight of the Risen One, and contemplate in all its power and extent the promise of which He has made us beneficiaries and co-heirs. *And the Star of the morning shall be his,* says Apocalypse 2:28—the very star which Lucifer's escape had left deserted and uninhabited. What is the morning star if not the cry from the tower, the trumpeting of the herald, the luminous call which calls up to existence—not like chaos but like an army organizing as it awakens—all of creation. This arousing power of initiative and order is put into our hands.[1] For eternity we are with someone *who has overcome the world*

1. *He rode out victorious, and to win victory* (Apoc. 6:2).

(John 16:33) and we share with Him this power which is superior to all resistance. *Whatever takes its origins from God* (I John 5:4) *must needs triumph over the world; our faith, that is the triumphant principle which triumphs over the world. He alone triumphs over the world, who believes that Jesus is the Son of God.* We should then rejoice with Him, as we are urged to in the Lesson of Christmas, as *when the booty is taken* (Isaias 9:3). *Thou dost mount up on high,* says Psalm 67:19, *thou dost capture thy spoil.*[2] And Saint Paul, recasting the quotation (Eph. 4:8): *He has mounted up on high; he has captured his spoil; he has brought gifts to men,* no doubt meaning by that, the gifts with which the bodies in glory will be invested and which we shall speak of later. *He has captured his spoil* means that, like Samson loading on his shoulders the gates of Gaza and leaving the other smashed gates *which shall not prevail against him* (Matth. 16:18), He carries off with Him to heaven those very obstacles of matter and flesh which held us prisoners and which arrested our sight and movement and action. This is the matter made to be penetrated, dominated and utilized by the spirit, and not the inverted spirit which groaning submits to this momentary violence. From this slavery of sin, from the false *liberty for wrong-doing,* which Saint Peter speaks of (I Peter 2:16), from the submission to limitation and exterior fact, we pass to an intelligent adoption: a view, an active, essential and total approbation of what in the heart of the Trinity is

2. The preceding verse is: *See when God comes, with chariots innumerable for his escort; thousands upon thousands.* With these words, I see a great ray of sun over the ocean crossing the entire circular extent from one horizon to the other, and thousands upon thousands of small flashes moving and lighting up, in the time of an acclamation, under a sudden glance, comparable to the flash of a glance immediately turned aside. This image harmonizes with the magnificent passage of Virgil, which describes for us the chariot of Neptune hastening over the waves and sending forth water under its sparkling wheels.

efficiently generative. We are no longer with the effects, we are with the cause. We are no longer with clay, we are with those two hands of the spiritual potter. We are no longer with time, we are with the source of time. We are no longer with the world, we are no longer in or under the world, we are with the One who surmounted the world. We have exhausted in the person of our Master all the power which death directed against us, and we can henceforth cry with the Apostle: Where is that famous *sting*?[3] It is over! and *death* definitively *is swallowed up in victory* (I Cor. 15:54). The Kingdom of Heaven is promised us, not in terms of subjects, but in terms of *thrones*, on which Christians, answerable to

3. To speak of the *sting of death* seems first a curious comparison. A sting is something which awakens, which pricks and arouses the consciousness, which urges up to effort in a determined sense. It seems that one might rather compare death to a numbness, to the penetrating and progressive action of a poison which gradually bargains with your faculties of resistance and ends by impregnating them, circumscribing and paralyzing them. But Saint Paul immediately gives us the explanation (I Cor. 15:56): *It is sin that gives death its sting.* Sin is in truth this secret sting—*I was given a sting to distress my outward nature, an angel of Satan sent to rebuff me* (II Cor. 12:7)—which comes to sound us under our hide and arouse the blind anarchic instincts of our nature. Death is a separation and sin is that sting which exasperates and accelerates the deep discord of our sinful nature, the strange subjugated union of the ass with the ox which Deuteronomy condemns. *Do not plough with an ox and an ass together* (Deuter. 22:10). The ox, patient and regular, attached to its rectilinear furrow, cannot support without misery the company of an artist like the ass, fanciful and a dreamer, recalcitrant, lubricious, an amateur of the wind and noise and who kicks in all directions. *Poor fools*, says Job 11:12, *that will have a mind of their own, and think they were born free as the wild ass!* And farther on (39:5): *Who gives the wild ass untrammelled liberty to roam the wilderness?* There are some, adds chapter 24:5, *like the wild ass in the desert.* Souls in perdition seized by the lion, says Ecclesiasticus (13:23), *as wild ass is to lion out in the desert.* Thus under the sting of Satan, the pair is broken. The ass went off to make the ass in the world and the bewildered ox did not know what to become.

153

Christ, *will judge*, will exercise intelligent authority, founded
on reference to a living text. *It is thou that dost curb the pride
of the sea, and calm the tumult of its waves* (Psalm 88:10).
For, as the Epistle to the Romans (6:9) says: *Christ, now he
has risen from the dead, cannot die any more; death has no
more power over him.*

What will be the consequences for the soul thus definitively
adopted and united with its Christ in the hands of the
Father—of this victory of the Spirit over matter, of this perfect domination of cause over effect, of what is superior over
what is inferior, of being over symbol?

The soul here below created the body on the other side
of the veil in blindness and night. Matter has been *shadow-
covered*; that is, there was between the light and the screen
the interposing of a drawing (or a plan), a contour, a particular idea reflected, translated and reproduced, the creation of
an opportunity, of a firm activity subjected to a suitable purpose. No text, no definition, no authority yet permits us to
imagine at what moment the idea passes to the other side
and becomes soul; at what moment being succeeds in attracting to itself, in absorbing to itself, in absorbing and reforming
its constructive and instructive program—in possessing, so to
speak, in itself what previously acted on it from the outside.
What is clearest is still the Thomistic distinction of the
vegetable, animal and intelligible soul, organs of individual
autonomy which support one another (without of course there
being three souls, but only one soul).

After death we know that the redeemed soul is put into the
presence of God face to face and made capable of interpret-
ing, of espousing divine will in conformity with the particular
intention which raised it up:[4] in all rightness, in full conscious

4. *Their birth came, not from human stock, not from nature's
will or man's, but from God* (John 1:13).

154

and intelligent possession both of its vision and its instrument—the eternal model; of working and following that model faithfully and lovingly. This is true of the amazing *amaeba proteus*, the drop of protoplasm which of its own will creates legs for walking and antennae for seeing and apprehending. Every particle of its vision and freedom is used to serve and that is why it is compared to the tongue of fire which the spirit animates and which reaches existence by vibration. *The servants that wait on him like a flame of fire* (Heb. 1:7). In order to express the intimate dialogue between the intelligent speaking lamp and the divine Word, Psalm 28 uses this image which today will seem familiar to the radio listener: *The Lord's voice kindles flashing fire* (v. 7).

This image of a being who reaches the fullness of his form by song and by a spiritual tension of his essential theme, with whom the realized sense has become the pure source of all the senses, will help us to understand the four dowries which according to theology, are the privilege of elected bodies: impassiveness, subtlety, agility and glory. Nothing of what we possess will be destroyed except the *fault,* but everything will be reestablished and raised to the highest degree, not only restored but inflamed, so to speak, transported from the domain of verification to that of lyric knowledge.

For example, the term *impassiveness* does not mean that henceforth we shall be dead to what is the sign and the means of an exterior physical action on ourselves, but simply that the sensation will no longer be imposed on us, that we will preserve in relationship to it all freedom within love and laws, that nothing will come before us with regard to which we will not nourish an inexhaustible resource of agreement and composition. Everywhere we shall carry with us the privilege of creation, and contact with the effects will be replaced by a dealing with causes; less impassiveness than extension to all

155

our being of self administration, less exercise and opportunity for sympathy, than endless duty which espouses justice, as the copulative joins with the proposition.

The virtue of *subtlety* is the transportation into the physical domain of that penetrating quality of the spirit, of that discernment which no texture, no obstacle can resist, against which nothing is more compact or refractory, according to this text of Wisdom (7:22): *Mind-enlightening is the influence that dwells in her; set high apart; one in its source, yet manifold in its operation; subtle, yet easily understood. An influence quick in movement, inviolable, persuasive, gentle, right-thinking, keen-edged, irresistible, beneficent.* It is by this quality that the glorified soul, as it is removed from exterior violence, becomes the absolute mistress of its inner instrumental domain. It is thereby that the risen Christ becomes suddenly present to His disciples, *behind closed doors.* Thereby so many saints even in this life have received the power to *put down and take back* their bodies, to dispose of them at the will of their charity (I mean according to their own mode of exterior manifestation, touchable or not, visible or not, according to whether the circumstance and love commend them). Everything is born in order to open up before this bearer of the Word. *Swing back, doors, higher yet!* the Psalmist (23:7) cries out. And Ezechiel: *In it came through the eastern gateway, the splendor of the Lord himself* (43:4). He profited from this intimate void, from this deficiency of every creature in the presence of the One who Is. Light is what passes through everything—as is shown by the modern discovery of the exploratory waves of matter. Now the risen one will be clothed with light, *amictus lumine,* the psalm says to us, *sicut vestimento,* and with the conscious intelligent light of all the qualities of light. *Clothing* does not signify the assumption of something exterior and foreign, but a covering intimately and closely united with that source which we constitute according to the text of Saint Paul: *it is not because we would be stripped of something; rather, we would clothe ourselves afresh* (II Cor. 5:4). We shall therefore be only one with grace, with that irresistible splendor, which nothing can stop because it is completely dedicated to the service of God, according to the text of Ezechiel (16:10): *oil I brought to anoint thee; clad thee with embroidery.*

As the virtue of *subtlety* is a victory over inert quantity, the virtue of *agility* is an indifference to space and distance. The magnificent text of Wisdom we quoted in part continues: *Nothing so agile that it can match wisdom for agility; nothing can penetrate this way and that, ethereal as she. Steam that ascends from the fervor of divine activity, pure effluence of his glory who is God all-powerful, she feels no passing taint; she, the glow that radiates from eternal light, she, the untarnished mirror of God's majesty, she, the faithful image of his goodness. Alone, with none to aid her, she is all-powerful; herself ever unchanged, she makes all things new; age after age she finds her way into holy men's hearts. . . . Brightness is hers beyond . . . all the starry host;*[5] *match her with light itself, and she outvies it. Agility* is therefore that gift by which one's being is capable of realizing itself wherever it wishes (if there was anything other than God expressing a wish); that is, to be constituted instantaneously in conformity with some exterior combination and in a harmonious melodic relationship constantly renewed with this conformity, and invented by the inexhaustible necessities of love. Distance is no longer a dividing or a remoteness, but what is called in music

---

5. This does not refer to astrology. Stars are indicated here like marks which serve for calculating space and time, that space and time which the spoke of the parousia, shot by the bow of the *strong man,* crosses in one projection from the east to the west.

an *interval*. It passes through all paradise in order to praise God with a marvellous sound like the bow on a string and you can't tell whether it is singing or making everything it passes sing.[6] And as there is agility in space (if the term "space" still fits this spiritual device), in this same way there will be agility in time; such that a being—with calculated acceleration or retard of which stellar rays give us the experience—will be attached everywhere to the infinite variety of causes and effects of which he has both the imperceptible and universal point of attachment. That is what the vision of Bethel shows us, where Jacob saw angels endlessly mounting and descending a ladder on which God leaned. From this also comes the comparison of the *net* as used by the prophets and Saint Matthew when he tells us (13:47): *the kingdom of heaven is like a net that was cast into the sea* and which lets nothing escape from its unfurling: the past as well as the present and future. This net of charity is dried and broken by heresy (Eze. 26:5-14). Everything, without exception, on every side, is necessary for our action of grace and cannot do without our presence and cooperation.

The first three dowries we have just studied concern principally the relationships between the risen one and the outside world. But the fourth, which is *Glory*, is attached in a more intimate way with its intrinsic institution. Throughout the Holy Books it is compared to a piece of clothing: *glory and beauty are thy clothing. The light is a garment thou dost wrap about thee* (Ps. 103:2). It is the seamless robe which Christ wore. It is an untearable covering, a principle of unification assembling all powers into a single act. *Brightness of the Lord's presence*, says Isaias 58:8, *close thy ranks behind.* And this principle, we know, is the fire which is kindled and

6. *See how he issues his command to the earth, how swift his word runs!* (Ps. 147:4).

continues with all materials, and unites everything it catches on into a single tongue of clear flame. *Glorify me,* is the prayer of Our Lord at the Last Supper. Now there is an inner light and an outer light. The inner light is that of conscience to which the texts of Matthew and Luke allude: *The eye is the light of the whole body, so that if thy eye is clear, the whole of thy body will be lit up* (Matth. 6:22). But our eye in the future life is *simple,* since it sees only one thing which is its first cause, and that simple vision kindles in the particular being a cooperation in a simple knowledge and a simple desire. In accordance with its principle, which the Bible calls its *sky above,*[7] it will become conscious of this desire, of this one soaring. And the outer light is the information concerning its nature which our own lamp furnishes as it burns outside, and the light also which it diffuses as a letter in a word is diffused over all the surrounding composition. This light formed us and now forms us again by illuminating us.[8] It is not a stranger to us, it is God in us who provoked it, but it is we who feed it from the deepest part of our substance. Thus Psalm 44:14: *She comes, the princess, all fair to see.* And in Ezechiel (28:18) addressing the devil: *such a fire I will kindle in the heart of thee as shall be thy undoing.* It is this glory

---

7. *Bright shall be the glory of wise counsellors, as the radiance of the sky above* (Dan. 12:3).

8. *Then God said, Let there be light* (Gen. 1:3). *Dawn of hope for the innocent, dawn of gladness for honest hearts!* (Ps. 96:11). *See how the path of the just grows ever brighter!* (Prov. 4:18) *That charge is a lamp to guide thee, that teaching a light to beckon thee* (Ps. 6:23). *God saw the light, and found it good, and he divided the spheres of light and darkness.* (Gen. 1:4). *Narrowly he scans the river's depths, and brings to light all they hide* (Job 28:11). *Now God has reprieved me from death's exile, I am to live still and see the light* (Job 33:28). *I, the creator of light* (Isaias 45:7). *The same God who bade light shine out of darkness* (II Cor. 4:6).

which Satan, struck by the Angel on his stomach, gives back to his author in a terrible vomiting which dirties the marriage gown: *how shamefully is that glory of thine bespewed!* (Hab. 2:16) and in the same passage: *This was to cover thyself with shame, not with glory; drink thou in thy turn!* The light which comes from us in that way, although kindled at the same source, when it is testimony given by one man, is infinitely varied. That is why the Holy Books can only compare the just with myriad stars which differ one from the other in quantity and quality and yet which God knows and calls, like sheep, each by its name.

Man is intelligence, sensitivity and action. On the state of intelligence in the glorified being, I can do no better than refer the reader to the treatise of Saint Thomas which is the sublime summit in the center of that Summa—brilliantly compared by Coventry Patmore to the Tibetan plateau. On his mode of action it is better to put off our hypotheses until the day when the contemplation of angels will have allowed us to behold something of the great spiritual laws, which, like those of music, astronomy, electricity and meteorology control the government of the high spheres. It is therefore solely to the realm of sensibility that I care to limit my research, which is less an original exposition than a diligent classification of texts.

The meanings which hold and communicate with one another like a seamless robe are compared to a piece of clothing which both limits our person and serves as means of communicating with the exterior: both form and information. It is this garment which in the Song of Songs is proposed to the Bride and before which she cried out: *Ah, but my shift, I have laid it by: how can I put it on again?* (5:3). This garment of *flesh and skin* of which Job speaks (10:11) has been eaten by the patient *moth* which is time (Job 13:28). The same prophet says that this garment hates the one who ill inhabits it. The moment has come for us to put on a new garment, for the strength in us (which has been able to constitute a field, a form and organs) is not exhausted now that, rather than working blindly and, if I may say, from inspiration and fashion, it has opened wide its eyes and feeds on the living model. *Firm as golden pillar in silver socket rest the feet of steadfast woman on the ground she treads*, says Ecclesiasticus 26:23, indicating thereby that the gifts of the Holy Spirit with which we feed our spiritual body depend upon the good will in us, all of whose merit consists in its unalterable purity. This will be set up the *holy candlestick* or foundation which will allow our raised light to shine forth. We know in truth that the body promised to us is a *spiritual* body, according to this text of Saint Paul (I Cor. 15:44-49): *what is sown a natural body, rises a spiritual body. If there is such a thing as a natural body, there must be a spiritual body too.* (Saint Paul here alludes doubtless to the verse of Genesis (2:7) where God breathed into the nostrils of Adam the breath of life.) *Mankind begins with the Adam who became a living soul; it is fulfilled in the Adam who has become a life-giving spirit. It was not the principle of spiritual life that came first; natural life came first, then spiritual life; the man who came first came from earth, fashioned of dust, the man who came afterwards came from heaven, and his fashion is heavenly. The nature of that earth-born man is shared by his earthly sons, the nature of the heaven-born man, by his heavenly sons; and it remains for us, who once bore the stamp of earth, to bear the stamp of heaven.* The opposition which the Apostle establishes between the *living soul* and the *life-giving spirit* is quite remarkable. In the first case, you might say it is a utilized resource, an exploited deposit; and in the second, a creative force whose disposition we receive. The spirit which was contained, now becomes the container (namely what holds together). The body was formerly here below what transforms the spirit into a face, but now the spirit is that which transforms the body through the face and above the face into a light, and through this effect, enveloped with rays and directions, it becomes breathable and intelligible to everything that surrounds it. Such is the meaning of the passage in the Apocalypse in which God promises to give the faithful *the star of morning*. For He Himself is in her the *root, the splendid morning star* from which emanates in all directions a life-giving ray. That is also why the prophets, speaking of the happiness of the purified soul, compare it to a light, and not to all light, but precisely to that of the morning which crosses its fires with the light whose name above the deserts is: *O Oriens*.[9] It is the happiness of being constituted at every moment at the source, of owing at every moment this source in us to a source outside of us of which the Apocalypse speaks when it says: *He shewed me, too, a river, whose waters give life . . . clear as crystal* (Apoc. 22:1). *The favor of the Lord our God smile on us!* says Psalm 89:17. The favor (splendor) of God in us which elicits (Bar. 5:3-Is. 62:1) and that which is elicited. *Until he, the Just One, is revealed to her like the dawn. He will fill thy soul with comfort* (Isaias 58:11). Not a changing light like that which illuminates our night: *From birth, princely state shall be thine, holy and glorious; thou art my son, born like dew before the day-star rises* (Ps. 109:3). These are different splendors like the reason for a particular illustration which called them to existence, and that is why they are compared to stars, explorers through Infinity of the inexhaustible number. For Eternity they give answer to the double commandment of Deuteronomy: *thou*

9. *Here is one takes his name from the Day-spring* (Zacharias 6:12).

*shalt love the Lord thy God with the love of thy whole heart
and thy neighbor as thyself* (6:5). *How fair to look upon,*
says Baruch (6:59), *are sun and moon and stars! Yet theirs
is loyal and useful service; and so it is with yonder lightning,
that dazzles the view.* It is a light, infinitely more delicate
than all the sensory organs, which has become the organ of
charity, of tact, appreciation, of brotherly communication
within the hive, by which they are made capable of giving,
not only something, but themselves. Nothing irreducible
is left which is opposed to our action and reception.

The last texts I have just quoted invite us to pass from the
realm of vision to that of hearing, from the realm of proportion to that of modulation; from the realm of the simultane-
ous to that of the successive and the values of timbre. *No
doubt all these different languages,* Saint Paul says to us (I
Cor. 14:10), *exist somewhere in the world, and each of them
has its significance; but if I cannot understand what the
language means, the effect is that I am a foreigner to a man
who is speaking, and he is a foreigner to me.*[10] This is the
language which henceforth for eternity the Holy Spirit put
into our voice, so that we might at last express ourselves, and
answer the affectionate invitation: *Shew me but thy face, let
me but hear thy voice, that voice sweet as thy face is fair* (S.
of Songs 2:14). The soul has completely become praise and,
the *echoes (daughters) of music faint,* according to the expression of Ecclesiastes (12:4), from that sonorous and mel-
odious sustained note of the breath or *pneuma* whose need
was communicated to it in the night (Job 3:6-10). It has completely become a musical instrument. It is not a harp in one's
hands, itself is the harp finding in itself the scale and from octave to octave the means, with an infinite variety, of rising
from the lowest to the highest. *Wake, my soul,* says David

10. *On a ten-stringed harp I will sound thy praise* (Ps. 143:9).

(Ps. 56:9), *wake, echoes of harp and viol. They will ever be praising thee*, says Psalm 83:6. It is not without reason that they speak of a *just* man (*un homme juste*) and a lute which is *just* (in tune) (*un luth juste*). Justice is on the severely stretched strings and makes on them attacks and phrases according to Psalm 48:5: *reveal, with the harp's music, things of deep import.* The word of God found this heart which was no longer of stone but of flesh, and awakened to His commandments, along our fibers, a tenfold answer.[11] If we wished to develop this, we could say that the strings, in order to resound, have to be stretched full length between desire and defense: so that the bow of love can play over them. They could be compared to the woof on which the sonorous shuttle establishes its fabric. Is not the psalter today and all the learned arrangement of the Divine Office, the framework prepared for the ingenious introduction and deliberate recapitulation of prayer?

But the gold ladder of that liturgical triangle called the harp does not exhaust in the soul—like a prey to the spirit—the realm of sonorous efficiency. Beside the eloquent, skillful concerted strings, there is the cry(!), the violence of intervening inspiration. *The Lord's voice kindles flashing fire* (Ps. 28: 7). The trumpet is the instrument of this flashing rape, the trumpet which from Exodus to the Apocalypse accompanies all theophanies. The prophet Zacharias (9:14) tells us that *the Lord God sounds with the trumpet.* The salubrious, life-giving, imperious, precise trumpet suddenly strips the soul of all the past and points out a new order. *God goes up, loud are the cries of victory*, says Psalm 46:6; *the Lord goes up, loudly the trumpets peal.* It is fitting that at all stages of our spiritual development we should hear the piercing cry of that

11. *Flute and harp make sweet melody; best of all a kindly tongue* (Eccl. 40:21).

tube which awakens in us the buried metal and calls it to that vibrant erectile state which can be compared only to a burst of flame. *Cry aloud, never ceasing,* says Isaias 58:1, *raise thy voice like a trumpet-call.*

To review the instruments of our mystical orchestra, such as the psalms show them to us in the hands of King David, we must speak of the organ and the cymbals. The official purpose of the organ is to permit a sonorous atmosphere to break free. It makes accessible to hearing the fullness surrounding us, it impregnates space with sound. In opposition to other vessels of music, it gives expression to what lasts rather than to what passes: it arranges the continuous. It is the soul's exhalation which evaporates; it is the long insistence on a single thought; while at different stages, separated by layers, timbres are effaced and drawn on clouds, like fugitive buildings and undulant stairways. It gives space, organizes levels, makes mountains dance around it, communicates to an entire crowd its gigantic impetus. It brays to God like the earth and the sea with all the force of its superimposed lungs.

And finally, the supreme crest on the top of the pyramid, the cymbals.—— At the back of the orchestra, in symphonic performances behind the mass of strings, behind the line of oboes and bassoons, flanked on one side by brass and on the other by double-bass, we see the heavy artillery in reserve, the shells and the trench-mortars and the entire ammunition depot. When the crescendo of the musical ode grows and swells, when from every corner of the orchestra the lines converge and culminate, when the gradual increasing of the base prepares the imminent fuse of the column—then movement begins in the percussion instruments. *For clapping of hand and stamping of foot* (Ezechiel 25:6). When the bass drumstick is in the air, you see the corybant preparing to dance on her casks and awaken with swift drum beats the deep echo of subterranean presences. The drum begins to roll, the drum-head in full drill enslaves the entire orchestra to its irresistible pulse. But you feel that the event, the ultimate fulguration is yet to come; it is in the hands of the baccant who at the back of the stage suddenly stands up and waves a double golden sun! When, from the height of a great cliff you see the huge waves in powerful lines coming one after the other under the gust of the north wind to break at last against the unshakable wall which the coastline presents to them, the first idea which comes to us is that of the impotent anger of the elements. But it is not really anger, it is enthusiasm! The watery monster, powerfully balanced on the arms of the sea divinities is hurled against a curtain of dark rocks, so that plumed giants suddenly surge fifty feet in the air and crash into an explosion of fury and snow as they are pierced by the curved sword of a fiery rainbow. They are not angry, they are drunk. Singing and dancing, they are happy to have found their limit, something solid which permits them to unfurl.——And here, the ecstatic frenzied cymbal exists at the zenith of that sea which throws it up to the stars, shattering it there into powder! But the cymbal is not only, at the triumphant peak of the chorus, that which bursts and resounds and bangs, it is also that which, in the most silent and attentive regions of our soul, begins suddenly to tremble. Is it an earthquake beginning? Is it the child Jupiter awakening under the foliage? What moved suddenly under that slow wand? *The complaint I made before him found a hearing* (Ps. 17:7).

And could I forget the elegiac gentle flute whose detours and flights, like water flowing and shining, leads us into the ways of peace: it both refreshes us and pains us like the sight of a child's cheek and the naive glance of affectionate eyes. As the Spartans once gave the care of training their troops not to the trumpet or fife, but to the flute (esteeming that their warriors needed less excitement than self-possession), so our shepherd makes us hear a counsel of sweetness and lets us see at our feet a path of light and azure. These are the *green fields* which an angel in dreams showed to former martyrs on the vigil of their martyrdom, and whose strange clarinet, in which the meaning of the past mingles with poignant anticipation, makes us nostalgic.

But after we have heard the sound of those instruments which, in the hands of the spiritual orchestra accompany, sustain and annotate the celebration of the Psalms, David and Solomon—and all the prophets and prophetesses[12] of the Old and New Testament—would be astonished if from under their words (which diverts the light for our eyes and mouth to use) we did not become more attentive to the continuum, the intonation of their voices, the holy use their tongue and lips, through angels, make of the breath their lungs have drawn up from the Trinity itself. For sound precedes the word, as Saint John the Baptist preceded Jesus Christ. (It was appropriate that the Church found in the initials of a hymn to Saint John the names for the seven tones of the scale.)

The word expresses ideas. The song, accentuation of tone, is what expresses sentiment. Through language which is a kind of sonorous writing, we offer to the mind of the listener those concepts which are words *(motus)*. Each word constitutes in itself a kind of fixed image and derives its meaning from impulse, in company with other words or rigid vehicles, which the sentence impresses on them. By song, on the con-

12. Like those prophets in the windows of our churches (as at Chartres), each carries an apostle on his shoulders. They are all here: from old Lamech to Zacharias, father of John; from Mary, sister of Moses, to the perfect Mary herself who was the mother of Christ.

trary (or modulated vowel), we ourselves, by an act of will on the emission of breath, enter upon a state of movement and passage. The first is in analysis, an interpretation by the medium of the luminous brush and the intellectual spurt which the desire of expression directs out of us. The second is a sonorous exploitation of our essential unity in time, the consciousness we have, in listening to it, of that line we trace indefinitely in duration. We exhale a breath, we make ourselves resound, we musically associate our soul with those words we are invited to utter, and it comes from between our lips moistened with our life. The spiritual reed attached to the back of our throat and the moist supple tongue, not only permits us to fashion in the trough of our mouth the vibrant air, but as the organ of our conscience, it permits us to enjoy the taste of the air as it passes through. Hence the expression found so often in sacred exclamations: *Honey itself cannot vie with well-framed words, for heart's comfort and body refreshment* (Prov. 16:24). Honey is the song and wax the word, the cell with the soluble walls, the mystical recipient containing the drop of edible light. Through song in the limitless realm of the spirit, and without moving, we are invested with the power of rising and descending, for such is the freedom of the children of God! From the base to the tip, from the foundation to the firmament, we climb—without omitting any step—like an angel swiftly flying, all the degrees of logic. We are the masters of our pace, we can at will increase or slacken it. We can weigh, insist, prolong, and we can also graze the ground with a prosody foot lighter and swifter than an elf's. We can multiply the points of contact, the guide marks of our sonorous flight, and we can also in one leap cover an immense space. Like a prisoner happily amusing himself with his chains, we have made out of our captivity a game. A furrow has become our only frontier, our wing has become a bond, our soul in delight over whatever it does, speaks ecstatically of the impossibility of escaping divine joy! We mount toward the sun like an arrow, we swoop down on our prey like an eagle, like a bolt of lightning! O arpeggio! O powerful unfolding of feathers! O roaring with all cylinders of our motor! O just and strong commandment! rising supported by weight! O radiant freedom of all that now, far from the ground, takes place in the air! We have at our disposal all space to cross it out victoriously with the sign of the cross! Our soul spreading its wings in measure with its inspiration, invents the translation outside of this rhythm which it draws up from the very foundations of its nature. It listens to itself speak to God, and soon the powerful release of clear pure thought follows the preparatory stammering. This is the mysterious *horn* the Holy Books speak of, that growth outside of us, that drawing which like a ray of fire we trace on the void by the modulation of our very existence. We needed a single cry to create silence around us and to invite as an echo the immensity which suddenly had become present. It is our very extinction, our continuous disappearance on behalf of a limitless advance which has become our means of expression. A figure, a melody is born from the instantaneous debate between what appears and what no longer exists, between what resounds in our ears and that note which our inner mind has never ceased hearing. Let us give to the musical angel in us the care of developing the scale, of prolonging around the altar the censer and the garland, and furnishing to that eternity which is our natural and acquired habitat the inexhaustible comparison of continuance.

It is thus, to use a Virgilian simile, "like a goose babbling in the midst of swans," that I tried to have you hear something of the glory of the saints and that sonorous habit which their *mother*—or divine Wisdom operating in them—prepared. What is—when I hear Cecilia or Theresa spoken of, or when I see Saint Maximian, the priest, raise in his hands the black radiant skull of Saint Magdalen—that odor of violet and balsam? Is it not usual and customary to hear said of a pious person that he died in *the odor of sanctity?* And since, if we can believe Genesis, it is through the nostrils that the life-giving spirit entered us, how can we contradict the blind patriarch who, in order to recognize his first born heir, trusts something other than his eyes? Is it not written (II Cor. 2:15) that *we are Christ's incense offered to God; as a deadly fume where it finds death, as a life-giving perfume where it finds life?* Holy Wisdom associates the perfume not only with the flower, but with the fruit. *No vine ever yielded fruit so fragrant* (Ecclesiasticus 24:23). This is the simple pure perfume of grace, the mingled odor of good works. *Josias, too, is still remembered,* says Eccl. 49:1; *a memory grateful as some mingled scent, pride of the perfumer's art.* (And he adds: *or the honey that tastes sweet in all men's mouths, or music over the wine.*) It is the odor which pleases God: this odor which consecrates His priests and His elect; this odor exhaled like a perpetual offering, mingled with our Christian flesh, with the character impressed on us by the finger of Christ; this odor which the Lord calls for in the Mosaic Law as the accompaniment and crowning of all sacrifices—the incense, the *thymiama,* which the Kings of the East hastened to offer as soon as their new-born Sovereign appeared. *The odor of sanctity* abated God's anger after the flood (Gen. 8:21), and made Him say: *Never again will I plague the earth on man's account.* It was the odor of paradise which filled the whole house when the heart of Magdalen broke over the feet of her Saviour. That odor the Christian, impregnated with his

Christ, brings everywhere he goes, in the manner, Saint Paul says, of a *knowledge* intimated by it. It is pleasant to smell a flower, but how much better it is to breathe in life, to take in through our nostrils that which will prevent our dying!

The preface to the Mass of the Dead warns us, in the words of Saint Paul, that *we shall all rise again, but not all of us will undergo the change I speak of.* So, if life remains—although transformed, one may believe that the functions which maintain it remain also—although transformed—in the service of the spiritual body. When the Holy Books tell us that the citizens of the eternal Sabbath use *invisible food,* one might think that this expression corresponds to a reality, that it is not, as nothing is in the Holy Books, a simple literary trope. If *in truth and in reality*—that is, preeminently, as we are invited to believe—the body and blood of Jesus Christ are for us *both food and drink*—that is, not only restoration to strength but satisfaction for the taste, if *man cannot live by bread only, there is life for him in all the words that proceed from the mouth of God* (Deuter. 8:3), how can one believe that in the other world there will be nothing to correspond to the eucharistic communion, and that the *bread of angels* will be lacking in our food? For in heaven exist the only realities of which the poor material contingencies here below are but the shadow and the shape. That is why *the table,* which established a level among guests is pointed out as an essential piece of sacred furniture. It will stand *on the north* (Exodus 36:35), which means unmovable fixity. Around it that eternal Passover is celebrated which the Saviour wanted to eat with us, the great feast on *the bread of heaven,* so often referred to in the Gospel, and which is a consoling thought in our trials. *Envious my foes watch, while thou dost spread a banquet for me* (Ps. 22:5). There it is promised our hunger will be satisfied. *When I wake up, I shall be well content with thy likeness* (Ps. 16:15). *His glory contemplating, thou shalt never have thy fill*, says Ecclesiasticus 42:26, intimating thereby that no satisfaction in us will be able to appease the desire. For, although the Epistle to the Romans (14:17) warns us that *the kingdom of God is not a matter of eating or drinking this or that*, you might say that the lower faculties have delegated their powers and rights to higher apprehensions. Thus it is that Psalm 103:11 tells us that *there shall be watercourses among the hills that give drink to every wild beast; here the wild asses may slake their thirst*, those to which the cool valleys of mercy open like the hollow of two joined hands.

Spiritual restoration is thus presented to us in a double form suited to our double nature of liquid and solid. And the first is drink, which is the desire for that water whose taste was given to us in baptism. It is Grace which is said to *abound*, or rather *superbound*. *We have all been given drink*, says Saint Paul (I Cor. 12:13) *at a single source, the one Spirit*. And Psalm 35:9: *bid them drink deep at thy fountain of contentment*. This is something direct and immediate, similar to the reflex of the new-born, a kind of liquid respiration, the mouth aspiring and breathing in. We have all seen a small child behave thus at his mother's breast, while with his outstretched arm you might say that he beats out the time and forbids any disturbance. Each mouthful refreshes us, fills, relieves, dilates and expands us. Deuteronomy (33:19) tells us: *The wealth of the sea shall foster them*. And the Song of Songs (8:1): *Would that thou wert my brother, nursed at my mother's breast?* We drank unity from the same breast, we draw from a common source in order to form a communion. *Weanling must be there*, says Joel (2:16). And Isaias (60:16): *thou shalt have nations to suckle thee, kings to foster thee*.

God provides us not only with the means of being free and active, but also the means of becoming strong:[13] not only water, but bread, according to the word of Saint Luke (14: 15): *Blessed is the man who shall feast in the kingdom of God.* Eating is not—like drinking—something purely passive, it involves an appreciation, a knowing of what is offered to our mouth and our heart. That is why it is said in Saint John (4:34): *My meat is to do the will of him who sent me. Your bodies,* says Saint Paul (I Cor. 6:13) *are meant for the Lord, and the Lord claims your bodies.*

It is possible to distinguish in spiritual nourishment what I shall call three *phases.* The first (which can be assimilated to taste and to that savoury pressing of the tongue against the palate), is that perfect act of knowledge by which, according to the expression of Saint Paul (1 Cor. 11:29) we *recognize the Lord's body (dijudicantes corpus Domini).*[14] We realize in the source and the details all the difference there is between God and us, between Being and Nothing, between the cause and the effect, between the general good and the particular intention of which we are responsible and which brought about our existence. In the bond of charity with our brothers (for a gigantic consequence and for our organic cooperation in the body of Christ) we are given possession of that *white pebble,* of that *morning star,* of that *new name* which is put in our mouth so that we will digest it in our heart. *The one bread makes us one body, though we are many in number* (I Cor. 10:17 and ibid. 16): *Is not the bread we break a participation in Christ's body?* The second phase is that essential act of our freedom and will by which, having

13. *Bread that will keep man's strength from failing* (Ps. 103: 15).

14. *As surely as the ear judges words* (Job 12:11). *For food, the discerning palate* (Job 34:3).

discovered, we accept: in the advancing of our lips, in the activity of our tongue and our teeth, in the infusion of our saliva, we reduce the fragment to a mouthful, and pass to the inside what had been until then on the outside. And finally the third *phase* is assimilation, the production by operation and, I might say, by the progressive directed relaxation of that mysterious food in us which we have received, and of that image by which the passenger imitates: from the very movement which is the confession of his nothingness, from that vibrating station where he is constituted, from the line he traces—what endures—because he is the only continuation outside of God who possesses the means of translating the permanent.[15]

Glory does not only radiate, it is not only in us and above us a victorious principle of illumination, of cry, conservation and action. It is also something still more subtly and essentially associated with the very foundations of matter, it is *weight*, according to this word which Saint Paul gives us for meditation (II Cor. 4:17): *This light and momentary affliction brings with it a reward multiplied every way, loading us with everlasting glory.* The weight in us is a much more subtle, general, intrinsic quality than all other accidents of sensibility. It is the center of our unity, the foundation of our person, the conscience of our individuality. And what is more remarkable is that, so intimate, and so inseparable in all appearances, it seems attached to being itself so purely that it seems to indicate the quantity, the proportion and value. Yet the law of gravitation teaches us that it is completely due to a traction controlled by something outside of us, and due to what is called *pull*. At every moment we are in a state of

15. This is perhaps the origin of the relationship between the two terms of *dur* (hard) and *durée* (duration).

comparison with the entire universe whose secret summons maintains me compact and one. We do not escape for one second from the careful balance of Justice, the one in which King Balthazar was once found wanting. This is the weight which stifles, oppresses and quarters the damned, which maintains the elect in their exact position at the center of eternal Mercy.[16] There as everywhere else the measurement of God takes possession of the measurement of man to enrich it and multiply it. It is somewhat Pascal's principle of hydro-statics.

And here in this delivery of His spirit into the hands of the Father end the Seven Words of Our Lord Jesus Christ on the cross.

THE SUPREME CRY

> Then Jesus cried out again with a loud voice, and yielded up his spirit. (Matth. 27:50).

Is IT permissible to confuse this great cry, this *powerful clamor* of which the Epistle to the Hebrews speaks, with the Seventh Word? I do not think it possible, in spite of Luke's text which seems, by the way, to indicate two distinct emis-sions. A cry is not a word. It does not come from the same region of the soul. It is not addressed to the same ear of the receiver. A cry invokes violence, a universality which does not belong to this precise testamentary arrangement. *Father, I*

16. *Scale and balance are emblems of the Lord's own justice* (Prov. 16:11). *He can weigh my offence with true scales* (Job 31: 6). *Who was it measured out . . . earth's mass poised on three of his fingers?* (allusion to the Trinity) *Who tried yonder moun-tains in the scale, weighed out the hills?* (Is. 40:12).

175

put My soul back into Your hands. Let a dying man at his last breath find strength to utter not only a cry, but a great cry, and it is enough of a miracle without our finding it necessary to add the spoken articulation of an entire sentence. The cry had to reach farther than the word. Among the infirm whom Our Saviour raised from their distress, the Gospel enumerates the blind, lepers, paralytics and the deaf in whom the demon seems to have occupied a particularly strong place—since it is at the very entrance of our intelligence that he mounts guard. And who is more deaf than that corpse tightly wrapped and closed within a granite sepulchre whom we read that Jesus called upon with a loud voice to *come out?* Once more, then, the voice which created heaven and earth spoke up! The word reaches the intelligence, but the cry triumphs over deafness. We see in Holy Scripture the Saviour coming to the soul and communicating to it uprightness and virtue by an appropriate contact. It is His hand touching you, His robe brushing against you, a bit of watered earth He places on closed eyelids. He needs only to look once at that gaper under a fig tree to turn him into an apostle. For that he needed less time to convince Nicodemus! Jesus did not always need a prodigy or a word. A certain stress was sufficient, an inflection, and something passed through the intervening fence, the lost sheep recognized his master's voice which was unlike any other and answered him with a weak bleating. *Clama et ulula, fili hominis* (Ezec.). The call is enough, the explanation will follow later.

Jesus at that supreme moment, exalted and strengthened on that altar of sacrifice to which all the centuries have delegated Him, assumed and appropriated officially and canonically so to speak, the Cry, the immense sacred clamor which from the day it left Eden, rises toward its Author from the depths of Humanity.[1] A clamor which often when mute, like that of Abel's blood, is not less piercing. There is the *offering of triumphant music* in Psalm 26. *All thy gates, now, must echo with lament!* says Isaias 14:31, *all thy cities ring with cries!* The opening up toward heaven of all misfortune and all human suffering, poverty of cities, prisons, schools, hospitals, the everlasting battlefield, are all fused into one roar of indignation and into one torrent of tears, an erupting toward God, as from a disemboweled animal, of our inexhaustible need! *Out of the depths I cry to thee, O Lord,* says Psalm 129: 1. *From the ends of the earth I call upon thee,* says Psalm 60, *thou will set me high up on a rock.* And Psalm 87: *Lord God, day and night I cry bitterly to thee. On thee I call, to thee stretch out my hands.*——Hear this supreme trumpet blast toward You from the neighborhood regions of hell. What I ask, what I want, I do not know, for if I were capable of speaking, I would not cry! You must see Yourself in it! *Listen to my plea,* says Psalm 5, *pay heed to my cry of petition!* For have You not called blessed the one *who takes thought for the poor and the destitute?* (Psalm 40:1). The invitation, Lord, which You made to Your bride to have her voice heard is now answered (S. of Songs 8:13). It is, the Apocalypse tells us (19:6): *like the noise of water in flood.* And Habacuc (3:10): *the depths beneath us roar aloud, the heights beckon from above.*——The creation, mute for so long a time, trembled on the lips of Jesus dying (Hab. 3:16). At last it found the means of expressing itself, it found the means of reaching God, the means of having itself heard. Jesus was silent before Pilate, but now He cries out and henceforth He will not keep silence. *For love of Sion,* says Isaias 62:1, *I will*

1. *He lives on still to make intercession on our behalf* (Heb. 7:25).

no more be silent! It is something fixed and penetrating like the pupil of the eye which is planted in the very heart of God. *Never let that eye weary of its task,* say The Lamentations of Jeremias 2:18. For in prayer the intelligence continues to grow with desire.

From the very womb of the grave call I, says the prophet Jonas (2:3), *thou art listening to me!* But God is not the only one to listen. The entire earth was obliged, and today it is not yet over being obliged to listen. *No word, no accent of theirs,* says Psalm 18:4-6, *that does not make itself heard, till their message reaches the ends of the world.* It is not only the ancient navigator mentioned by Plutarch, over whom the clamor of panic passed. And it is not for nothing that the author of the Apocalypse compares the voice of the angel proclaiming the Gospel to that of the lion. *The Lion that comes from the tribe of Juda* (Apoc. 5:5). It is like Achilles in Homer, rising up on the edge of the moat and whose voice was strong enough to hurl back the assaulting hordes of warriors and enemy chariots. *Here is a lion growling over his prey,* says Isaias 31:40. *So it will be with the Lord of hosts, when he comes down to war.* And elsewhere (11:6): *Wolf shall live at peace with lamb; calf and lion and sheep in one dwelling place, with a little child to herd them!* The calf which is sacrifice, the lion which is strength and victory, the sheep which is gentleness, are all together on the cross in the person of Our Lord. Travelers have noticed that when the voice of the lion is heard, all other animals keep silence. This happens to the false gods and all pagan philosophies as soon as Christ appears. One of the treatises of Plutarch is called: *Why the oracles stopped.* All the great mythological and philosophical systems of Asia precede the arrival of the missionaries. You might say that the pure vision of truth is enough to prevent the hydra from forming new heads.

Hell also heard! *Why dost thou meddle with us, Jesus, Son of God?* (Matth. 8:29).

THE DESCENT FROM THE CROSS

JESUS was silent. His body hung between heaven and earth.

In keeping with the practice recommended by the Fathers of the Church, let us turn to the Bible and see if in the pages of the Holy Chronicle, we shall find some analogy with this raising and this vertical inscribing of a man on the horizon.

In Genesis there is the story of Pharao's cupbearer to whom Joseph predicted his destiny. We have spoken of this elsewhere.

There is also the story of Absolom in the Second Book of Kings. An illustration in the large book of de Sacy shows him hanging with his hair from a branch, while a rider, armed with a spear, pierces him. Let us see if there is something to find in this episode.

We should not be disconcerted by the sinister hateful trait of this character whom it would be more natural, I confess, to compare to Lucifer the first-born and favorite, who becomes Satan the apostate and parricide. Yet it is not the first time that the prefiguration of the Saviour animates for a moment the traits and gestures of a criminal, for has it not been said of Him (Is. 53:12) that He *would be counted among the wrong-doers,* and that He *will come upon thee like a thief* (Apoc. 3:3)? And is it not written in the Law of Moses (Deuter. 21:23), in a passage which the Epistle to the Galatians recalls (3:13), that *his body must not be left to hang there on the gibbet,* for it seems that neither heaven nor earth wants Him and that He will be excommunicated from both? Is He not the eternal anathema whom the Fathers, in common consent, see in the image of the scapegoat? Throughout the ritual texts the lamb and the kid seem to be equally valued.

It would be useless, as has often been pointed out, to try to find in the prophetic documents an absolute system of tracings or numerals. It often happens that the intention is unquestionable and the meaning clear under a transparent veil, and still more often it is only a question of an obscure proposition, of a careless trait, of an unfinished drawing, an allusion, an analogy, a suggestion; sometimes less than that: of a *word*, such as initiates say to one another, of a reflection, an intonation which is enough to quicken the faithful heart. When Christ appeared on Thabor to His three apostles in company with Moses (who is the figure of the law), and Elias (the figure of direct prophecy), we read that *a shining cloud overshadowed them* (Matth. 17:5): something which both manifested and hid, which separated and joined, which showed the essential gesture and blurred the detail. Thus from the Old to the New Testament we see the fog clearing and sparing our weak eyes, and prophecy becomes parable.

Now through this fog a form already trembles as we approach and prepares to recover its pendulum movement. No, it is not yet Judas, patron of all the desperate and the hanged, it is Achitophel the deceiving counselor of the usurper for whom the hook and rope were prepared. He goes from left to right—for a time—and then from right to left. He is watched by an old mustached rat shouldering arms in the corner of the barn. His slippers have fallen down and his loosened belt drags on the ground.

The leader is young handsome Absolom who, after listening to Achitophel's astute advice, turned to Chusai, forgetting that collaboration with gentlemen is not always without risk for knaves.[1] *Famed for his beauty,* the chronicler tells us (II Kings 14:25), *from the sole of his foot to the crown of his head was no blemish to be found.* But the most curious trait of his personality was his extraordinary hair. It was by nature more abundant than Louis XIV's wig. This hair grew so thick and rapidly that each year he was obliged to sell this hyperbolic harvest whose value or weight—the name suggests both—was two hundred sicles.

Hair is what comes from the head. Around the human face, it is a kind of material radiation and physical halo, a cloud out of which the face emerges. It is a tuft in back of us as multiple and inextricable as thought. It is human foliage. It is an atmosphere, a flag, our vegetation capable of splendor, a glory at the summit of the person! It is the equivalent of that spiritual mane which makes the nondescript crowd tremble at the appearance of a genius. Magdalen took it in her hand to dry the feet of the Saviour. In it Samson's power resided. It is the clue of our consecration. It is like the oil, says the psalm, which flows over the garment of Aaron. It offers to destiny a way of seizing us. The bride of the Song of Songs uses it to win the heart of her bridegroom, and by means of it the Angel seized Habacuc and his soup bowl to take them to Daniel. It is by keeping the razor from his head that man, according to the prescription of Moses (Num. 6) concecrates himself to God and deserves the name Nazarene. The natural hair of his flesh falls back as a benediction over his shoulders.

Was it then on the branch of an oak that Absolom was so strangely caught, or might it not have been the justice of God, to which the senseless mule which served as his mount

1. *Lovingly wilt thou treat those who love thee, with the loyal keep troth; pure of heart the pure of heart shall find thee, the cunning thou wilt overreach* (Ps. 17:26-27).

and which he had forgotten to hold fast in hand according to the precept of the psalm (31:9), suddenly gave him over? There he was between heaven and earth exposed as on the wrist of an angel, while Joab leisurely discussed his fate. And into the heart of this trembling body David's general—whose name means *paternity*—three times thrust the spear. The Centurion, later, inspired from above, will take upon himself to consummate this act on Calvary.

It has been said that events project their shadow before them. This shadow is not only the one which accompanies on a sheet of parchment the prophetic calamus moving quickly, it does not only fill the ink-horn which Ezechiel (9:2) saw at the girdle of a man clad in linen, it draws all kinds of figures, a cross, a crown, a spear; or rather, it is not a shadow, it is light: it illumines with an intention superior to the fact, like a Rembrandt ray which suddenly enters the pitch to stimulate a piece of glass-ware or a breast-plate, like a sub-ordinate character of the long preparatory drama. So, in the midst of a confused brushwood, appeared the handsome face of Absolom and the suspended body proposing its heart to the point of our investigating spear. What Joab sought was found by the Centurion, the inexhaustible source of blood and water in Jesus Christ. It seems that the word Absolom means *peace of the Father* and thus suggests the contemplation by the Begetter of that face in which He put His complaisance. The Book shows us Absolom who had risen very early.[2] He stood at the entrance to the gate and when a solicitor appeared, he called him, learned of his business and complained that between him and the king there was no delegated intermediary: *Ah, if only I could be appointed as judge in the land, so that all who had matters to decide could bring them to me*

2. *Thou art my son, born like dew before the day-star rises.* (Ps. 109:3).

for a careful hearing! (cf. *Come to me, all you that labour and are burdened,* Matth. 11:28.) *And when men came up to greet him, he would put out his hand and take them to himself with a kiss* (II Kings 15:3-5). Can we not find there an indication of that kind of simulated conflict which arose in the heart of the Trinity between the mercy of God and His justice? Must we believe that finally this just judge did come to the earth, the judge who is knowing and able to sympathize with our weakness? Thus the legal Sovereign in his legitimacy allows himself to be forced back by the Usurper. We see Absolom established in his father's place in his city, in his palace, on his throne and taking his place even in his bed. All Israel was called to witness in the light of the sun the mystery of his intercourse (II Kings 16:22). Meanwhile the old king withdrew and traced backwards the future itinerary: Jesus on the night of Maundy Thursday will have only to follow those footsteps. He crossed the Cedron and wet his lips, as he passed, with the water less transitory than the favor of men. He reached the Mount of Olives, and went still farther, across the Jordan with all he possessed, leaving nothing behind. And it was only after crossing back again over that river which means baptism, that, with the consent of the Twelve Tribes, he regained possession of his fortune and concluded with his own a new pact based on a general pardon. For there was in the interval some one *destined to bring about the fall of many and the rise of many in Israel* (Luke 2:34). Uselessly Israel complains of injustice and partiality: *How is it that our brethren, the men of Juda, have stolen from us? By what warrant did they escort the king, and his household and the warriors of David's army, on their passage over Jordan? . . . And the Israelites replied, We are ten to one; our rights with the king, our claims upon David, are ten times as great as yours* (II Kings 19:41-43). The King's place henceforth for all centuries is solely in Jerusalem impregnated with the blood of His Son.

The Cedron and the Jordan will no longer suffice to contain the majesty of an outraged repulsed God, nor the accumulated waves in the desert which return over the ungrateful land with the fierceness of a tidal wave or a geological upheaval. The nine rivers of hell with their windings will have no effect. While Joseph of Arimathea completed his transactions with a worried nervous Pilate who decidedly preferred the open air to the damaged shelter of his administrative palace (in such a moment he was on the verge of granting anything they wished!), the blood of a slain God penetrated the earth through all its fissures, and like a corrosive destructive liquid it passed to the nest of Satan's avarice, to the central lair on which the foul badger had hooked himself. O the disgust and explosions behind the sombre walls of Dis! The Christian soul should listen, on the sorrowful afternoon of Good Friday, while the last yellow candle of Tenebrae is put out, to the muffled trampling of the crowd in the side-aisles as they come to worship the crucifix on the floor! Listen and you will still hear the echo of that subterranean commotion. There is something hellish which has not yet recovered from the deep blow of the axe! Hear the noise of the doors pulled off, of the walls collapsing, of iron being smashed, of gigantic crowds of bottled-up demons, lashed by the whip of the angel and grunting like a pack of boars! Someone is approaching in a clap of thunder! Yes, he is coming, someone who is irresistible! Someone formidable who will pass over the body of the entire swarming pack of beasts! The very root of everything is horrified. It is as if someone with both hands is shaking the tree of creation. Are the stars going to fall down like hail on our heads? Terrified Caiphas tried in vain to find shelter. Through the hole of the cistern you saw sinister shapes, and if you opened that door, the room was filled with corpses standing up waiting for you, like those rows of manikins in the show-window of a department store! THE VEIL OF THE TEMPLE WAS RENT! The bewildered animals fled in every direction and bellowed as they knocked against one another. A great cry came out from the Holy of Holies and filled the entire city from Antonia to the valley of Hinnon: Let's get out of here! And during this time, the moon all black, like pious Veronica with her cloth, wiped the blood-stained face of the sun. On the right and the left of Christ, the good and bad thief hung hideous and broken. No one was left on Calvary and on the winding road down below, you could see only one figure, a small man all alone running away as fast as he could.

On Calvary there remained only the liturgical personnel attached to the thirteenth station: the Virgin, Magdalen and the other Marys, John, Nicodemus and Joseph of Arimathea who had just come with the shroud and the aromatics. The ass which brought him, was down below waiting, a servant holding its bridle. At some distance, in the burial garden which we overlooked you could see men already busy moving the heavy stone which closed the entrance of the sepulchre. There was not much time: the Sabbath was about to begin and its atmosphere was already merged with the gloomy March twilight.

And now the scene which for all time the brush of Rubens has immobilized, rose up and appeared as in a frame.

From time to time in artistic compositions there is, as in animal species, a conclusive event after many attempts: the emergence of a perfect type after an exhaustive number of proposals. In the Cathedral of Antwerp, for example, on the Gospel side, the painter, despite the focussing of all the resources of his genius, has not completely succeeded in exalting the Holy Cross. The ropes pulling together, the display of muscles, and the large crowd directed by a man in armor and all the pulling of shoulders and bent backs, are not enough! The entire effort of the populace below (without mentioning the man in red who with his arms outstretched is tackling the work and trying to foist himself up on the human flesh) gives only the impression of something unsteady and suspended. The great diagonal, the gigantic bird raising itself and taking flight, the Man they are hoisting up to meet His Father, with His hand raised in a gesture of conquering and testifying to heaven, the labor and grinding of teeth which from the left side ends in seizing the full arm on the right side, the enthronement of the right hand, all this forms a scene of terror and hope, making us lose our balance; almost like the group of witnesses squeezed together in the left panel who stare wide-eyed (and the rider on the prancing horse in the right panel who is already preparing for the cavalcades of the Apocalypse)! It is one of those paintings in which devotion gives over to eloquence.

But if we go to the Epistle side, then in front of that sublime square of canvas our expectation is in perfect accord with our contemplation. We feel that it is just right, that the Saviour is taken down not for us personally but for the entire peaceful kneeling Church and received willingly into our hearts and minds. To realize its great superiority, this interpretation should be compared to that of Rembrandt which can be seen in the Museum of the Hermitage. The painting of Rubens resembles a ceremony where each performer plays an indispensable part, but in the Rembrandt it is a vision of the spirit materialized by an insistent luminous ray, while in the increasing darkness obscure figures move about. The Virgin is not in her place at the feet of her Son. She falls backward, her eyes closed. The Divine Corpse pulls with all its weight and draws away from the two topmen way up on the gallowsyard who hold it by the arm and release it notch by notch. Jesus Christ was not let down to be administered to us, He was dropped. And if that fellow had not been there to catch Him in his arms (the one whose head is pressed against His stomach), He would have fallen. He is seated, hunched over on His abdomen, completely turned inwards. His head does not turn, it falls to the side. He pays attention to no one. You might say He gives over to His center, to something more inner in Himself than the spiritual light in the middle of the picture is to the surrounding zones of shadow. At the foot of the cross there is a shroud carefully prepared, and they are going to have Him disappear in that, as truth disappears into writing.

Compared with this sinister operation, revealed in the darkest charcoal of thought, illuminated as by the headlights of an auto, the great page of Rubens appears to us consoling in its majesty and tenderness! A page between its two margins: on one side the radiant triumphant Virgin who is paying a visit to her cousin Elizabeth; and on the other side the delegated waiting of the old Law in the person of Simeon who receives the Newcomer. On one side the old hands stretch out, and on the other side they grasp. But it is still only a promise. In the middle is the accomplishment, the solemn total delivery of the human-divine species. The rest of us are down below, full of confidence in the Virgin, in Saint John and in the kneeling women in whom we have delegated our first rank. Let us try to tell what we see and what the painter has realized for us, probably without knowing what he was doing.

The essential object of the composition is the long sacramental linen, like communion linen, which joins all the actors and all the parts of the scene and which makes around the august body, which the Angels themselves would tremble to touch, a kind of luminous halo and shining path between heaven and earth. On every side there are hands which stretch out and which dare not touch. The arm of the man above is almost parallel to Christ's and more adhering than sustaining. It is with his two arms disappearing under the ritual tablecloth that Saint John prepares to let the entire body glide down to the soul and the anguished heart of Magdalen who waits below. Someone else is careful to raise the end of the cloth so that it will not drag. The only contacts there are in this picture are the arm on high adhering to the arm of the Father, and below, the naked foot which tenderly rests on the bare shoulders of the sinful woman. In the two men high up on the bar, one old and one young, who are giving Jesus Christ over to us, I can almost see the two Testaments, the New and the Old. The latter holds a corner of the cloth between his teeth. From his mouth flows the immense luminous river, a cataract with great waves of prophecies, analogies and testimonials, in the midst of which the figure of the Redeemer is presented to us, freeing itself as from a wrapping. In its descent the body is accompanied by two venerable personages, one on the right, the other on the left. I imagine that these are the figures of doctors and ecclesiastical authorities whose hierarchy is suggested by the two ends of the ladder which appear, one high up under the feet of the young man almost in flight, and the other at the very bottom touching the loosened sentence-scroll which is held by a heavy stone, and a copper bowl which has received the blood-stained nails and crown. The Pope, with prudence and consideration, watches from below, but Saint Paul derives from heaven his gesture and inspiration. The group below is composed of four: the Blessed Virgin in blue, the two kneeling women in green, and Saint John in red. The first who entreats and whose two raised hands follow the direction of her eyes, is Faith. The two figures in humility represent Hope, and the ardent young man whose right foot both props up the ladder and prepares to climb, is Charity. The body of Christ with the full sweep of its arms and with the powerful simple curve which extends from the toe to the lofty hand giving an affectionate blessing, forms the liaison between heaven and earth. He has nothing left for Himself. He gives Himself to everyone. And it is on the bare shoulder of Magdalen that He wanted to reach the ground.

THE HARROWING OF HELL

LOWER! still lower! it is not only the sinful woman whom God chose for a footstool and placed on her shoulder that foot which calms the sea. The time has come to visit sin itself, within which God has asked Death to lead Him. Between the cross and Easter there are thirty-six hours during which Jesus will profit from this freedom which His deserted body gives Him and this timed distance between the soul and the flesh which is the privilege of Adam, the *stipendium peccati*, the salary of sin which the Son of Man loyally earned by the sweat of His brow.

The body remains with us. Hundreds of sculptors and painters have piously taken it upon themselves to perpetuate this body among us. Yesterday we put it into the grave in the midst of candles and flowers which for us replace the Asian aromatics, and which tongues and tribes come to venerate until the moment when the clergy in procession comes for it to take it to the high altar and consume it there.

189

Here is the body. It belongs to us. We possess it and understand it, even lifeless and cold. But what has become of the soul during this time? It is able to move since we are told *Jesus descended into hell,* which means that He passed from one place to what we are forced to imagine is another place. But how then are we to imagine the soul, the breath which our nostrils have drawn in from the very lips of the Creator, which our lungs have appropriated, and for which the images of flame and light are too coarse or of that ψ which on the day of baptism the priest traced on our forehead—the lamp of Psyche with its triple point balanced on our essential unity? How can we be surprised by the heavy laughter of the medico who claims he never came across it under his scalpel? What discoverer will betray it? What electric file, what precision balance will be capable of capturing its trace? What field can we attribute to this volatilized butterfly?

This explains the embarrassment and disapproval of our naive and dull-witted ancestors of the eighteenth and nineteenth centuries with regard to this phantom who always eluded their ten outstretched fingers. Whatever lay beyond measurement lay beyond their intelligence. From then on they had only to let their ears stick up majestically and fix, with a sharp tooth, on solid articles, on all those comforting things you find on the ground, on succulent thistle, for example, which grows abundantly between our feet. And the dismay there was when under our more and more solemn attentive examination and under our fixed mathematical microscopic eye the material in which we had placed our hope and confidence began to give unmistakable signs of decay and when the texture grew thin and gave way between our fingers! So there was nothing resistant! There was no way left to stir up, in a sensuous Epicurean manner, a universe obtained from grains of wheat. The concept of law was replaced by a ridiculous system of statistics. The law of necessity, pushed to its last retrenchments, escaped from us along the road of absurdity, and nature answered this anxious investigator with the most colloidal of her smiles. There was little point in making such fun of the *substance* of the ancient philosophers to reach that universal-material concept of something undifferentiated, foreign to every definition and every distinctive quality. We had to grow accustomed to replacing the idea of permanence with that of duration. We were advised to listen to things rather than look at them. We had to admit, as basis for everything, pure movement; namely, the passage from nothing to being, a certain pulling on the unknown immediately qualified by rhythm or a closed form, the passage from being to quality and finally the use of quality by the individual and the soul: an appeal practiced on matter by an idea and a name, which establishes a point of convergence between lines and series of causes. These very striking texts of Holy Scripture are thus justified: *My life is nothing in thy reckoning* (Ps. 38:6). *Earthward I looked, and all was void and empty* (Jer. 4:23). *He poised the earth on nothing* (Job 26:7). *One who has spread out the heavens like gossamer* (Is. 40:22). According to these verses weight and mass, as well as space, are elements drawn up from nothing and the effect of a continuous creation. The deeper one descends, the clearer the void, according to this passage in the Psalms: *O'erthrow it, o'erthrow it, till the very foundation is left bare* (Ps. 136:7). Thus in the second book of Paralipomena (33:5) it is a gate in the Temple of Solomon, an opening, to which is given this name: *the shrine of his name forever.*

Now, if from the physical we pass to the spiritual world, it is not possible for us not to see between the two a certain community of form and appearance, which is testified to in the language which is metaphor and continual reference from one to the other. There is nothing surprising if we remember that God created all things at the same time, according to the same plan, and moreover the soul is *the form of the body*: its workman, modeler, artist, and the matrix which prints its character, as the end does for the means. The body is for the soul simultaneously an expression, a permanence, a capital, the costume suitable to its role, the construction of its identity with itself in time, and its means of action and communication with the outside. The correspondent of this permanence in the soul is the faculty of acquisition and capture, the power of transforming duration into space, melody into simultaneity in an establishment of proportions, a photographic sensitivity, a filtering and an arresting of sensation by the screen and the attainment to fixity which is design, memory, conscience, an explanation of ourselves, a provocation to meaning which out of an inner object makes a state of knowledge, a registering, food furnished to our intimate unity and the test of our possibilities. And on the other hand our spiritual being, as well as our physical being, is submitted to the law of rhythm, our body is the effect of a clock which ticks. The lungs, heart and brain itself are all penetrated and animated by a law of inflation and deflation, of absorption and repression. And likewise we do not think continuously, but by utterances, by a series of spurts and verses. Our perceptions themselves, our attentiveness to various kinds of work, are conditioned by tension and remission, according to Job's remark (14:2) that man is *changing all the while*. The body is not only an illustration, a concrete exposition of the glory of God,[1] it is also an analytical and logical instrument. When we extend our arm, we put into action an entire apparatus of comparisons and measurements. It is articulated like a syllogism. It is a system, at our disposal, of axes, extensions,

1. *Glory and beauty are thy clothing* (Ps. 103:1).

directions, comprehensions, pulleys and levers. Its unfolding is an explanation, a marvel of truth and grace, a commentary in movement which is revealed to the smallest detail, to the hand, to that fivefold arpeggio, to the sharp transparent finger nails which end on points of light. It is possible to see in the preparations and efforts of our will and energy an analogy with the interweavings of our muscular cords, with Samson blindfolded who with his back and shoulders pulled up from the earth the cemented gate of Gaza, with that powerful machine of our body which made the prophet say: *his bow rests in the strength that does not fail him* (Gen. 49:24) and Zacharias (9:13): *Bow of mine is Juda.*

Here, then, in the document we are holding, is the portrait of a living individual (or any known object), form and matter. Of these two elements, which has priority? It is beyond doubt the first, because pure matter, foreign to every quality, specification and definition, is not distinct from nothingness. It escapes our understanding. To exist, it is necessary to be something. You might even say that matter is made of superimposed forms in the sense of an increasingly rigorous individuality. Nothing exists alone. Everything is, in order to satisfy an ensemble. No thing can any more exist by itself than a horse can remain standing on one foot. But the ensemble exists only in relationship with the interior of a figure, or what is called a form. And form, to be detached from confusion, can exist only by definition, by a purpose, by the exclusion of all that is foreign to its design or plan, by a limitation of its possibilities. This steadfast and resistant element is relationship. You can continue indefinitely to sustain an *a* or an *e*, but the harmony between the two notes remains the same. You can indefinitely prolong the radius of a circle or the sides of a triangle, but the geometrical formula of these two figures, the inner computation of which they are the expression, will remain the same. Within, there is relationship and number, and without, there is unbreakable unity.

Whether it is physical reality or spiritual reality, one always returns to the basic verification which is movement. But movement itself is submitted to a relationship, either inner formula or form, and this form is the vibrant palpitating expression, enclosed within a certain rhythm or figure or cyclical number, of the mysterious duty of resemblance which divine Being communicated to it. All movement is language. God alone is constant act. But everything that exists concretely, or lives, is the result of a certain intersecting of being with nothingness, or, if you prefer, of fullness with the void.[2] Consequently the soul, even separated from the flesh and from the clothing of the senses which adapted it to given surroundings, preserves in itself that resonant power, that elocution of language which permits it to utter the name which God asks of it: the theme which it is instructed to furnish is the competence and the means of knowledge and gratitude.

But if we wish to consider things more closely, and understand each individual being in its root, and not simply state what according to its own mode created it, we shall have to discover behind being, the reason for being.

All created beings exist in order to give testimony of their author, in order to produce, by existing, a certain means of having Him known, of translating Him into the domain of the concrete. We can respectfully suppose that this is what the Gospel language means by the expression, *the achieved glory. All I have is thine, and all thou hast is mine; and in them my glory is achieved* (John 17:10). Now we know that all things in heaven and on earth universally belong to the

2. *The Lord's voice kindles flashing fire* (Ps. 28:7).

Son of God, and that consequently they have no other reason
for being than to manifest Him, either symbolically by their
form, or parabolically by their operation. The difference between material beings and living beings, and between living
beings and intelligent independent beings, is that these last
translate themselves by knowing what they are doing, within
the limits of freedom and of an activity constantly widening.
Man at the summit of the hierarchy of beings knows what
he has received as a mission to reveal. He is not the serf of
the law, but a free worker. All things are given back into his
hands and he serves by using them. Representative of God,
as he translates God to things by acting upon them, he translates things to God by language, he presents them to Him,
makes them present to Him, makes them pass from the
realm of the visible to the realm of the intelligible, from the
realm of hearing to that of understanding, from the realm of
the transitory to that of the eternal. The testimony he is capable of, with regard to what does not have an ending, I mean
his aptitude for the cause, is one of the essential conditions
of his existence. This is perhaps what Ezechiel wanted to
suggest to us when, speaking of those spiritual creatures placed
very close to Divinity, he described them as *covered with eyes*
and like a frame of eyes and wheels: as if meaning that in
them sight is the immediate condition for operation, the
necessary ignition of the cyclical motor. But in this world
and as long as we are implicated in the bonds of flesh and
deranged by the defect of original sin, our knowledge is veiled
and our operation is uncertain. Illumination is more rare in
us than deduction, and *divination* (success) more rare than
proposition and experience. Under the direction of angels
who are constantly leading us, the result is obtained only after
long confused wanderings. But in the other life when we shall
be able to live the text of the open book, we shall translate it

and *glorify* it according to all its power and energy in the idiom which is appropriate to us. We shall know by the very act which gives us existence; that is, no longer by an interpretation of signs[3] but face to face by a certain opening, adaptation, aspiration and respiration of all our being, transmitting a message, an indication, around us, like a signaling star. There will be no covering to hide us. Everything in us will have become clear, sonorous and legible. And it is by being born fully and directly with them, that we shall know other spirits, thanks to this interruption of being, as we have seen, whose image is this physical vibration on which every sensation is inscribed. It is insufficient to say that we shall be incorporated with that numberless Christ of all our brothers (as the word—with accent and comma—is incorporated in the sentence), but we shall have found the distinct means—by looking at God—to have them understand that, in a certain way, we exist only by them and they exist only for us. Each shading introduced into their essential spiritual composition will react instantaneously on ours. Our fundamental difference will happily propagate around us an invitation to unity. Together around God we shall do something that will have no ending. We shall create a cause. The cause directly coming from every direction will harmonize with *the* cause.

Thus we understand that the soul is not, like so many parrots squawking morning and night on their university perches—a kind of fluid fabricated somehow or other which the body yields like a gas-generator. On the contrary, everything takes place as if there were a motor-directive principle governing our organized matter, and as if there were in us

3. That is what is meant by the text: *No longer wilt thou have the moon's beam to enlighten thee; the Lord shall be thy everlasting light* (Is. 60:19). And the psalm of Vespers (109.3): *From birth, princely state shall be thine, holy and glorious.*

someone who is master and who knows what he has to do with everything. It is not our body which makes us, it is we at each second who make our body and who compose it in that attitude adapted to every situation which we call sensation and perception. It is not movement which drags us along in an irresistible flow. Movement is at our disposal. We can exploit it. We who are able to oppose and stop it, and, by using a free and limitless choice, impose on our perceptions the firm pattern of a concept, of a figure, of a will. Therefore when death comes, the body does not abandon the soul, since it has no right over it, and since it owes the soul the fact of its being a composition rather than a juxtaposition. The soul abandons the body. The body then is immobile and cold and each of its cells listens to the counsel of decomposition which begins throughout it. The soul is somewhere else.

Let us profit from the holy hours between Thursday and Friday, when the clergy in procession, after withdrawing the body of Christ from the tabernacle, went solemnly to bury it in another place, in order to consider our own remains, and judge, in a detached fashion, their appearance, like documents which the language of the law courts designates as "exhibits," flattened and lying on the mortuary marble. There at the end of the prescribed number of years, is the form we made for ourselves, the matter we shaped and organized through the night, the machine for snatching the soul, which the father, at the moment of conception, asked for in the deep immemorial resources of a mother. There is Peter. There is Mary. There is, before our eyes, the completed statue, the definitive result. The heart stopped, and there, finally before us, is what was obtained. Taken from off our shoulders, our cross is there on the ground. The intimate part which our soul had plotted with the body, that apparatus for fabricating the person whose condition we had to submit to all our life and whose openings we had to exploit, the heritage from our parents and the argument of heaven, a learned complex of invitations and refusals——is there in a state of collapse, awaiting the resurrection day when we must again put on the armature either heavy or light, opaque or radiant. We are now, once and for all, rid of that unreliable shifty servant, that demanding associate, obstinate and dishonest, who is at times ominously patient and at other times ridiculously recalcitrant. But if it could speak, Master Body would have something to say. In his coarse language, he says we have given him spicy and half-baked things. It seems that, if we had been able to interpret it correctly, an intestinal trouble was only a delicate reproach for a misunderstood resource and a neglected chance. Little wonder that our surveillance weakened at the sudden flaring up of all the accumulated grievances and domestic quarrels which from time to time left such a painful memory, and at the brace which a tireless specialist put on the right spot with a skill which was really virtuosity. Like a clock of which we see only the face and the pair of mustaches ceaselessly moving and slashing the enamelled visage with their conventional angle, we look at ourselves in the mirror or oppose to the abundant exhaling of thought that other mirror which is the sheet of white paper, and we do not realize the infinitely multiple complicated work which is being accomplished, connected with some act (or some omission) of our intelligence and will, with some program going on inside of us, which is a closet filled with wheels around the central pump, with test tubes, wires, coils, and tools. As I advance along a difficult road, from major premise to the conclusion of my syllogism, each of my resolutions, each of those mouthfuls I snatch from reality to deliver to spiritual digestion, is appreciated, transcribed, registered, stored, incorporated by the triple formation of my pulmonary and alimentary balance. There is in me, synchronized with desire and thought, an entire laboratory whose analytical selective activity never stops, a factory functioning, the working together of an entire system of valves, filters, compressors and fuses, at times accelerated by flushings, at times retarded by the slow impregnations, like that of one's conscience, of meters and faucets. And just as the chauffeur can see the daily mileage of his auto added up on the speedometer, we can see that our body (as it is the organ of our mobility) is also the witness of our duration, and that as it has boxed everything in, it has also registered everything. We deliver to the shrewd judge a document he is capable of appraising line by line. There is not an event or an act of our life about which a note has not been recorded somewhere with classification and reference. It is this *Liber scriptus* which will come out of the grave with us like a complete file. This is the explanation of the beneficial efficacy of relics, the bones of saints which do not cease sending forth, like a vial filled with a strong perfume, that love which presided over their edification, that anointing oil which, from their head, penetrated to their marrow, that power of communication which, in death as in life, is the privilege of the obedient. *Joseph left his bones*, says Ecclesiasticus 49:18, *to await the day of God's deliverance, in death prophetic still.* Thus it is that the foundation rock[4] in us reabsorbs the flesh (*a people whose bones lie scattered at the grave's mouth*, Ps. 140:6), but however far our remains enter the novitiate of dust, they do not escape the accounting which their Creator continues to keep. They cherish a promise of resurrection, according to Psalm 15:9 and Acts 2:26: *my body, too, shall rest in confidence.* It was through this door, through this opening made between the flesh and the soul that Christ wanted to

4. *Dost thou care for me more than these others, Simon Peter?* (John 21:15).

199

pass first, but within His tomb blessed under the broken epi-
taph which revealed the destroyed name, the future citizen of
the stars knew that He was not abandoned. *He, to whom I
have given my confidence,* he says with the Apostle Timothy
(II, 1:12), *is no stranger to me, and I am fully persuaded that
he has the means to keep my pledge safe, until that day comes.*
Why worry? We have learned from His own lips: *Could you
not tell that I must needs be in the place which belongs to my
Father?* (Luke 2:49).

Let us keep our own places peacefully while Jesus Our Lord,
in order to visit the most hermetically-sealed part of creation
and deal with that knot, the supreme lock of which the
Leviathan forms the latch,[5] profits from the removed garment,
as on the day when, bending down in order to wash the feet
of His disciples, He took off His outer habit. Soon He will
show Himself in His flesh to the world of the flesh. Today it is
in spirit that He is showing Himself to the spirits: demons
who, in their refusal of God, made for themselves an appropriate habitat. And to the numberless people, the generations
after generations of disincarnate who, around Adam and Eve,
the root taken from Eden (to which the swarming vegetation
of Original Sin attaches them), have been waiting for milleniums for the ray of deliverance or the confirmation of punishment. *Descendit ad inferos.* He descended into hell, to the
inhabitants of the underworld. What does this mean? What
category of ideas can emanate from these words?

Let us try first to clarify our vocabulary. Every movement is
translated by a change of position. In its turn the position is
defined by the relationship of one point to another point, or
to several other exterior points. These relationships are evalu-

---

5. *Hard and heavy and strong that sword is which the Lord
carries: shall he not wreak his vengeance, in due time, upon the
monstrous serpent that bars the gate?* (Is. 27:1).

ated in distances, namely in a certain estimation of time which is necessary to cover them. All these positions together form a composition, or in the words of our senses, a figure whose root or intimate power is that action, comprehension, desire and unifying will for the realization of a common end, and which the different parts of the whole exercise with regard for one another. This action, by reason of our human constitution, is easier for us to realize in the world of material solidity than in the world of spiritual substances, but we have known for a long time that one is the faithful and ingenious translation of the other. Therefore we should have no scruple in using the resources of language furnished us by our material surroundings. This is a legitimate metaphor. On both sides the same forces are at work, the same ideas are being expressed, the same obedience is being manifested. From one to the other column in the text, endless references are being explained.

Therefore when Scripture speaks to us of the high and the low, of descent and mounting, when Saint Paul says (Eph. 4:9): *The words, He has gone up, must mean that he had gone down, first, to the lower regions of earth,* we are invited to consider not so much a concrete fact as a *meaning.* The "high" means for us attraction and effort, the "low" means meditation and weight. One is felt by violence and appeal, the other by persistence and advice. The way of one is our direction and end, the way of the other is for us the point of departure and the principle. The way of one is appetite, that language in us which aspires, according to the invitation of the spirit: *You must be heavenly-minded* (Col. 3:2). The way of the other is conscience and humility, that feeling in us for the earth from which we are made. God is equally in both places, according to this word of Deuteronomy (4:39): *the Lord is the God who reigns in heaven above and on earth beneath,* and the verse of Psalm 138:8, *If I should climb up to heaven,*

201

thou art there; if I sink down to the world beneath, thou art present still. But He is above us in the way of love, and below us in the way of issue, credit, paternity. Our Christian life is a perpetual coming and going between these two poles. How is it that the good is identified in current speech with the high, and evil with the low?

It is quite simply a question of reversal in the perception we have of *meaning.* Rather than going to the Father in a linear movement which Saint Thomas, following Saint Denys, defined for us, as either moving in an oblique direction, or returning complacently toward our principles, we look at ourselves, we are curious about our starting point, we desire to take possession of it, we derive benefit from it. And such is the root in us of pride, concupiscence and avarice. With incestuous delight, we lean upon this one point[6] which is our essential holding: namely our nothingness. In other words, rather than going straight ahead, we begin to turn,[7] and this is called to *turn bad.* We begin to gravitate in an unbreakable orbit around that ideal and non-existent point in us, and in that deadly study we involve everything that belongs to us and everything that has with us a relationship of weight. We create a figure of revolution. Rather than being a center of effusion, we become a nucleus of opaqueness and mass. And that doubtless is what can be called *Hell.*

Hell is what is below, not *per accidens* but *per se,* of a fundamental lowness which excludes all capacity for ascent and

6. *If I abandoned thee, it was but for a little moment* (Is. 54: 7). *They go down at last without a struggle to the grave* (Job 21: 13).

7. *Beaten down, bowed to the earth, I go mourning all day long* (Ps. 37:7). *Turned away, like a bow that plays the arche false* (Ps. 77:57). *See where they have laid a snare, to bring me low* (Ps. 56:7). Remember all the bent backs in the Gospel which our Lord straightened.

whose physical reality condenses the image under our feet. As it is movement which creates space, so it is the study of the fascinated soul around that void in itself to which it is chained which creates the domain of its captivity and the endless circle where it is caught. That is the place which the prophet calls the soul of hell.[8] *The toils of the grave were all about me,* says the Book of Kings (II Kings 22:6), *deadly snares had trapped my feet.* It is not only the assuming of a situation, it is a pact of the will. We have made a pact with hell (Is. 18:15). There, freedom is not, there is only the law, accuracy, both penal and mathematical justice. The appeal from on high is replaced by inflexible severity, by the impossibility of escaping one's inner examination and agreeing with it. The Ancients unanimously, all the great seers and poets, believed that the punished souls dwelt within the earth.[9] It is true that we cannot easily understand the attraction which pure matter compressed on this globe can have for the soul which is a spiritual principle. All that can be said is that the physical forces which tighten and maintain in a strict blind cohesion the materials of our planetary ball, have a certain resemblance, a certain homogeneity with the attraction for the void, an inner suction, which makes of demons and outcast souls a single compact mass.[10] The soul straining in an effort against God finds support in all that is resistance, all that is coalition for resisting an outside will. Like the scientist who holds in his hands the figure he built, the apparatus made by his intelligence, the soul

8. *That is why the abyss hungers for you, opens its greedy jaws* (Is. 5:14).

9. Eccl. 17:19: *A day will come when he . . . overwhelms them in the depths of the earth. Our pride is bowed in the dust* (Ps. 43: 26). This is Sion capsized about which it is said: *Walk about Sion, make the round of her towers* (Ps. 47:13). The Serpent is represented as eating dust, as feeding on it.

10. Job 41:6: *The body of him* (Leviathan) *is like shields . . . so close to one another as to leave no vent between.*

can approve, inhabit, integrate with the primordial crystal and make of it the seed and the support of its own condensation. It finds therein a geometrical seduction which serves to *precipitate* it. On this subject there is a provocative passage in the Gospel (Matth. 8). I refer to the episode of the Gerasenes. Cast out by Jesus Christ, the demons who *possessed* the two creatures begged for another physical recipient and the Saviour released to them a herd of swine which they entered with apparent ease. It would seem that between spirit and matter there is, outside of the hypostatic union, a certain ability and perhaps a need to unite, to which corresponds some porosity in matter. Psalm 103:2 tells us that for the blessed *The light is a garment thou dost wrap about thee.* Perhaps the bad spirits also need over them an opaque covering, an armor against light: *The deep,* says Psalm 103:6, *once covered it, like a cloak.* And Genesis tells us that as soon as evil is committed, there is an impulse to hide, to cover oneself, to withdraw from sight.

If it were thus, we might think there is a kind of perpetual pact between sin and pain, and that at the very heart of Justice the soul is maintained in an exact suspension according to its specific weight. Through the power of some intrinsic necessity, it marries as it blasphemes the Justice of God. Directly under the wine-press, it is face to face subjected to such a demand. *Soul, art thou still downcast? Wilt thou never be at peace?* (Ps. 41:6). And Job 22:11, *left benighted when thou thoughtest to see day* (the writer means that the absence of God has become for him a matter of positive appraisal), *overwhelmed by the unexpected flood.* Such is the *substance* spoken of in the Epistle to the Hebrews (11:1): *It is that which gives substance to our hopes, which convinces us of things we cannot see.* Such is the operation of the winepress *(torcular)* so often referred to in the Holy Books: the millstone that grinds, the pressure of society, the eagerness for quantity, the loveless unanimity of which the large modern cities give us a picture, the atmosphere of extravasated blood in which the horses of the Apocalypse sink up to their breasts, the putting outside of that inner measure of grace which God had given to us to provide for the sustaining of our resemblance.

For within the lost soul the constricting action of Justice caused the flame to shoot forth! *Such a fire I will kindle*, says Ezechiel 28:18, *in the heart of thee as shall be thy undoing.* And Isaias 9:19, *Fiery vengeance of the Lord of hosts, that ravages country-side and devours citizen!—A new Topheth has been made ready; this, too, made ready by a king. It is deep and wide, fed with flaming brands in abundance* (the brands given to it each day from the supply of the human forest); *and the breath of the Lord comes down like a stream of brimstone, to kindle it* (Is. 30:33). A terrifying revelation of the Holy Spirit blowing on the penal fire in order to increase the burning! This breath, taken back by the priest on the day of our baptism, which the Creator breathed into the nostrils of Adam, a fire ignited in us over which our plastic form has been fashioned, is now at grips with the invincible corpse, the irreducible idol which our own will has constructed and shaped in the ironic resemblance with God! In the place of liquefaction and clarification of love, this is calcination, demonstration, the pitiless detailed accusation of Justice.[11] Isaias in terrifying chapters (34 and 24) describes for us the cursed land which sin has made: *Pitch they shall be henceforward, the brooks of Edom* (pitch is the soul's attachment to itself), *its soil brimstone; a land of burning pitch, never quenched night or day, its smoke going up eternally; age after age it shall yet*

11. *Fire will test the quality of each man's workmanship* (I Cor. 3:13).

be desolate. (What is, in truth, this fruit of error each generation passes to the next? Saint Paul tells us that there is no alliance between the wicked, every alliance being founded on the desire for a common good). *Untravelled for ever by the foot of man* (for evil leads nowhere). (Is. 34:9,10). *Earth drained to its dregs, earth ravaged and ransacked. . . . Earth woebegone and withered, a world that withers and grows feeble.*[12] . . . *Poor earth, polluted by the men that dwell on it; they have broken God's law, traversed the decree he made for them, violated his eternal covenant with men; cankered it lies by a curse, peopled with guilty men. Woe-begone the vintage, withered now the wine, hearts sighing that once were merry. . . . Ransacked and ruined lies yonder city, where every house denies entrance* (Isaias 24:3-7,10). . . . *When that day comes, the Lord will hold a reckoning with the hosts of heaven, there above, with the kings on the earth, here on earth; huddled together, as captives are huddled together in a dungeon, they shall remain prisoners; so, at last the reckoning will be held. And after many days they will be visited. Plotted with the Lord's measuring-line, an empty void, tried with his plummet, a hanging ruin. . . . Devils and monstrous forms shall haunt it, satyr call out to satyr; there the vampire lies down and finds rest. Hedge-hog makes a nest to rear its young* (Isaias 34:11, 14-15). And Isaias warns us so that out of these unrelated images we shall derive a common concept: *Turn back, when the time comes, to this record of divine prophecy, and read it afresh; you shall learn, then, that none of these signs was lacking, none waited for the coming of the next. The Lord it was entrusted me with the prophecies I utter; by his Spirit*

---

12. The lost soul, an eternal Tantalus, tries in vain to recover the earth, the former taste of the good earth; *his enemies will be humbled in the dust* (Ps. 71:9).

that strange company was called together. For each in its own dwelling-place; in his hand was the line that measured it out to them; there they shall live on for ever, to all ages undisturbed (Isaias 34:16-17).

Such is that *death*, such is that *interior of death* which the Son of Man came to visit, such is that root under the earth to which He had to manifest Himself, that invitation of the cross which He found it just to accept, that end of the road which He reached by going through the opened door of the sepulchre. He had first to be recognized by the Lord below, by Satan both individual and collective, the first among the living, the one whom Job (18:13) calls *death in its primal guise.* He had to open the door and show that key against which no lock prevails. Lucifer had not hidden so far away that God was not able to find him. Again they are face to face. Oh! he went to a great deal of trouble, and the moment came at last when he fully realized the result of that occult collaboration. The scandal, which once in heaven involved the protest of the first protester, is over. The Man-God is here, and it is Satan himself who for eternity attached his mark, as principal collaborator, on this exploit of divine mercy. It is he whom divine Wisdom from beginning to end reduced to the role of unconscious associate. However deep the devil is, there is a certain grain of salt deeper still than he.[13] *With Wisdom the topaz from Ethiopia and the finest gold-leaf cannot compare. Whence, then, does wisdom come to us; where is discernment to be found? . . . The shadow-world of death claims no more than to have heard the rumor of it* (Job 28:19-23). This is like the avowal of bewilderment. Men tamed the dragon and put a bit between his foaming jaws to direct him. *I shall be your*

13. *It is a covenant* (of salt) *between the Lord and thy race* (Num. 18:19).

bite, hell! cries the prophet Osee, try your teeth as much as you wish on this piece of iron! And the angels surrounding Christ began the song of triumph (Job 18): *Nay, the hopes of the wicked man are a light that shall be put out; a very will of the wisp; darkness shall fall over his dwelling-place, and the lamp that shone there will shine no more. The boldness of his own stride takes him prisoner; his own devices recoil against him; into the trap he walks, struggles vainly with its meshes; now he is laid by the heels! Mounts ever higher his burning thirst. The ground sown with snares, pit-falls about his path. . . . His strength brought low by famine, hunger gnawing at his sides . . . , death in its primal guise shall devour those limbs. Gone the security of his home, now its master lies under the heels of tyrant death; in his house strangers shall dwell, on his lands brimstone be scattered, root never grow beneath nor harvest rise from it. Gone the fame of him, gone the name of him, from street and country-side, eclipsed in utter darkness, lost to the world . . . he who lived here, lived a stranger to God.*

Jesus descended to the substructure of the creation to confirm it, to consolidate hell and give it its full meaning, to transform the implicit negation of Satan into an explicit refusal, to perfect the appearance of this absence by going there Himself. He went also to free the people there who were waiting for Him under the *shadow of death*. We must understand the meaning of this expression. There is *death*, the *second death*, spoken of by the Apocalypse, which is precisely hell; and there is the *shadow of death*, which is not death but the shadow it projects, the physical effect which its proximity produces, the interception of light, the impotency in movement which comes about in us from the obliterating of our direction, the meditation on the awareness of our weight. We read in the Book of Acts (5:15) that the shadow of Peter was enough to bring healing and life, just as the shadow of Satan, the area without light which his intervention determines,[14] is sufficient to spread paralysis and freezing. Interposed between the soul and its Creator is all the density of committed and inherited evil. It is an atmosphere, and night itself is combined with what we breathe. There our guilty flesh, inherited from Eve, is admitted, in order to taste the bitterness of this word from the Song of Songs (2:3): *shade cool to rest under . . . such is he my heart longs for.* Now they have become capable of answering the question of Job (38:19): *Tell me, if such knowledge is thine . . . where darkness finds its home. Shadows,* the same patriarch tells us, *protect the shadow* of this captive and merge with his own darkness. It is the darkness of Egypt, described to us in the Book of Wisdom which the professors of Holy Scripture agree on finding "graphic" (Wisdom 17), the dwelling of all those *bound together by the same chain.* This chain is that of original sin which, distributed and proliferating in every direction like a cause, binds generations one to the other, this *chain in our midst,* attached to our navel which the prophet Isaias invites us to get rid of. But our own strength is not enough. We need the hand of Him of whom it is said that He *listened to the groans of the prisoners, delivered a race that was doomed to die* (Ps. 101:21). If there are among my readers some unfortunate ones who have been placed alive in hell, who without losing their faith, have done evil, in full knowledge of what they were doing, and who for years, with hearts and minds intact and devoted to Christ, have had the leisure to consider their bound limbs and measure before their eyes what it was impossible for them to accomplish, since they were during that time given over to the work of Satan, they will understand the sweetness which

14. *Shelter us, like the shadow, dark as night, that gives shelter at noon-day* (Is. 16:3).

the promise of the Psalmist has for them. *But when I betook me to the fruit garden to see if . . . pomegranate (walnuts) had budded*, says the Bridegroom of the Sulamite (S. of Songs 6:11). What in truth is more hermetically closed and compressed than a walnut? Inside, it is attached with all its strength to its own shell. To open it, you have to break it, in order to bring out from its wooden coffin the edible mummy. The avaricious heart is like this, adhering to its own prison which no desire dilates and which the dew of heaven cannot moisten. It is the same with those eyes, or rather those balls petrified by natural or acquired blindness, rolled at random in their orbits by the blind man who henceforth depends on the animal verification of his smell and touch, while waiting for the merciful voice murmuring the omnipotent *Ephphata*. The eyes of God do not rest on that hard stone, on that perfect spherical resistance whose sharpest point would seek in vain the defect and the hinge. *Gone the heart of stone*, says Ezechiel 11:19, *and a human heart theirs in place of it. He . . . bidding . . . the chastened soul, rise and live!* (Is. 57:15). In the deepest part of School the father does not forget his son, the fisherman will laboriously fish out the lamb fallen down through the hole of the cistern. *I will go down mourning*, says the patriarch of Genesis, *to keep my son company in the grave*. In the place of the compact walnut which has to be imagined inside its bitter husk, behold all the fruits of the orchard and the profusion of the basket, all the varieties of sweetness, all that is born to melt in our mouth: the pear and the apple which satisfy all the promises of the flesh, the peach, the apricot, the purple plum, the small bunch of bitter currants, the blue and white grapes and the weight in our hand of that translucent bunch, the fig of concentrated honey, the lemon for the slaking of that thirst, which so gaily attacks our taste buds, the pomegranate, honor of the fruit-bowl, whose scarlet treasure bursts under its leather jerkin. All that juice which comes forth when we bite! And I almost forgot the melon and the royal mango, and that pure snow of the mangosteen in its purple cell—the mango which we can't put aside, any more than the ferocious wasp will give up clinging to the sticky opening of the greengage . . .

A single glance of Christ was enough to make us forget the taste of all that; and the apple, hardly bitten into, rolled at the feet of Adam.

He understood, in truth, that these were only insipid ridiculous fruits by comparison with those tasted once on the banks of the river Hevilath which produces emerald and gold. No earthly tree will be able again to furnish them until that miraculous water once again reflects the heavy branch. It is the fruit which the *Father who sees what is done in secret* (Matth. 6:4) creates by looking at it, and which adorns with a double inexhaustible garland the banks of this living and life-giving river of crystal which John after the four great Prophets saw flowing from the throne of God (Apoc. 22:1). The torrent of delight which will cover us is close by and will soon be here! The *store-house of fresh water* has opened up under the resounding rod of Moses (Num. 20:6). It is not a weak trickle oozing out, but the plug of the abyss which gave way. It is the deep cavity of the Void which has water for drinking! On every side you hear thunder and the leaping of geysers on high which explore the Void! *Peace shall flow through her like a river,* says Isaias 66:12. This is not the *aquaduct* spoken of by Ecclesiasticus 24:41, one of those rivers like the Mekong or the Nile which feeds a limitless network of irrigation. It is an irresistible sea mounting, filling and submerging everything. *From me rivers flow, says Wisdom, deep rivers* (Eccle. 24:40). I come in and stop up all the ponds of Tartarus and swell them instantly with that increase whose origin is in the depths of the stars! *Can it be a river that comes up in flood?* (Jer. 46:7). *I am the Lord thy God, ever ready to teach thee what it concerns thee to know.* . . . *Then had a flowing stream of peace been with thee, a full tide of the Lord's favor* (Is. 48:17-18). *As our fault was amplified, grace has been more amply bestowed than ever* (Rom. 5:20). Everything is submerged by it, filled, raised, cleaned and carried away.

Reader, this is about you. I am not a professional guide with the task of leading you before old frescoes almost obliterated where a bit blasé and tired you look for a moment at some "amusing" detail. If you do not believe in hell, you had better leave me and listen to the other guides who fight over your patronage. You have only to let them take over and follow them. They are all here: the prostitute, the materialistic philosopher, the man of letters, the demagogue, the cocaine pusher. They know the way, and the right door to open. There is no need even of dying in a formal sense, because the living are admitted. All you have to do is to spend a few weeks in that place praised for its picturesqueness and comfort. It is true that they don't give you a round-trip ticket, but once you are there most of our clients like it so much that the question of departure is put off.

It was really hell, the hell whose gates the Son of Man opened. (Arthur Rimbaud).

For hell is not only outside of us, it is within us. It is not only tomorrow we shall be there, it is now, whenever an act of mortal sin is committed, whenever grace has been lost. I recognize only too well the symptoms as described by the prophets, the characteristics of the climate: the stupor, the itching, the disgust, the bond and the oppression, the void, the sharp point, the darkness, the pitch which clings, the sulphur which corrodes, the two hamstrings cut, and in our mouth the stopper of vitriol and lime; and the entrance to the lower stages of our temperament where we hold rage, hatred, the need to laugh and the need to vomit! Happy is the man who in this hideous place began by losing both eyes, but what of the man who remains awake and clairvoyant?

It is into this rotting den, this cadaverous larder and morgue, this storeroom for caskets, this *garden of walnuts,* this region which is *under the shadow of death,* that Jesus Christ suddenly brought His presence, His superior force and poignant gentleness, His harsh and sweet majesty, His invincible pardon, His irresistible light which is both cruel and desirable! Once already, just previously, the door of the sepulchre had been violated, and under the command of the piercing cry and the formidable right hand they had seen a Lazarus half eaten away rise up out of the tomb! But now it is not death coming to confront God and present to Him face to face that thing which He had not made, it is God Himself in His Second Person who, profiting from the opening, descends towards death and sin, and comes to question the Void. As at times night is suddenly illuminated, so a flash now fills the concavity of the firmament. *In the twinkling of an eye, when the last trumpet sounds,* says Saint Paul, (I Cor. 15:52), the man struck down on the Damascus road. It is like the immense arrow which the sun shoots when its burning eye appears on the sea horizon, over the numberless furrows of the swell, when all the distance of the sky from end to end is crossed! But also light may proceed for us by a slow impregnation, a progressive digestion of our opacity. Nothing is seen at first, but birds have begun to see everywhere in the fog. And suddenly the white spot on our right which gradually thins out, the branch greener than enamel appears before us shining with dew. Oh! this time, there is no mistake, it is the sun we have heard about! Continue on your way, holy pilgrim!

There are still many marshes, many bogs to cross before you reach the end, many tenacious rivers where something which has the consistency of pitch and lava darkly flows—before you are able to put your hand on the shoulder of Adam, in the center knot of your personality, almost incorporated with stone, rooted with all your roots like an oak through the geological strata!

When Jesus crossed the public square of Capharnaum, or when, leaving the Synagogue, He came upon that bazaar clinic of the blind and paralytics and the sufferers from convulsions who had been brought carefully by their families and placed before Him, what a shout was heard in the markets and the back kitchens, when all of them, still a bit shaky . . . but healed, began to walk behind Him! But here there are not just a few dozen poor wretches, a few samples taken from the swarming poverty-stricken population of an Eastern city. All eyes are opened, suddenly myriads of them, generations one after the other He penetrates and animates, like the sun appearing at the Eastern gate and illuminating an entire continent at the same moment. It is a general onrush of humanity, the vast pocket of darkness evacuating its crowds! All meet and become acquainted. The huge family of humanity is reconstructed under the gaze of God. It is like the platform of a beehive when the swarm newly organized around its Queen is instructed and prepares to leave. Each new-born bee learns to function for the heaven the Queen represents and to use its own wings, antenna and olfactive nerve. All who now are going to take flight in a great uproar learn about what has happened. It will not be possible to hold out for long against the irresistible heavens! The moment has come when the first human supporters emerge triumphantly in the uninhabited heaven and mingle with the perfume of angels the last of their animal mustiness. All that was superimposed in time is now juxtaposed in space. The rest of us will find up there a part quickly recognized, explored and divided where countless landmarks and familiar faces await us, but all those who escape from hell on Easter morning form the eternal site around us which each newcomer learns to utilize. Let us leave them to their work. With one hand over our eyes, let us follow each group one after the other who, farther off than the nebula, hover, turn and obey the pigeon house. We shall remain attached to Jesus Christ, as close as we can to the group of patriarchs and prophets who prepared His advent and who now cannot separate from Him.

Part Three

Prayers

FOR many years now, O Lord, each day at five o'clock in the afternoon, I have been the client of Your blessed cross. A disappointing client. The air which this sluggish character displaces when he moves would not be enough to turn the sails of a windmill. It doesn't matter. He likes to be here, he likes to feel totally dissolved and ignored here, to accept his part of silence and general immobility. Most of the time, nothing happens, at least nothing perceptible. He is happy when, after long repeated periods of watching, he feels deep within himself something as important as the falling of a grain of sand. But is it nothing just purely and simply to exist? Is it nothing just to coexist with that lamp, with that tiny particle of red light which at times diminishes and at other times abruptly flashes out, as it testifies to God over yonder in the sanctuary? Passion has become patience. It is You, O Lord, and it is the cross! Is it nothing to have for one instant espoused Eternity in the abdication of time, and to participate in the patience of God?

Above me the sad stream of memories, images and ideas

continues its whirling iridescent course. I am somewhere else, below, a little lower down. I am substantially myself where the principal function is purely and simply to continue and to breathe. I look at nothing. I ask for nothing. I am here, and I wait. It is good to be here.

Age has weakened my ears and my eyes. I am beginning to feel around me all the symptoms of that period of life spoken of by Ecclesiastes. *The street-doors shut, muffled the hum of the mill, bird-song for waking-time* (I know only too well the incessant bird-call!), *and all the echoes of music faint!* (These are the syllables which lose their consonants.) *Almond-blossom matched for whiteness; the grasshopper's weight a burden now.* (The grasshopper, mad woman of the house, forever needing to chirp, is now a little heavy!) *The spiced food untasted.* (The capers and mysterious pimento are now beginning to spoil!) *Man is for his everlasting home.* My everlasting home! Why, Lord, that is what I want, but after all, am I not already here? Only here do I feel really comfortable. I am like one of those old men in a General Store of the Far West. He doesn't speak. He doesn't buy anything. But they let him stay there because he's no trouble. He doesn't listen to the conversation going on around him, but he follows it from time to time when it coincides with his own thoughts. He is there as if he didn't exist, and someone seeing him close to the stove might think that he has nothing else to do in life but warm himself at that inside sun.

The stained glass windows all around me are only a scattered variegated pattern, and as daylight fades they look yellow and dull. But by bending my head back and looking way up, I see my Lord on a huge crucifix which is hanging from the ceiling. The other day in the Louvre I was visiting the new galleries of Ancient Art. (There is also the frieze of the dog-headed monkeys, barking at the rising sun and that handsome plain casket of black diorite, inflated like a human form where the inhabitant must feel very comfortable in the arms of the goddess Internatamattit.) In the middle of a room so highly lighted that it dazzles you like a concentrated sun, there is exhibited a column of white stone. Probably Demeter's stalk of wheat. But high up, on this vault above me, between heaven and earth, I contemplate another stalk of wheat, the first shoot, the royal impulse which an hypostasized God gave to mankind. I am alone here below (in company with that harvester of chairs whose operations my presence somewhat impedes) as I meet this endless presence. From time to time in the dark nave a woman rapidly crosses herself or an old man painfully genuflects. I have taken hold of the horn of the oak ox under the pulpit, which, joined with the lion, the eagle and the angel, represent the third Evangelist. And I think of the sacrificer in Leviticus who was charged with providing the high priest with the blood which he was to take *behind the veil*. It gives me a feeling of security to hold on to the horn of this strong animal. And I think of the two victims consecrated by the same high priest on certain days of the year: one sacrificed on the altar, and the other, the emissary, sent into the outer darkness and laden with curses. It is still there galloping madly down the streets of our cities. Beast of steel today bellowing everywhere and racing madly.

I see, fulfilled before my eyes, the promise of the Gospel: *Yes, if only I am lifted up from the earth, I will attract all men to myself* (John 12:32). He said: *all men*. All men, in an absolute sense. Since Christ was lifted up, there has been a continuous uninterrupted action. A movement opposite to that of matter which tends always to fall. It is an appeal, an invitation to each being to separate himself from the world. This recalls a thought of Saint Augustine who reminds us that Saint Paul teaches that Jesus Christ is the *corner-stone* (Eph.

2:20) and the *foundation* (I Cor. 3:11) on which is built the
spiritual temple which all Christians form. Since Christ is
the foundation, the entire construction must lean on Him.
But Christ is risen, He is in heaven. "Therefore it is in heaven
we must seek our support. When it is a question of construct-
ing a building on the ground with materials which their weight
constantly pulls downward, the foundations have to be placed
at the bottom, but it is the opposite for us: the Rock which
constitutes the foundation of the building was placed on
high:[1] it therefore attracts us upward by the charity which becomes our very weight. *Amor meus, pondus meum.*" (S. Aug.,
Serm. 337, c. IV.) It is not therefore any outer violence
ravishing us, but a quality in accord with our substance. It
is a magnetic action. A duty. The determined consciousness
in the heart of a subject that he belongs to some other plan
than his own.[2]

—O Lord, I understand now that it is no slight thing, I don't
mean carrying Your cross, but simply accompanying it, mea-
suring it with my eyes, at once attracted, astonished and terrified. Now, up there where it has flown high, it beckons to
me. What do I do to join it?[3] I feel I am engaged in too difficult an enterprise! I don't know what to do to adapt to my
own shoulders those wooden wings. And here on the ground,
where would I get that heave of back and shoulders, that
enormous strength of will necessary, I don't mean for transporting that incomprehensible machine, but simply to budge

---

1. *His own sacred trophy themselves shall be.* (Literally, "they
shall be like stone of sanctification that are lifted up as a standard
over his head.") (Zac. 9:16).
2. *Wait till you see the signal raised on the mountains, till you
hear the trumpet sound* (Is. 18:3).
3. *By the full light of heaven above earth, my dealings are
higher than your dealings, my thoughts than your thoughts* (Is.
55:9).

it. I feel that each step ahead could be made only by some kind of fundamental violence comparable to an eruption in nature. Now since I am earthbound, since I can neither fly nor make any headway, my one hope is in my ability to shout! Only by shouting can I cross that immeasurable distance! I am like those shapeless creatures flattened out on the fossile shores when, after centuries of striving, they utter their first cry: a kind of monstrous braying. *Let me but hear thy voice, that voice sweet as thy face is fair* (S. of Songs 2:14).

Yes, if only I am lifted up from the earth, I will attract all men to myself. Lifted up—that is the word. I should like first to understand the meaning of *lifted up*. Immediately I thing of that *elevation* which is the central moment of the Mass when the priest, successor of the ancient sacrificer, shows to heaven and earth the victim, the beating heart which is alive in his hands.[4] At that sign, raised up in that way, from the back of the church the crowd of the faithful swarms up to the steps of the sanctuary.[5] And I associate their entreaty with the strange episode of the *brazen serpent* (Num. 21), that mortal devouring principle which the hand of Moses picked up from the sand in order to make it, as soon as he hoisted it at the end of a staff, the means of healing a terrified people. What was concealed on the ground that bit and killed, is now visible and exhibited, and it is that which saves. The minister of death became that instrument of salvation. What else is the serpent save a simplified diagram, the breath in a sheath, the root of the soul in the flesh, the humiliated spirit grovelling on the ground, the spirit which incessantly schemes against the heel of our mortality and keeps us from subsisting? What

4. *The breast of the ram . . . thou shalt remove, and sanctify it by holding it up in the Lord's presence* (Exodus 29:26).
5. *Up, up, Jerusalem, bestir thyself!* (Is. 51:17). *Sursum corda! You must be heavenly-minded* (Col. 3:2). *Gloria in excelsis!*

form was more suitable to the Word in His final abasement when for us he bore sin and mire. *But I, poor worm, have no manhood left* (Ps. 21:7). It pleased God to pick that up and give him a *name which is greater than any other name* (Phili. 2:9), so that we should see interwoven on the cross in the same calligraphy the root of our fault and the root of our salvation. This is the Tree which for our wonder produced the *Kingdom of God*, the *seed* which the Gospel speaks of, so small that it is the smallest of all and cannot be perceived by our senses. It has now become this tremendous tree.⁶ *Pith of the tall cedar I will take and set it firm, young branch from its crest of branches I will snap off, and plant it on a mountain that stands high above the rest. High in the hill country of Israel I will plant it, and there it shall grow into a great cedar-tree. . . . Learn that I the Lord, bring high tree low, raise low tree high, wither the burgeoning trunk, give life to the barren. What the Lord promises, the Lord fulfills* (Ezec. 17:22-24). *Word from him for crag and hill, ravine and valley and barren upland.* (ibid. 36:4). And Jesus Christ tells us that the measure of His exaltation is the measure of His abasement. There is nothing so low but what He wished to know it. He is not only in the slime like the serpent, and in the rotting earth like the worm, He is at our feet. It is our very foundation, the alternating principle of our movement and equilibrium that He came to verify, sanctify and baptize. It is at our feet that the Creator took the posture of suppliant, and He washed them with tears and kisses. (And He is perhaps still there. We have to be careful not to walk on Him.) So these are the feet which henceforth have to be ready for the ascent. But we can forget them if we remember the two

6. *Grew a tree from the heart of the earth, beyond measure tall* (Dan. 4:7).

224

strong arms above us which have just raised up. *Arise,* they say, *and come!* In Asia I have seen those inert idols, those compact Buddhas, some, as in Ceylon, flattened out full length on the ground like slugs. And others, as in China, seated, their eyes closed, blended with their own weight. But the God we worship is not only standing, He is raised, all His body stretched, an active power visible in each fiber! He is above everything and holds on to nothing. But it is He who holds us, and we who depend on Him, the two of us indissoluble. He is here forever between heaven and earth, suspended, intermediary. He is a God fully functioning. He is not only raised, but with His eyes fixed on His Father, He is totally absorbed in an effort to elevate everything, to raise us up to Him.

Son of Man! Son of David! hear me in my turn. In this hour of diminishing light, as I hold on to the horn of the Gospel animal, I cry in lamentation toward You, with my head bent back: *Son of man, can life return to these bones?* (Ezec. 37:3). Where is that wind, coming simultaneously from the four shores of the sky, that will reanimate me and make a new man in Your resemblance out of this pile of dry disjointed bones? *They are complaining,* says the prophet (Ezec. 37:11) *that their very bones have withered away, that all hope is lost, they are dead men.* (There is no better description of the cemetery which once I shared with so many living dead and where since then I have lived from time to time!) *Drained of strength, like grass the sun scorches,* says the Psalmist (101:5-6) . . . *I am spent with sighing, till my skin clings to my bones. As will chase a wisp of straw,* says Job (13:25). But immediately I hear the same patriarch say: *Hope rests within my bones!* I have not lost consciousness of my essential design. Something irreducible in me knows *that his redeemer lives.* The foundation remains, the sacred bone, the Creed, the pebble remains and the stone that cries out! (Luke 19:40). The wind coming from all directions at the same time which created heaven and earth and man is not exhausted, this I know. There is something in me bound up with the entire universe which remembers the way in which we were taken from the void. It was not a flick of the finger which, according to the philosopher, started the machinery, it was a spark, a sting, like the hidden pinpoint of genius, which assembled and created a scaffolding of propositions. And in the place of a vague eruption, a precise question, something which carries out a plan rather than a questioning.[7] At first desire, at first a blind cry, and then, around me on all sides, the hands—eager knowing hands—my own hands searching—choosing and performing.[8] It is the word *raised* or transcendent which excites latent energy in the individual. There would be no ascent, no rising up everywhere which make out of several a single thing, if THAT were not above us, which provokes and attracts, that end which allows the transitory creature to listen to eternity. *Each bone,* the prophet tells us, *sought for its joint* and found it. Then the supple strong machine of muscles and ligaments, which is capable of propelling form to autonomy and movement, leaned against this armor and took root there. Over it like a piece of cloth, the flesh and the robe of the senses were extended. But all that would not have sufficed unless from the four corners of the heavens the Spirit had not breathed, that more or less obscure conscience which the *animated* being derives in breathing in from himself and from his vocation. *Veni Creator Spiritus!*

7. *The depths beneath us roar aloud, the heights beckon from above* (Hab. 3:10).

8. *Cry aloud, never ceasing!* (Is. 58:1). *All thy gates, now, must echo with lament, all thy cities ring with cries* (Is. 14:31). *When he calls upon me, I will listen* (Ps. 90:15).

This spirit with which God created the world by breathing on it, like the priest who with his lips and from the bottom of his lungs draws the letter ψ on the baptismal fonts, has not ceased moving over us. They are the great trade-winds which since the day of Pentecost have been swelling the sails of the Church. At times it is the tempest uprooting oak trees, and at other times it is the enameller's blow-pipe, or the sudden irresistible scent of the rose. A word, even less than that—the form of a word—was sufficient.

Long ago it was the Spirit which elicited Christ in the womb of the Virgin Mary and it is the personal Christ, in His turn, who draws, assembles and promotes around Him that Church which is His collective body: that which is called forth, bound, formed and animated by faith in the same head and by participation in the same sacraments.

The cross is not only the abstract symbol but also the mechanical expression, in a certain sense, of that ceaseless energy of Christ who draws all to Him, of that fourfold[9] desire which is felt both on the left and the right, at the heights and at the depths, for unifying unity. Christ on the cross does not cease working. It is a machine before our eyes functioning endlessly. It is the irrepressible leaven which does not stop operating on the three measures of wheat. It is the poignant

9. One could find a representation of the four lines of effort of the crucifix in the traditional emblems of the Evangelists. John's eagle is vertical flight. Matthew's angel, executor of divine will in time, scientifically looks for the foundation of the cross in geneology and at the frontiers of Israel. Mark's lion is that swift triumphant right hand carrying baptism to the nations. The ox of Luke is that power of *conference* of a triple stomach, the ruminated and enlivening digestion of divine truth, the operation of breathing and of the heart over that matter which memory brings. *In the very heart of the fire, was a glow . . . that enclosed four living figures* (Ezec. 1:5).

grasp, the fundamental traction, the "tug." The arms of the cross are not only the abridged expression[10] of complete man realized in Justice, they are levers in action. They form the winepress of Japheth, described by Anne Catherine Emmerich *(Life of Our Lord,* VI, 19): "The winepress had the form of a Y.... The funnel had a leather bag at the top. Two movable arms, similar to levers and penetrating the trunk on each side, squeezed the grapes enclosed in the bag and the juice flowed out through the holes that had been made in the lower part of the machine. It was therefore both a cross and a winepress."[11]

The cross is God at work. It is not only His instrument, it is His active form, His extracting unifying operation, His extension between the four cardinal points: the north of zenith which is the root in the *firmament;* the south or nadir which is matter warmed by grace on which force is exerted; the arms to the right and the left are the instruments of His temporal energy.

Thus it is not only of the creature that one can say, as Saint Paul does (Rom. 8:22), that *the whole of nature . . . groans in a common travail all the while.* It is of the Creator Himself (similar to Samson in the power of the Philistines, deposed and "put to work"). This is what is given us to realize and feel and understand, at Mass or in this Eglise des Sablons where, as my head is turned back and as I clutch the animal's horn, I look at the suspended cross. That is what keeps the mass of surrounding things from being at rest, that is what torments them and secretly upsets them in their balance. It is a solicitation revealed in an ever expanding area by all

10. *The Lord is making up his reckoning and cutting it short in his justice* (Rom. 9:28).

11. This representation can be found, I believe, in various iconographical documents of earlier times. In a stained-glass window, for example, of Saint-Etienne-du-Mont, in Paris.

kinds of swellings, explosions, ebbings, destructions, and also by momentary coalitions and trials in an attitude of resistance, but soon reduced by innate incoherence and the irresistible temptation of weight. Since God was crucified in the middle of everything, the world now is concerned only with paying attention deliberately to that heart which beats and attracts it.

And while our noble athlete at the junction of the two worlds struggles and labors for us, let us join with the solemn supplication by which Mother Church, on this Good Friday, tries to push, one behind the other, into the area of her activity, the ponderous and recalcitrant peoples.

FOR JEWS

IT IS written in the prayer book: Lord, You are witness of all the beaters who today are at work on this trembling harried people.

FOR MOSLEMS

THIS is the realm, under the sign of Abraham and Ismael, of my friend Louis Massignon. It is for them that my friend Charles Henrion endured for twenty years fire and desolation in Sidi Sâad. May Miriam one day in the middle of the desert enter that demolished sepulchre!

229

FOR PAGANS

AND especially for the multitudes of the Far East with whom I lived twenty years, the silent walk of the Chinese and the clicking walk of the Japanese. Europe is a country of slopes and valleys, a restless ill-matched people endlessly tormented by threats and temptations, whipped by rain, burned by the sun, at grips with an always changing climactic program, stirred up, bruised, poked by the sea winds in constant battle with the continent winds, an element of anger and prey to hidden ferment which suddenly, with various whirlwinds and surf, rises and rips in furious lashes and foam the gigantic breakwater which divides it into all manner of ingenious compartments and contradictory slopes. But China is the country of rice: the entire occupation of man is to build frames and partitions, to arrange endless levels in order to contain something, to watch over the growing plants mingled with human excrement which gently cook in their boxes. It is all so vast and homogeneous that despite any moving about of man, nothing changes position. And for Japan, the ocean surrounding it keeps it in the presence of eternity and the horizontal line, and there is always Fouji pointing toward heaven like an altar exhaling its streak of smoke. Lord, I give You these imprisoned peoples. Profit from all those enclosures and the hidden umbilical cord which like a lotus stalk ties together in the deepest part of the generations one multitude with the others existing miserably in mud. Lord, whose name is the Orient[1] and who came to us like a lion, the moment has

1. *Here is one takes his name from the Dayspring* (Zach. 6:12).

come to turn around like a dove and touch with Your wing this immobile people. Like a dove—or like a small child in the arms of this woman whom poor wretches call by the name Kwang Yin, so that he will strangle the Dragon in his small fist. Their artists have trained them to look up and transport their contemplation from one level to another. Descend upon them in a flood of peace,[2] like one of those great rivers collected by gigantic mountains which feed with the network of their subdivided waters all the endless ruminating of the provinces, all those large and small groups of houses like buffalo on a level with the straw. And if the rivers do not suffice, there is the sea, there is the ocean which is both their ending and their source. Oh! great people! that water which *you shall drink deep from the fountain of deliverance!* (Is. 12:3)— *Ah! if thou too couldst understand . . . the ways that can bring thee peace!* (Luke 19:42). That compact Buddha will not give it to you, nor that early incubation which your philosophers recommend, nor that striving of your conscience to reach the void. Use rather that remarkable attentiveness you have cultivated for so long and that gift of silence. Your ears were made for something other than that bell in the middle of the forest or in the mountain valley which says so starkly NO. Listen rather within your heart to that buried seed of a faint answer, the possibility of a humble Yes, or to the proposition of a preference in that hollow of the non-existent within you. Here on the threshold of your soul is some one who came not to dissolve but to fulfill. Welcome this woman with the

2. *Such a harvest his subjects shall reap, peace on every mountain* (Ps. 71:3). *The wealth of the sea shall foster them* (Deuter. 33:19). *Peace shall flow through her like a river* (Is. 66:12). *Then had a flowing stream of peace been with thee* (Is. 48:18). Something abundant and quiet but which knows where it comes from and where it is going. *And I, I am a wall; impregnable this breast as a fortress* (S. of Songs 8:10).

Child in her arms who destroys death! *Peace is my bequest to you, and the peace which I will give you is mine to give; I do not give peace as the world gives it* (John 14:27). *I, the fashioner of darkness, the creator of light, I, the maker of peace, the author of calamity* (Is. 45:7). For now when you see only the good, you realize evil. Take from looking on Me that forgetting of self which until now you had asked of a deadly discipline. *I am the way.* It is I whom old Loa-Tzeu went to find on the other side of the west mountains. I am the Tao, the forgotten road he tried in vain to reach in the obscure coils of the old Dragon. It is I whose presence Confucius felt in the midst of everything.

FOR PROTESTANTS

THUS far, O Lord, I have prayed to You for those born blind, but what can be said, what can be done for those who blind themselves, who, free to see, keep their eyes shut through a persistent action of their perverted conscience? I have lived for so many years among them! Who can reach their soul and pass through that wild stubborn covering of darkness, melancholy, pride, of sinister coldness and limbo? It is of them that the Blessed Virgin pointing them out, said with compassion: *Wine they have not.* And how could they have any, what fruit could they bear, separated as they are from the one Vineyard of which the Bride of the Song says to us: *Thy breasts challenge the clustering vine* (7:7). The sacred poet compares this wine to music (Eccl. 40:20). Its odor was strong enough on the day of Pentecost to enrapture the Apostles who had collapsed like workmen during the grape-harvesting. They have never put their lips to the cup which teaches man to forget himself, which takes away our self-possession, and which makes us light and free, ready to answer the deliberated invitation which Our Lord promised aging Peter. Theirs is a sad freedom which makes them shrunken and deaf, which attaches their feet to the ground and keeps them from graciously accepting all the outside invitation of music and dance! For they did not understand that *he who lost his soul because of Jesus Christ, truly found it.* They did not understand that all we receive is not to own and enjoy alone, but to give immediately, like the dancer who laughing goes to take from the hand of his companion in that dancing ring an offering which he quickly passes to his next neighbor, joyfully follows at the same time the un-interrupted cadence of the dance!—Jealous like Cain, of the shadow they themselves make on the ground, they do not know how *gracious the sight, and full of comfort, when brethren dwell united* (Ps. 132:1).——Protestants, do not re-main so stubborn! Forget your science, your tidiness, your virtue, your invaluable superiority, forget your propriety and the self you speak of so constantly, *forget the house of thy father* (Ps. 44:11). God's grace is not a piece of meat you have to eat in a corner like an ill-tempered dog growling and showing his teeth to everyone! The characteristic of grace is graciousness, gratuitously received and gratuitously given, with joyful humility, with irresistible authority and the triumphant transport of joy, reason and love! Accept the universe! The entire universe is yours if you wish it, freely accepted and embraced. Make one effort! You have only to hold out your hand. Learn, my friend, that *only one thing is necessary* (Luke 10:42). Alone you will never succeed in being one.[1] So give

1. *Over all the earth the Lord shall be king, one Lord, called everywhere by one name* (Zach. 14:9).

up protesting. There is only one way of abjuring this greatest
of faults, and you know it, which is to be Protestant, and
that is to become Catholic, to accept the universe triumphantly in the heart of Jesus Christ. For *he who does not
gather his store with me, scatters it abroad* (Luke 11:23).

To gather. To gather is an active verb. It does not indicate
the result of an action. It indicates the action itself. We are
invited to participate, not only in a unified body but in a
unifying virtue. We make only one in Christ with the desire
and the convoking of everything to Him. We are incorporated
on the cross by an arrangement of the creative instrument,
with an insistence on the perpendicular and a passion for
the vertical, with the operation of lever and pump which
breathes in the Church, which is interested in everything and
draws everything to One. In annihilating ourselves, we have
espoused the need for everything. We do not suffice for what
we are asked and we bear down on the mass which surrounds
us with all the force of suction from our void. We involve
something with our life. It is perfectly certain that by adhering to God with all our soul we have provoked something
gigantic and indivisible. We have become conscious, sensitive
and energetic in our right to existence. We receive and trans-
mit on all sides commands and suggestions which themselves
are the conclusion of numberless series in space and time. We
have become church conscious in relationship with Jesus
Christ. We have vigorously put on in relationship with Him
that robe which allows us to embrace Him and be completely
possessed by Him. We know that we cannot reach union
with Him save in communion. And the body, that Church
to which we belong, is not only a total but an infinitely just
and delicate compound. We suffer instantly from the slightest
displacement which upsets movement and keeps something
from passing. It is not only with all our strength, it is with the

strength of the entire Church past and present and the Church ahead of us which through us asks to be, that we embrace Christ and try to understand and realize what He wants of us.

We pray then for the Protestants who have forgotten all that, who claimed from the Father their personal share of the inheritance and who since wander like the Prodigal *wasting his fortune.*[2]

FOR UNBELIEVERS

AND now let us pray for the Unbelievers. Let us pray for the immense dispersed confused people of Unbelievers, for the shepherdless flock, for the degenerate humanity around us returned to chaos, of which it can only be said as of that collective creature on whom shone the dawn of the first day, that it was an *empty waste.* But the Holy Spirit has not left it and that mystical bird, not knowing where to rest, has not ceased brooding and warming with its heart and wings these

2. Certain Biblical figures might represent the Protestants. The first is Ismael, the nomad, desert dweller, without house and home, always wandering from one cistern to another, from one opinion to another, always searching for tomorrow's idea to exchange it with today's. And yet he shared with Isaac the baptism of the Old Law which was circumcision and God promised *to make him fruitful* (Gen. 17:20). Ismael was the son of Agar the maid-servant, namely the son of the human faculties whose role was to serve Sarai who conceived in faith. The second figure is that of the Ten Tribes who perpetrated the schism after their Lord, as later the nations of the north did, while remembering Jerusalem nostalgically and replacing Solomon's temple with that amateurish building on Mount Garizim, similar to the Mormons' shanty at Salt Lake City.

desolate stretches which are a prey to the future. *Thy very name spoken soothes the heart like a flow of oil* (S. of Songs 1:3). *Like a flow!* This expression may be looked upon as having two meanings: the oil which pours over Aaron's head, the oil *of joy* which sinks into our bones (Ps. 108:18) and of which it is said that we are given *the very marrow* (Num. 18:12); the royal priestly oil which confers on us our eminence as of Christians and which is incorporated into the sacraments of baptism and confirmation, the oil with which we receive our name which appropriately *is anointed* and with which our forehead is marked. Today it is split, forgotten, lost under the sand and ashes or even under ulcers. It seems diffused, evaporated and strengthless (Joel 1:10). *I am spent as spilt water*, says Psalm 21:15 like those flocks without shepherd which are dispersed. *All you peoples of the world*, says Isaias . . . *wait till you see the signal raised on the mountains, till you hear the trumpet sound. . . . Be you a thousand to one, yet at the challenge of five men you shall take to flight; nought left of you but a remnant, lonely as flag-staff on the mountain-top, as beacon on the hill* (Is. 18:3, 30:17). This might well be the exact picture of the ravages which heresy and the frenzy over an exact meaning like fire on which alcohol is poured, have caused in the Christian city, and the contagious cowardice which makes a thousand men flee for fear of five. The first come—a Voltaire, a Renan, or even less (if this is possible), a columnist, a tyrant of some city precinct, a miserable instructor or a bookworm—that is all that is needed to upset and throw into an inextricable dilemma, thousands of young men. And by degrees everything perished. Nothing remains except a calvary at the crossroads (insulted by automobiles), and that sign high up in the middle of a deserted church before which I weep alone—while waiting for it to appear in heaven (Matth. 24:30). An earth without

236

slopes has absorbed the great baptismal river directed toward it, and rather than giving life to it, it has rotted the earth. It is now soft treacherous mud into which you sink, an odor of corruption, a mixture of mildew and reeds, rampant wildness which, opening the irrigation canals, assults the ruins. *Outstretched these hands of mine, all the day long, to a nation of rebels* (Is. 65:2). It is worth while to develop this idea at greater length.

Genesis teaches us that on the Third Day, God separated the dry land from the water and that He called the first, Land, and the congregation of the other, He called Sea *(Maria)*. These are the two elements of natural life, the image of supernatural life, and their distinction lies at the base of the entire structure of creation. Like heaven and earth, previously taken into account, their intimate reciprocal relations are strengthened *(firmamentum)* by their difference. The idea of transcendence, exchange, operation and charity replaces the idea of indwelling. There is a marriage here. The earth ceases being a vague sponge and becomes a clearly shaped body, provided with hills and directions, watered with streams which give it movement and meaning. For the earth, the sea under the sun gives forth a blessing in the form of clouds, abundant rain, showers, snow, dew, fog—and those messengers of wrath—storms which beat down everywhere like blind giants. And the earth, in all of its possible shapes gives answer at the four cardinal points in the effusion of an endless vow. Together the land and the sea form a couple, united by a sacrament, joined in the same propulsion of love. It is written (Matth. 19:6): *What God, then, has joined, let not man put asunder.* One is tempted to say: what God separated, man should not join.

As there are two elements in the physical nature of man, there are two in his moral nature. The first is an element of stability and permanence: it is called earth, matter, substance, form (in the concrete sense). The second element is fluid, subtle, mobile, intelligent, penetrating, dynamic; and it is called, depending upon the various images it takes, water, blood, breath, spirit. The Apostle John refers to this: *We have a threefold warrant on earth, the Spirit, the water, and the blood, three witnesses that conspire in one* (I John 5:8). Blood, according to Deuteronomy, is the support of the soul of living beings: *it is the blood that animates living things* (12:23). For it is from the very mouth of God that this moving element, motor and fluid, received impetus and propulsion. It is the pulse counting and probing in the deepest part of us. In us the blood has received a mission. It knows what it has to do, whence it comes and where it is going. This element, coming from God, cannot find its end in any created thing. What it cannot penetrate like water, it attacks and destroys like fire. That is why one of the earliest orders of the Old Testament is not to mix flesh and blood: they must be eaten separately. God said to Noah in Genesis: *This creation that lives and moves is to provide food for you; I make it all over to you, by the same title as the herbs that have growth. Only, you must not eat the flesh with the blood still in it* (Gen. 9:3-5). God follows, so to speak, that blood of which He is the inspirer in us, the liquid bond which attaches Him to us. He watches over all the various operations which He pursues by means of those beings around us which have been given over to us as food. He takes back and jealously asks again for what in our work comes from Him and belongs to Him. To consume blood in the flesh is to confine holy sustenance within a created role, to imprison it for an immediate end when it should have none other than its own source. This is the sin spoken of in the Second Book of Paralipomena: *he set . . . hands to work stopping up . . . the stream that*

flowed through the open country (32:4). As soon as water is
made captive, as soon as it is cut off and hoarded, rather than
used to fulfill its role of canal and emissary, it stagnates and
corrupts everything around it. The earth becomes saturated
and ferments in its own water. A glass of water cheerfully
given will be returned one hundred fold, but the water we
refuse to give, destroys our conscience. Water is nothing else
but movement put at our disposal, and which we must deliver
to its destination. Sin is what stops this circulation. It is that
aneurism which blocks the organ and brings on congestion
and a series of inflammatory and local disorders. We stop
breathing water and make fire from it, and we stop breathing
fire and make light out of it.

When it does happen that water extravasates rather than
circulates, when entire spiritual regions under the grievous
level of a falling of souls and personalities are transformed
into crevices and hollows, and when digestion has taken the
place of all other vital functions, what does the wise engineer
have to do? To purify he has to dig. Below the epidermic reactions, below the range of tickling and surface reactions
with the outside, he has to appeal to the deep sentiments and
pierce to the region of causes. As Jesus taught Zacchaeus
(Luke 19), you have to teach man to descend into himself,
into that place where his author waits for him. That is where
the hidden treasure accumulates, and which sooner or
later under the instrument of pain or penance will gush
forth in a flood of tears. There takes place the *congregating
of waters,* which is Mary.[1] For the deeper we go into ourselves, the closer we come to the pure man, to the common
foundation, to the resemblance with God and with everything which in us and in our brothers is made in resemblance
with God. We have become capable of communion and com-

1. *Jesus said to her, Mary* (John 20:4).

munication, and from the very fact of our increased humidity we attract into ourselves the surrounding superficial seepings of water. *Nay, drink, and drink deep,* Solomon tells us (Prov. 5:15), *at thy own well, thy own cistern.* Agar in the desert called this *a well that had water in it* (Gen. 21:19). It was one of the wells of Abraham which the Philistines had closed up and to which his son Isaac gave back their depth and their name. *Like waters from thy own fountain flowing* (Prov. 5: 16). Under the vain sheet of water, under the superficial rapid flow they found the living water. It was one of those walls, one of those curb-stones on which the Saviour was leaning when the woman of Samaria asked Him for that water which destroys thirst, which was one day to come forth from His opened heart. Wherever there is a little water, the flocks *(jumenta)*, tired of licking the sand and the fodder of thorns and cacti which the professors furnish them, assemble, and the halt gradually turns into a city.

But it is not enough to find water under the soil, it is not enough to put it passively into one place by utilizing its properties of freedom and weight. Then you have to purify it of stagnation and give it a freshness it had at the source, and give it a direction avoiding every level of pestilence. There are two ways of accomplishing this.

The first, and the only one within our capacity, is to dig a trench, make a canal, a network of flushings and drains which is grafted on a sewer. This is the work of apologetics, the beneficent chain of reasoning, the temptation of order which is incorporated into chaos and which enlivens sloth, indifference, bad faith, acedia. How slow, unending and difficult is this work of the steam-excavator, digging in a barren hard earth! It is as if we tried to suck the whole sea through a straw!

But God proceeds in other ways. He makes us remember

that He the Lord built the earth by taking mountains as the basis of His manifestation and the means of our salvation, for without mountains it would be impossible for water to reach the sea. *His own building*, says Psalm 86:1, *amidst the inviolate hills*. And Psalm 71:16, *The land shall have good store of corn, high up the hill-sides. Yet there shall be torrents flooding the glens* (Ps. 103:10). The formidable mountain on the horizon which suddenly the convert sees, covered with snow and light on its sides, is the Mountain of God. The *high* hill, says Psalm 67:16, the hill whose wealth is shown and whose abundance is inexhaustible—the *rugged* hill. How better can be characterized the conservation, the reserves and the condensation of purity and blessing which are, for our use, the source in heaven of all rivers? This is the store-room, *so well with corn and wine furnished, both man and maid shall thrive* (Zach. 9:17).[8] The convert sees all that comes into view, not only a mountain, but the entire range huge like rams, like a row of enormous white lambs! (Ps. 118:6). It grew all at the same time in the midst of the barren desolate plain. *I lift up my eyes to the hills, to find deliverance* (Ps. 120:1). And suddenly that vision takes away from the plain, the desert, the ordered flatness around us, their importance. The point our toe reaches only to reject at once and put behind us is no longer a prison, it is a temporary carpet our impatient feet tread on, something not to inhabit but to cross. So it is true! Finally those *eternal hills* we have yearned for since the creation of the world and with which we feel joined in secret are made real before our eyes. We do not come upon them, we recognize them. For we know that the *fluenta evangelii* in the liturgy which are now at our disposal in the blue of the heavens, are the same as the *fluenta putei* toward which long

2. *multiplying, with soft showers, the grain* (Ps. 64:11).

ago, as we followed the patriarch Abraham, we guided our flocks in the darkness. Everything is purified and exchanged around us. Everything circulates. Once from the vast swamps you could hear only the croaking of frogs. But now rather than that cemetery verbiage, I hear on all sides the clear melody of obedience, the cooperative speech of water proceeding to its unanimous duty,[3] that movement around us which is the varied and multiplied expression in time of the universal plan. The desire within us has found a way out. The drop uses its weight. It falls in search of another drop which a distant horizon reserves for it. It knows it has something to measure and nourish. It has to nourish the sea and draw from the resources of the field. *The wealth of the sea shall foster them* (Deuter. 33:49). *A river of peace*, says Isaias. And the same prophet (66:12): *the wealth of the nations shall pour into her like a torrent in flood.* And another passage: *his breath like a mountain stream that floods over till it is neck deep* (Is. 30: 28). (This means that we are left the freedom to turn our necks in whatever direction we wish.) No swamp can resist that powerful flood. *The voice of the Lord is heard over the waters!* says Psalm 28:3. For He uses the water to purify and consolidate the earth, *the Lord thundering over swollen waters.*

It is the hill which comes to help the pit and with us leans over that chance fissure into which so many wretches have fallen. The cistern where the ox and ass have fallen represents our capacities for patience and work and commerce and song. Since the older painters used to depict the donors on their knees and holding the votive image of the chapel they built, why should I not provide my prayer with the rough reproduction and the relief map of the world where I have been called to live? This will by my ex-voto!

3. *Procedamus in pace in nomine Domini* (Liturgy).

242

FOR MY FAMILY

ANNE-CATHERINE EMMERICH tells us that all the sufferings of the Saviour in Gethsemani the hardest and most painful was the realization of His impotence over the hardened sinner, of His ineffectiveness with Judas and with the numberless crowds untouched by the coming of their Lord. It is this vision of the spirit which the cross of Calvary interprets and transforms into physical quartering, the formidable hoisting of love caught on relentless resistance. All of you angels, look on this! The Almighty is vanquished. He is powerless. He created heaven and earth, and He cannot convince a simple human being who says no! This child, for example, will never be convinced. Here is a rebel in whom our Lord will never recuperate that small part of Himself. He is not wanted. He shows them hell and they laugh. That threat has been overused.[1] He proposes heaven and earth, and no one wants them. He Himself descended and offered Himself. *He laid His garments aside* (John 13:4) and prostrated Himself at our feet. He took them, kissed them and wept on them. He was repulsed with horror and hate, with irony, and what is worse, with boredom, with a tired languishing gesture. There is no point in discussing the matter. We've had enough of the whole story. Leave us alone! And now the Son of God is on the cross. He is on the testing stand. From all sides they pull hard on Him. Under this terrible frame He cracks, His flesh is torn and His heart is almost squeezed out from the viscera. But on the face

1. *How it shines in his wake, as though ocean itself had grown hoary with age!* (Job 41:23).

243

of the spectator, one of those faces we know, this spectacle brought only a sneer of disgust. *What time is it?*

This is the scandal which all Christians, small and great, share, proportionately with their faith, with their leader. *Is anyone's conscience hurt?* asks Saint Paul (II Cor. 11:29). *I am ablaze with indignation.* The pious mother sees her son join free-masonry. A Christian wife lives forty years with an unyielding husband. The convert son is treated by the entire family with scornful pitying indulgence. A friend has with his closest friends conversations like those you have with the dead in your dreams. There is a metaphor which says that our words "fall into the void." That is exactly it.

It is not surprising that the saints before that stone confronting them are seized with a feeling of horror and despair. It is not merely twice like Moses that they struck it with the prophetic rod, it was their own flesh, as they constantly lashed it, that they bruised to the bone. They cry profusely and sob like a child wearing himself out before a closed door. And then the conviction gradually grows in them that it is their fault. They did not do enough. They betrayed Christ in their personal inadequacy. They kept something for themselves to which they had no right. And what they kept for themselves prevents truth from reaching them. As in the parable of the sower, it is that superficial part of the soul, the hardest, which keeps the seed from entering. How shall I reach the heart of that poor fellow who is here in front of me, if my resistance is harder than his? I give them not merely one hardness to overcome, but two, theirs and my own. If I have no power over theirs, I am not disarmed against my own. And that is why we see in books the saints whipping themselves mercilessly and placing in their mortified flesh the prick of horsehair and nails. They have taken arms. At any price they had to break the armor, crack the selfish carapace, open up a

244

passage for grace, communicate with all of their flesh with the consciousness of their insignificance, destroy in themselves everything that prevent charity from emanating, that hinders the expansion in us which is the presence of God. In this way we shall finally understand, from within, the man whom the psalmist calls *egenum et pauperem,* or the sinner. For we shall no longer attack him from the outside, it is within him that we have means for understanding. Already we have conquered something deep within us to which he was not a stranger. This is what Saint Paul means when he exhorts us to become *Christ's incense* (II Cor. 2:15). *Making manifest,* he adds, *both those who are achieving salvation and those who are on the road to ruin.* We fight against reasoning, and even against a face, but we do not oppose perfume. We are invaded suddenly, our land is taken, and we breathe the spirit. *Now, while the king sits at his wine, breathes out the spikenard of my thoughts* (S. of Songs 1:11). And Saint Paul again, *as a life-giving perfume where it finds life* (II Cor. 2: 16). The house of the Pharisee was filled with it and it was the sinful woman who broke the pot of ointment. We listen. Yes, that is the right word and the irresistible intonation. Let us hear it again!

That is the way the saints behave, those sons of Benjamin, the violent ones to whom the Kingdom of God is promised, those ravishers of a country without boundaries. (For that *Kingdom of God* which is promised to them is compared in another parable to a grain of mustard seed, *of all seeds none is so little*—Matth. 13:31—which we cannot hold because it has no dimensions.) There are not only heroes and knights in the world, there are obscure inconspicuous people, without wit, but who try in their own way to hold on where there is no chance of doing otherwise. After all, we are Christians, and it is impossible to be a Christian without releasing something new around us, without our beginning to smell of *Christ's incense*. Whence the exasperation of the world with us (not without a hint at times of secret pity), is justified by our own mediocrity still more than by our aggression. Pharao grinds his teeth and furiously asks what gives us the right to smell of God. Nothing, Your Highness. It is natural. Or rather, it is supernatural. At any rate, that is the way it is. I am sorry, but you cannot easily get rid of us. We are here, and that odor we exhale through our pores could not be exterminated by all the waters of the Red Sea. You can try to push us out, but we are here, and what we have begun to undertake, we don't have to begin over, for the Christian is the man who does not cease continuing. Even if the mediocre Christian has not put on the *helmet of salvation* described by Saint Paul (Eph. 6:17), at least you can say he fills the role of a kind of living gabion in the enterprise for which he intuitively knows he is somewhere designated.[2] He has received the privilege of a latent but fundamental incompatibility which makes him both dangerous and invulnerable. He enjoys, not without some degree of bantering, a privilege of exterritoriality. His organic system of defense is so compact that no attack from the outside can cut into him. It's worse than the testicles of Behemoth and the close-pressing scales of Leviathan. *Nor fears he the archer; sling-stones he counts as straw* (Job 41:19). You can absolutely count on him, on condition that you ask only a very slight effort each day when the routine contributes as much as duty does, a second zone service, something for which it is necessary to put on—not the shining breast-plate of Diana of Ephesus—but the threadbare coat of the clerk, a kind of signature on the time sheet, accompanied by a veiled complacency with progress. For in his

2. *Does he not know the number of the stars, and call each by its name?* (Ps. 146:4).

246

affiliation with catacombs, in their subterranean set-up, to which immediately after his conversion he received a pass-key from an angel, it did not take him long to realize that as the guest of a prison secretly troubled with all kinds of scratch-ings and codes, he was in correspondence with a multitude of invisibles on all sides, engaged in a general conspiracy whose purpose and means he has no need of knowing because it began before him and will continue without him. It is a con-tinual training of the attention, a disposition—and I do not mention the circumstance along our way which engages our direction and our gait. Something of this can be found in Kafka's novels *The Trial* and *The Castle*. I myself composed a parable along these lines, called *La Pension de Famille*, where there is an engineer in need of concessions, who had taken a room in a boarding house administered by a large old lady. This *pension* housed a cosmopolitan miscellany as variegated as Jerusalem at the time of Pentecost: *There are Parthians among us, and Medes, and Elamites; our homes are in Mesopotamia or Judea . . . some of us are Jews and other proselytes; there are Cretans among us too, and Arabians* (Acts 2:9-11). Something of which an analogy could easily be found in the neighborhood of the Etoile or the Val-de-Grâce. But our newcomer was not long in realizing that among all those boarders, men and women, sick and strong, there was a secret bond, a practical understanding of which it was not absolutely necessary, on the faith of his own experi-ence, that they were even imperfectly aware. The way in which this encompassing plot, this progressive invasion of an unknown scenario, succeeded in affecting my personal nego-tiation of a loan for a railroad, the kind of attraction which this composition I gradually learned to become a close part of, exercised on my writing and my movements, is what I shall leave to the imagination of my readers.

Christian philosophy teaches us that true science is *to know by causes*. Is it not true that the true cause is not *how* but *why?* That is, not the means or the ensemble of means (this one or that one!) by which a given result has been obtained, for that is only for curiosity's sake, but the *raison d'être*, or what provoked that presence before our eyes, and to what drama and composition it is attached. The second of the great commandments enjoins us to *love our neighbor as ourself*. This is called solidarity. That means there is not a single one of those people whom chance puts in our way and proposes to us, with whom we do not have everything in common, and with whom we do not inherit, as children of God, a certain indivisibility. Providence made them holders of a part of our own destiny, depositaries of a certain amount of possibilities. They bring us something from Providence, a pass word. It is worthwhile to look at this fellow, to study him, to understand him, and moreover, to try him. With him he brings something we needed and also something for which our help is needed, an action from both of us for which the time has come. But I am aware of the business he came to consult us on, without realizing it, and for which he submits his files in bulk, and the matter at hand is none else than his eternal salvation and mine along with it. Yes, the leathery faced peasant, the alcoholic, the timid and cantankerous bourgeois who looks like the fat dog of the concierge, the business woman with the awful gaze putting lipstick on her wizened lips, are our brothers and sisters. Jesus Christ died for them. There is a star deeply hidden within that flesh, more deeply driven in than the legal coin in the carp of Gennesaret. It is a long distance between heaven and earth, and the adventure that leads all those obscure figures to me would take a long time to tell. But there is no gainsaying it. They are in front of me, as clear as corpses, who will win the victory. *I will . . . give him a white stone, on*

which stone a new name is written (Apoc. 2:17). The new
name, or rather the ancient name, is obliterated under nick-
names and the surname. I see them and own them, I know by
causes. Beneath them I speak to their guardian angel, in them
I have dealings both with that cork, the habit, which obstructs
them, and with the blind effort of that child in us, uninterrupted from beginning to end, who asks to be born. I have
access to everything and even to that black hole, to that corrupt place where lies an almost half-dead soul freeing itself
bubble by bubble. I know enough to understand, alas, but not
enough in order to help. Between me and my subject there is
a glass blade which is my insufficiency. I am like someone on
the bank who grieves at not knowing how to swim.

This is the anguish, this is the hope against judgment and
fearless faith against the fact, which each day restores thousands of priests, missionaries and religious. This is the patience
of the countless crucified, this is the monstrous rigid cross at
their backs which they do not see, but which they impregnate
with their sweat and which they penetrate with their justification. For them there is a cross overhead to look at, but there
is another at their back, which shapes their posture and which
they do not know. If I am not able to bring to the work of salvation the contribution of very much heroism, I have an insipid patience, a bureaucratic faithfulness, an inert but
unshakable resistance to displacement, and the daily unpack-
ing at your feet of this colorless prayer. *See how . . . the eyes of
a maid . . . are fixed on the hand of her mistress* (Ps. 122:2).
Yes, Lord, I still have my eyes to question You. They are still
alive! They are close to Your face.

The Creed speaks to us of a communion of saints, but there
is also a communion of sinners. It is impossible for us to study
that instrument high up on the church ceiling (or should I say
that grip, that hook, by which someone maneuvers the enor-

mous living net which absorbs and scrapes the depths) without becoming conscious of the mesh which I constitute; or rather it is not tarred rope, but the weight and the effort. of the living net around me to which I am painfully rooted with all limbs and the four parts of my person. It is Christ's work in which we have to participate whether we like it or not, it is the work of salvation that is so strong within our very viscera: the Christ to furnish to Christ! I am almost tempted to identify it with what is called the instinct of conservation.

We do not in fact pray only by means of our own words. The woman who comes to light a candle in front of the Sacred Heart is replaced by the wax burning for a few hours until it is consumed. The heart of the Levite who raises the censer at the foot of the altar suddenly dilates in the full clouds of smoke. When we rise on a summer morning, at five o'clock, is the flashing of dew and birds ourselves or is it all the earth praising God with irresistible cries? And as God surrounds everything, other souls are united with ours as yellow is with blue, and the flower with the bee, and to whom existence is sufficient for them to need us and speech sufficient for us to be understood. We felt on us the work of all those agile fingers, and at times, coming from somewhere, a blessing which does not know where to land, a child kissing us blindly on our eyes and lips. Everywhere around us we feel the atmosphere and the demands of a choir and of a public we are obliged to supply with provisions from our own resources. Lord Jesus, have pity on this invisible system, on this city of prayers which furnishes its services from the same budget, from all the counters which work for me, some within reach of my hands and others beyond the horizon. Kindly listen to this sentence we, as we are joined together, are so painfully trying to articulate.

The man who once did me good has lost thereby his independence. I have taken a permanent interest in his affairs which we have not the means of liquidating. With regard to him, I am henceforth a part of those works of which it is written that they follow us, that they are inseparable from us. I furnish something of his capital. We breathe at the same time. We think together. We pay attention to each other in all the elements of our constitution.

It is therefore right, Lord, that as I willingly look up toward Your cross and hold the horn of that animal stipulated by Moses, I pray to You for all of my family, my father and mother, my two sisters, my wife, for my five children and my five grand children. It is right that I pray to You for Arthur Rimbaud, without whom my eyes would not have been opened to Your face. There was a man covered with glory, called Ernest Renan, shining, resplendent with all the bourgeois virtues and all the flatteries of fortune. And he proposed all the science and malice and talent he had in order to extinguish You. He wrote that *Vie de Jésus*, a disgusting compendium of infamy and lies which a publisher put through several cheap editions. It was the same publisher who bought for 1500 francs the rights for all the works of Baudelaire. There was that wild adolescent, that frenzied vagabond, intractable, exiled, desperate, mystical, whose errors and crimes some new fool every month undertakes to tell us. But there is also someone who thinks of him each day with a total faithfulness, as of an older brother and master. There is someone obstinately testifying to God that he owes him everything, that he saved him from hell and from the university. There is someone speaking for him as best he can to God, and who never ceases asking for pardon and justice.

At times I think of how I might have met him, when in 1891, he crossed Paris, between the Gare du Nord and the Gare d'Austerlitz, a tall white-haired Celt, full of tears and blasphemies, who had dragged from Voncq to the Hospital of the Assumption in Marseille the stump of his leg eaten away by cancer. Now I have no communication with him except the will of God, in whom he dwells forever, and this cold ransom of prayers with which I try from time to time to make some payment on account. But what could he have said to me which would be worth the sudden pull on my heart which often I feel in the middle of a conversation and the interruption in some continuity or other which wakes me up in the middle of the night. He knows that long ago we met *in the shade of some poplars in Germany*, somewhere in the north, under the portico of Bethseda crowded with phantoms! And now far away, at the feet of an immobile judge, and waiting for that hour which no humanly-devised clepsydra can tell, he inhabits a mournful silent realm of which we are told, if it is not death, is like *the shadow of death*.

That is the realm which Philippe entered the other day, at the moment when he closed his eyes and his great heart stopped beating. *Siccine separat amara mors!* Yes, that is how death separates two hearts strongly united, not through any monotonous habit, but in a virile understanding, in the kindness of two minds which discovered one another and smiled affectionately at one another. There was just enough time to raise my hand to his noble brow, and he had moved far away from my reach. He was transplanted. The hand he raised did not reach his mouth, and now he is in the presence of God! Lord, with all the tears of my broken heart, I pray You not to be harsh on Philippe! You who understood friendship. You whom the Gospel shows weeping, shaken even in Your hypostasis by the death of Your friend Lazarus who had fallen asleep when You were away, it is to You I tell my complaint and my grievance! You who are faithful, I fervently ask of You, because my hands are empty, to pay in my place what I owe and what I was not able to settle. You had made him my manager in temporal affairs. He was my wise and good guide. He never left my side. The mission You entrusted to him for me, he carried out scrupulously. And I did nothing in return. Not one of those stammering words, which at times I tried to say and he brushed aside with an indulgent smile, reached his hearing. Lord, I pray to You for my brother Philippe who was asleep when You were away! Wherever he is, in this moment of prayer I share with him, I testify and I join my cause with his. Remember that during his life time You were not deprived of all communication with him. If the façade were rigid and hardened by a rationalist Protestant education, under the varnish of Parisian irony, the heart was warm and loving. If he was unable to raise his eyes to You, his heart always beat in unison with Yours. And after all, that is what You ask of us. As Saint John says: *I have a new commandment to give you, that you are to love one another* (John 13:34). When the Gospel depicts You speaking to Your elect and thanking them because they came to You, and fed, clothed and comforted You, we can imagine that nothing could express their amazement. They wondered if they had heard correctly. They looked at one another and they looked at You without understanding. "But when did we do all that for You, Lord? We never saw You! It is true we heard of You at times, but it was so vague that we never waited to learn any more about it." And the answer came immediately: *When you did it to one of the least of my brethren here, you did it to me* (Matth. 25:40). After all, why couldn't I be, as well as any one else, the least of the brethren?[3]

Lazarus our brother sleeps. That is true. But don't we read

---

3. The power of prayers for the dead is suggested by the story of Elias (III Kings 17). *Three times, he measured his whole length upon the child's body . . . the boy's life returned to him and he revived.*

in Genesis (45:26), that when Jacob had heard the voice that spoke to him explaining all to him in a marvellous and powerful communication, that then in the arms of Joseph he had *the look of one just awoken from a heavy sleep.*—— *The man who claimed me found in me a bringer of content* (S. of Songs 8:10).

Lord, it has been said to us, and I believe it with all my soul, that *Your mercy is boundless.* It is like a man of genius who makes fun of all the rules. What better opportunity will You find to show this sublime independence than in helping this man who at the foot of Your altar brings not a fatted calf or a pair of pigeons, but a drop of rancid oil and a handful of dust?

FOR MYSELF

AND now that I have spent so much attention on others, perhaps the moment has come for me to pray a bit for this man swallowed up and formed by countless downstrokes of the pen which I call myself. Don't I have a better imitation of the cross to offer than that of the swimmer who peacefully floats, his arms stretched out on the inert soft surface of abstract contemplation? The fundamental invitation is first addressed to me: *If only I am lifted up from the earth, I will attract all men to myself* (John 12:32). There are many things in me which need to be unified. To that poignant profound call of God, what a stammering and embarrassed answer I make, what a confused obscure beginning of a person! It is not by remaining seated[1] that I can be seized by divine action: it is by getting

1. *What, thou wouldst sleep a little longer, yawn a little longer; a little longer thou must pillow head or hand? Ay, but poverty will*

down on my knees. All that a mistress[2] can read in her servant girl's eyes, I have furnished; now I have to take the posture of my humility and bend[3] down like those victims long ago which were all trussed offered at the altar. I pray that my faculties, the feet and hands of my mind, all that in me is capable of distraction and wandering to the right and the left, be thus bound for a few happy moments and reduced to impotency! The treatises on asceticism tell us that is not enough and that, as shown in the example of Elias on Carmel (III Kings 18), fire must be prepared by water, we must present to God a heart searching, purified, softened, illuminated both by the faith and penitence of which the material sacraments are the vehicle. So here I am on this prayer-stool and all that is alive in me is my mouth breathing,[4] and my heart beating and my ear listening.[5] It listens to the voice which says: *No man can*

---

not wait, like an armed vagabond it will fall upon thee! (Prov. 6: 10-11). The lazy man who puts his hand under his armpit in order better to enjoy his own warmth is not totally unknown to me. This hand is "not applied to the mouth." It does not ask what work is to be done. There can be a great distance between speech and action. You can't say that my right hand is disposed not to know its left hand! On the contrary, it is always slyly seeking out that comrade to insert itself comfortably between its finger joints and derive the elements of that beatitude, that satisfaction with self, that intimate contact, that self-consciousness which is the paradise of men of letters. During that time the imagination is a prey to all kinds of sterile dramas and poverty overtakes it on the road of the wanderer. Meanwhile, habit, like an armed figure, settles down in the center of the rusty machine.

2. *Whence comes Ágar . . . that was Sarai's maid-servant?* (Gen. 16:8).

3. *The low-born must fall, the high-born abate his pride* (Is. 5:15). *They bowed down and worshipped with their faces close to the ground* (II Esdras 8:6).

4. *Rises ever a sigh from my lips as I long after thy covenant* (Ps. 118:131).

5. *Which of you will listen to this, and mark it, and give a hearing to prophecy?* (Is. 42:23).

*enter into the kingdom of God unless birth comes to him
from water, and from the Holy Spirit* (John 3:5). Around me
the "upper chamber" has spread out and coincides with the
entire world. I am in contact not only with this stone church
which encircles me like a hollow organism, like a harp with
stretched strings, but with all the souls who at this moment
desire and pray, with all men of good will who are trying to
find their words, with all that supplicating patience. Personally
I am sorry I am able only to offer as combustible that *puddle
of water*, that "thick water," spoken of in II Machabees 1:20.
And how could I hope for the same miracle which accompanied the offerings of Moses (Lev. 9:24) and Solomon, if
from my birth on, You had not nurtured in me the seed of a
secret complicity? Under me I have gathered enough hay and
straw, or paper, to start a fire. There is no lack of fodder! If
nothing in me justifies love, I do not lack things which can
serve as fuel for anger! I am like a bad artist who never grows
tired of showing his master a bad statue, a work at first coddled by his unskillful hands, and the result later of many disparate attempts: with the secret hope that at the end his indignation would be kindled and the cumbersome monster
would be thrown away. Lord, if I am not a saint, at least I can
always resort to being intolerable! I pray You, who commanded us *not to carve images* (Exodus 20:4), help me be
done with this grotesque body—and supplement the work of
time and worms! I detest this dried skin of mine, this face,
this flesh which is being abandoned by life as it separates from
me and from itself, this broken down chassis which has driven
me around too long. Oh! if all that could only disappear or
light up in a clear fire like a puff of alcohol! For it is water
which unites nations, but it is fire, the draught of the fire,
which unifies the person, that person in us created in the
image of the Holy Trinity. The Holy Books, on every page,
cannot show the direct action of God on the soul better than

by the operation of fire (Deuter. 4:24; 9:3). Ezechiel goes as far as to compare it with an electrical phenomenon (1:4). It is this fire which descended on the twelve Apostles on the day of Pentecost and made them into inextinguishable torches. What suddenly exploded over their heads on the feast day, was the emanation of their own soul which had reached a supreme state of vibration and which caught fire by contact with the divine spark. This is the way an ember, when blown upon, first gives out an intermittent blue flame and then a rooted flame.[6] *Such a fire I will kindle,* says Ezechiel (28:18), *in the heart of thee as shall be thy undoing.* And Isaias (33: 11): *your own impetuous spirit shall be a fire.* And also Isaias (50:11): *For you others . . . that your own fire would make, with fire your own brands have kindled light the path if you can.* The river finds its outlet in a broad delta, but fire does not descend, it mounts! It is in this burning point, at the call of God, that, from our body and the joints of all our bones, all our physical, moral and intellectual faculties are consumed. A flame which, in burning us, testifies to us, for the Epistle to the Corinthians says (I Cor. 3:13): *fire will test the quality of each man's workmanship.* A flame takes root in what is inextinguishable in us, and gives expression and eloquence to our natural totality and sheds our light in all directions. It is a voice, and a tongue, or rather a cry, a song, the modulation of a phrase, a word beginning in us and kindled by the Word with which our own breath is mingled, according to this sentence of the Psalm (28:7): *The Lord's voice kindles flashing fire.*

New York, April 1933
Brussels, April 1935
EXPLICIT
LAUS DEO

6. *At the rumour of it my lips quivered with fear* (Habacuc 3:16).

APPENDIX

THE KISS OF JUDAS

WHY did Judas, doubtless on the order of the officers of the priests, walk at the head of that cohort they had sent to take Jesus? He was *their guide*, says Saint Luke (22:47). And Saint John: *There, then, Judas came, accompanied by the guard. He was in command and led them.*

Mauriac says he was there to recognize Jesus and to point Him out to the executioners. And he concludes that there was nothing remarkable about the person of the Saviour, that it was easy to confuse Him with the disciples, bearded as He was, who accompanied Him.

I do not share this opinion. I cannot believe that there would not be in the person of the Son of God something particular and extraordinary which would make one say immediately: "There He is!" Moreover, there were many people those last days in Jerusalem when He had spectacularly shown Himself to the crowds, able to identify Him. The Holy Shroud of Turin has given us a photograph of the Saviour. The exceptional face and the above-average size of the stature characterize a personality which could not easily be hidden or confused.

Then, why Judas and why the words which Saint Matthew records? *It is none other, he told them, than the man whom I shall greet with a kiss; hold him fast* (26:48).

258

I think that the subconscious idea of the Pharisees was to have not only the handing over of Christ, but a handing over authenticated by someone who would have correct qualifications and power, an apostle, someone who had received from Christ Himself the authority to say: It is He, do not look further. On another occasion, Peter, another apostle, declared: *Thou art the Christ* (Mark 8:29). And Judas, in his turn, said: *Ipse est.* He is the man. He is Christ. He is yours: seize Him. Do not let Him escape.

We should not forget that earlier Christ had escaped in the most surprising manner. In Nazareth He had passed through the midst of His enemies who had wanted to throw Him over the brow of a hill. *But he passed through the midst of them, and so went on his way* (Luke 4:30). Still more recently, in the midst of the indignant Pharisees, He made the same incomprehensible escape.

There had to be someone familiar with His ways, who would have the qualification to seize Him, and hold Him, to stabilize Him and keep Him from moving on, and to force an identification. Someone to propose to His lips, other lips, apostolic lips which He Himself had consecrated. *Ave, Rabbi,* Judas said. He acknowledged Jesus, pointed Him out, took possession of Him by his breath. He breathed the Word and it was that same breath which he took from Jesus that he used in order to say: it is He.

Thus for the last time, in the contact of an unspeakable horror, the renegade's mouth pressed against the mouth of His God! He brought Him the willed firmness of his being, the definitive refusal. The apostle testified to his source, and at the same time took leave forever, and separated. Now, he said, take Him and do with Him what you will.

A kiss from those lips! says the Song of Songs (1:1).

BENJAMIN'S THREE HUNDRED SILVER PIECES AND FIVE GARMENTS OF THE CHOICEST SORT

ON REREADING the proof of this book, I see there are many points I did not have the time to elucidate, but why not trust the insight of the reader who is now very much on the alert? However, the noble story of Joseph and his brothers would not be complete unless I tried to elucidate the *three hundred silver pieces* and *the five garments of the choicest sort* of which the patriarch, when he reveals himself, makes a gift to the youngest of his brothers, the son of suffering whose appearance cost his mother's life, and in whom we see a figure of the future reconciled Israel.

Three hundred is three times one hundred, and one hundred is ten times ten. Ten is the figure of the perfect sum returned to unity, and ten times ten, or one hundred, is the sum multiplied by itself, not outer fullness, but unlimited fecundation of capital by interest. It is the illustration of the principle of Genesis: *Increase and multiply.* But it is not solely a question of natural richness. God blesses it. He touches it, and the sum, multiplied by itself, is once again fecundated by the figure three. This time one can say that *All is consummated.* The promise of the psalm is fulfilled: *thou shalt have the nations for thy patrimony* (2:8). *She who was reproached with barrenness is now in her sixth month (Jesus died at the sixth hour)* (Luke 1:36). We know that silver is the word of God made liquid, purified, restored to its full value and endowed with a power of limitless gain.

The three hundred silver pieces remind us of the three hundred concubines of King Solomon, and, by way of contrast, of the three hundred foxes of destruction (with fire at their tails), which Samson sent into the harvest of the Philistines.

But what are the *Five Garments of the choicest sort?* I realize I will startle many by declaring that they are the *Five Wounds* of the Crucified. You will ask what is the relationship between a garment and a wound? The mystics have understood this and have an answer. In order to penetrate the inner meaning of the God-Man, they have not hesitated to use all the openings made by human justice in His sacred covering. Our Lord Himself invited us to put into each of His wounds, not only a finger, but our attention and our heart, and find there, as Saint Paul says, both baptism and burial. The catechumen receives at baptism the water which regenerates him, and the white robe which signifies the new being. In speaking of the Elect, Saint John says: *Blessed are those who wash their garments in the blood of the Lamb* (Apoc. 22:14). And again Saint Paul invites us, in the sacrament of baptism, to *arm ourselves with the Lord Jesus Christ* (Rom. 13:14). It is the *shift,* spoken of by the Bride of the Song of Songs (5:3), the garment mentioned by the apostle: *rather, we would clothe ourselves afresh* (II Cor. 5:4).[1] To put on Christ must mean to assimilate Him by Grace, to adapt to that activity which is His and of which each of His members and organs represents a particular form: the right hand, which is action; the left hand, which is preparation, reserve and assistance, the left foot which is solidity; the right foot which is movement and conquest, and finally the heart which is love. All these wounds are sources: from each of them we draw up a new being. In

1. *Well may I rejoice in the Lord, well may this heart triumph in my God. The deliverance he sends is like a garment that wraps me about, his mercy like a cloak enfolding me* (Is. 61:10).

them the Christian becomes an *alter Christus*. As at the game of dice we have won a seamless robe. To each of us is attributed some part in His eternal role. We are in His employ. At the extreme of our being there is trace of our attachment to the same cross; we have been clothed with the same purple and crowned with the same crown. Each of us has received as a religious habit and clothing, the *habit* par excellence which reveals only our face and our hands for daily tasks.

JACOB'S PEREGRINATION

FROM the top of the hills of Moab, the setting sun projects a gigantic shadow. It is the shadow of the Patriarch Jacob who soon will receive the sacred name of Israel. From the banks of the Dead Sea, it stretches across the desert to those banks where the Euphrates joins its waters with the Tigris which originated in the same paradise. From there, long before, his ancestor Abraham set out, at the command of the Almighty, to reach that narrow corridor between the sand and the sea, between Lebanon and Egypt, where he had been ordered to prepare a throne for the Messiah of Nations. It is in that direction now that the Supplanter, exiled by the anger of a brother he cheated of his blessing, has to turn in order to resume contact at length with his origin. Thus he conformed to the advice which Deuteronomy (32:7) will give later: *Cast thy mind back to old days*. The Psalmist answers (76:6): *I reflect upon days long past, the immemorial years possess my mind.* It was fitting that the Founder Israel, all of whose steps[2] were

2. *So jealous a record thou keepest of every step I take* (Job 14:16). *How dainty are the steps of thy sandalled feet* (S. of Songs 7:1). *Still in thy paths my steps were firmly planted* (Ps. 16:5).

directed by the Almighty, should move in the direction of the east.

On the road the vision of Bethel occurred: the foundation rock and the steps of the ladder, climbed by the angels, which led to God. Jacob consecrated it, as his Son later will consecrate the other Rock.

At that time, and like the Anointed later, his mission was not *to have service done him, he came to serve others* (Matth. 20:28). The master he chose was Laban, brother of his mother Rebecca, and nephew by Nachor of his grandfather Abraham. A verse of Genesis tells us that the God of one was also God of the other. But whereas the Father of the People chose the Living God to the exclusion of all the idols, the bourgeois of Mesopotamia, below the first and distant summit, seems to have reserved for himself a whole collection of little portable gods which he doubtless found more convenient for use and family worship.

I will consent to feed and tend thy herds, Jacob said (Gen. 30:31). There he inaugurated his role of guardian and assembler. The Good Shepherd in the midst of His flock. *Feed my sheep,* they said to him, as later to Peter: *Feed my lambs* (John 21:15).

But it was not Laban who attracted him and retained him. It was Rachel, his daughter (*What a wound thou hast made in this heart of mine,* S. of Songs 4:9) when she went to the well to preside over the watering of his flocks. And Jacob himself raised the stone which closed the opening. At this point, memories and allusions flood our mind. Jacob is the Holy Spirit, moved by love for mankind, for the sister, the daughter, the bride spoken of in the Song of Songs and chapter 16 of Ezechiel. Seven years, prolonged by the supplementary week, those Seven Days occupied by the interlude of Lia (lapses which later Daniel's prophecy will resume), seven years of

263

slavery which is little enough to acquire the right to that glance which penetrates my heart. It is on the mountain of the Vision that the Almighty will want a temple[3] erected to Him. And the well around which the flocks assembled and waited patiently for it to be opened so that they could draw life from it, reminds us of that incomparable water of Bethlehem (I Paral. 2:17) whence sprang an inexhaustible source to water all humanity gathered under the sceptre of Rome, and of Jacob's well where Jesus spoke with the woman of Samaria, and the large stone which closed the tomb of Lazarus, and not only of Lazarus, but of Christ, less heavy and less hard than our hearts.

But Rachel had an older sister, Lia, whom the Vulgate calls "rheumy-eyed," and the Hebrew simply "dull-eyed." These are not the shining eyes, sensitive and deep for which, as the Apocalypse says, *he rode out victorious, and to win victory* (6:2), and for which *he restores thy youth, as the eagle's plumage is restored* (Ps. 102:5). Rather they are the eyes, spoken of in Psalm 122:2, *of a maid fixed on the hand of her mistress,* eyes weakened by outside irritation or by some infirmity. There has always been a Church which sees, and a Church which listens, a Church of pastors and one of flocks, *homines et jumenta* says the psalm, a Church we ask only to obey, and whose eyes immediately serve her mouth. Martha and Mary have always existed, one active and the other contemplative. The Bride of the Song of Songs (ch. 8) also has *a little sister.* Jacob first married Lia, through the wiles of Laban, in the darkness as was fitting for that near-sighted girl. Rachel, the object of a longer desire, was also longer in giving her two sons, Joseph and Benjamin, whose names mean *growth* and

3. *Take thy only son . . . to the land of Clear Vision* (Gen. 22:2).

suffering. As for Lia, she was not long, with the help of her servant girl, in peopling the earth.[4]

Jacob's long years of sojourn and service with the relatives of his ancestor were not in vain. He carried out a return to the Promised Land, not alone, but at the head of an army of flocks and servants of whom his descendants still repeat the example or think nostalgically of repeating it. From under the feet of the immense speckled bleating flock, a column of dust rose up in the midst of which asses and camels could be distinguished.

4. There is much to say about the generations of the two sisters and their servant girls, Zelpha and Bala. But their interpretation is related to the very difficult interpretation of the mystical meaning of the twelve tribes to which is applied the double blessing of Genesis and Deuteronomy and to which have been added the blessings of the Apocalypse. I should like simply to say a few words about the fruit of the mandrake which Lia's son Reuben found in a field at the time of the harvest and which Rachel bought from her sister at the price of a night with her husband.

If this story is limited to its literal meaning, it is not very interesting and not very worthy of being the expression of the Holy Spirit. But this name of *mandrake* which is included in Solomon's horticulture (S. of Songs 7:13) makes us pay attention. The mandrake, doubtless because of its strange form and because of its narcotic properties, and aphrodiasiac as well, to which the Orient adds that of helping in childbirth, has always been considered by all peoples as adapted to magical operations. *Give me*, Rachel said to Lia, *some of the fruit thy son* (Reuben the first born) *has found* (Gen. 30:14). This secret tuber with the double root* which blossoms and matures at the same time as the harvest may well be that plant swollen *with all the blessings . . . in the depth beneath us, all the blessings that enrich breast and womb,* spoken of in Genesis (49:25), nourished on the testimony of Scripture, and which gives love and fecundity to the woman who bites into it. Lia, first, according to the flesh, who doubtless represents the Synagogue, and then Rachel, a figure of Eve generated during sleep, and who also represents Mary and the Church.

* *His command to me was that I should find my home in Jacob, throw in my lot with Israel, take root among his chosen race* (Eccl. 24:13). *I, the root* (Apoc. 22:16).

It was an incessant noise of bells and hand-bells, and dogs, eager on all sides, rallied the lame and the stragglers.

Why speckled? This was the result of the ruse of Jacob and the strange bargain he concluded with Laban. He scorned the sheep and goats which were black or white, and kept for himself only those which were spotted or speckled or gray. And to obtain this, he used the method of partly peeled branches[5] exposed before the eyes of the flocks so that when they came to drink they should conceive in full view of them (Gen. 30).

The peeled branch or the wand is of course the cross, and also the Crucified; and its double color of black (bark) and white (showing through where it had been stripped) indicates the double nature which is human and divine. And our souls also, in that baptism symbolized by the running water, lose something of their native covering and become divine while remaining human. The complete sinners, complete from head to foot, black or fawn-colored, not only do not appear among the elect, but neither do the just who are just only in their own justice, and *who have received their reward*; the *great and wise* who intimidate the Holy Spirit by their cleanness and shining appearance, so white a page that it refuses to be marked. We inherit bastards, half-breeds, blacks stained with white, and whites stained with black; not to mention those with the savage color of Esau, the crowd of all-comers whom later Divine Wisdom will recruit at the gates of the city and the crossroads![6]

5. *The sceptre of thy royalty is a rod that rules true* (Ps. 44:7). *I see a star that rises out of Jacob, a stem that springs from Israel's root* (Num. 24:17). *The Lord will make thy empire spring up like a branch out of Sion* (Ps. 107:2). *Shaft that galled the shoulder* (Is. 9:4). *A branch of a tree, I told him, with the eyes already open* (Jer. 1:11).

6. *My people grown strange to me* (literally: *Has my people become a speckled bird to me?*) (Jer. 12:8). *Clad thee with embroidery . . .* (Ezec. 16:10).

Rachel, the text tells us, *stole*, or as we would say in common speech today, sneaked away, her father's household gods (Gen. 31:19). The good man was annoyed. But the divine Master often posed *as a thief*, as a professional whose trade was to take what did not belong to Him. It is He in secret who steals and makes disappear without our realizing it, those small figures sculptured in our own image which we have coddled for so long, within ourselves. In vain Laban demanded them back from his daughter. She deliberately sat down upon them. They made one with original sin. It was up to him to try to recover them, if he could, under the *camel's harness*, in the hollow which the hump leaves, symbol of greed and pride of that mountainous animal.

Jacob meanwhile continued that pilgrimage which was a flight. Behind him was his father who wanted to recover his fortune, and ahead of him his fierce brother who was preparing to defend his fortune. The text says: *a message came to Laban, three days too late, Jacob has fled* (Gen. 31:22) with Rachel, his heir and depositary of the promises made to humanity. *He had been on the road seven days before he overtook him* (Gen. 31:23). This is comparable to the Jewish people whom the Messiah defrauded of His presence on the third day and who succeeded in catching Him only on the Seventh and last day of the week which is the Sabbath. It began with reproaches on both sides. *What meanest thou, by thus tricking me, and carrying off my daughters. . . . Tell me then, why hast thou carried away my household gods with thee?* And Jacob answered: *For what fault, what guilt of mine, hast thou so hotly pursued me? . . . Was it for this that I spent twenty years in thy service?* It all ended with a communion meal, like the one Joseph offered his brothers, and by the erection of a monument or heap of stones, which Jacob called the *Witness-heap* and Laban the *Cairn of Record, each according to the usage*

267

of his own tongue. And Laban said: *Let the Lord keep watch, and see justice done between us, when our ways have parted. . . .* Then he *went back to his home.*

Now Esau was soon warned of the return of this brother who formerly had taken his place. Esau, who had just concluded an alliance with a descendant of Ismael, that son of the servant-girl and patron of all wanderers, was the Separated Brother par excellence, the figure of all separated brothers, living in the desert, homesick, in anger and in a passionate love for property, for that mess of pottage so dearly paid for long ago, and who are called schismatics, heretics, nationalists, moslems. It is the hard negotiation of Abel (whose name is *breath*) with Cain (who is *gain*)! Jacob prepared for this, at Jacob's ford, not without harming his thigh muscle, when he triumphed over the angel who tried to stop him. But at times it is easier to win over God than over man! Jacob did not assert himself over Esau, he crept in. He divided his people into three parts: in the first rank the *servant-girls and their children,* in the second rank Lia and hers, in the last he himself accompanied by Rachel. And we remember the Master of the Vineyard in the parable, who sent to the bad workers successive detachments before He Himself went. The servant-girls[7] are the prayers, the books, the arguments of apologetics, all those things which belong to us and which we gratuitously

7. They were Bala and Zelpha. Bala, according to the gloss, means *inveterata, turbata,* Zelpha means *distillatio oris.* The first means penitence. *Grief has dimmed my eyes . . . so many are the adversaries that surround me* (Ps. 6:8). *In the enemy's land,* says Baruch 3:11. *While I kept my own secret, evermore I went sighing, so wasted my frame away,* in Psalm 31:3. The second means prayer, that stirring of rosary beads throughout the universe, the incessant movement of the lips of an old woman, as if she were drunk which is noticed by the High Priest in the Book of Kings. It is true that the mouth distills the soul when it makes words out of sentiments.

put at their disposal. Then Lia comes who is already the Church, in so far as principle of all kinds of material blessings: cows, ewes, she-asses, bulls, and those listed in the text, animals of all species: namely, works of education, science, assistance, schools, hospitals, day-nurseries, nurses etc. Such as missionaries in China, Japan and IndoChina. Like Our Lord, preceded by various cures and miracles, sending out devils and multiplying loaves of bread. His words preceded and concealed Him. And finally, in His Glory and accompanied by that Bride who will henceforth always be at His right hand, Christ the King comes, surrounded by His hierarchy.